CATCH MORE WALLEYES

Mark Romanack

Published by

**krause
publications**

700 E. State Street • Iola, WI 54990-0001
Telephone: 715/445-2214

Please, call or write us for our free catalog of hunting, fishing & outdoor publications. To place an
order or receive our free catalog, call 800-258-0929. For editorial comment and further information,
use our regular business telephone at (715) 445-2214.

Library of Congress Catalog Number: 99-67651
ISBN: 0-87341-826-3

Printed in the United States of America

CONTENTS

THE POWER OF FAMILY

I make a good living in the fishing industry. Writing magazine articles and books, shooting photos and conducting seminars keeps the bills paid and leaves enough extra to pursue a passion for fishing. Hard work and a drop or two of talent has helped a career blossom, but mostly a handful of people are responsible for the life I lead.

The list starts with my parents who encouraged me to find a career I was passionate about. I don't think they had fishing in mind when they gave me this advice, but the confidence I enjoy today came straight from the faith they showed in me as a baby, a boy and a young man.

My father wasn't a "fisherman" but he found time to take his youngest son fishing. My mother didn't live long enough to see her baby graduate college, but her love and guidance has never left my side.

The fire I feel for fishing may not have burned so brightly if it weren't for two other special family members. My brother Mike made time to take his little brother fishing often enough that a tradition was born. When Mike couldn't take me fishing, brother-in-law Les took over. Throughout my grade school and high school days, Mike and Les saw to it that little Marky got to go along.

Marrying into a fishing family didn't hurt my desire to fish for a living either. My father-in-law Don Parsons saw to it that his own sons, Gary and Doug, went fishing and his new son-in-law wasn't left out either. Add in Keith and John, two more brothers-in-law who share the same passion for fishing and the framework was pretty much set.

All these people and more encouraged me to polish my talent for writing and passion for fishing into a common goal. Now that the goal has been met, it's my loving wife Mari and sons Zackery and Jacob that remind me why working passionately is worthwhile. They also remind me how I got started and why time spent fishing is one of the greatest gifts parents can give their children. Thanks to God for the pleasures of fishing and the power of family.

ACKNOWLEDGEMENTS

No project as large as this book happens by itself. The information pertaining to walleyes contained within this book has taken a lifetime to collect. Along the way countless individuals have contributed to my education. Some of the most influential anglers have been tournament professionals, other guides and charter captains. A few tackle manufacturers and fisheries biologists have also been very helpful. Some fellow outdoor writers have contributed, as did more weekend walleye warriors than can be listed.

The knowledge of walleye fishing I've accumulated over the years has come from all these sources and more. Fishing is an ongoing lesson that only stops when passion for the sport wanes.

Some key people deserve special recognition. A handful of tournament professionals including Mike McClelland, Bob Propst, Sr., Gary Parsons, Keith Kavajecz, Rick LaCourse, Ted Takasaski and Bruce DeShano have shared with me both a walleye boat and countless brainstorming sessions. The passion these men have for fishing has rubbed off in many ways.

My longtime friend, confidant and tournament partner Dr. Steve Holt is one of the great minds in fishing. Despite Dr. Steve making his living in the emergency medical field, his knowledge of fishing and desire to refine and improve everything he does on the water makes him a constant inspiration.

A host of tackle and marine manufacturers deserve praise for working with anglers like me to produce a variety of products ideally suited to catching walleyes. Just a few of the companies that have helped my journey include Off Shore Tackle, Riviera Downriggers, Zebco/Quantum rods and reels, MotorGuide electric motors, Mercury Outboards, Fisher Boats, Lowrance Electronics, K&E Tackle and Storm Lures.

I would also like to thank the entire staff at Krause Publications. They are the faces behind the scene. These tireless individuals deserve recognition for the hours of editing, layout, design and marketing required to make this possible.

FOREWORD

Everyone who chases walleyes can benefit from the exchange of ideas. Such information sometimes changes hands when two or more anglers gather to talk about this magnificent fish. Unfortunately, many walleye fishermen are not known for honestly reporting their exploits. It can take a long time to get any real information out of a dyed-in-the-wool walleye angler.

Thankfully, Mark Romanack has done the research for you. He's cut through the fog and spent more than a decade sifting facts from fancy when it comes to finding walleyes and convincing them to bite. Finding and catching these elusive fish is always a challenge, but this book takes some of the guesswork out and allows you to narrow your search and prepare your presentation before you even take to the water.

Information is the best tool any angler can have and it's all right here on the pages that follow. Sit down. Flip through the book and get ready to start catching more and bigger walleyes than you ever thought possible. This book will put you on the road to success.

Kevin Michalowski
Editor

CHAPTER 1
WALLEYES, THE ANIMAL

I'm forever a student of walleye fishing. The more I learn about walleyes and fishing for this member of the Percidae family, the more convinced I am there are no absolutes. When I say no absolutes, I'm referring to rigid standards of finding or catching these fish that always apply.

The author is a student of walleye fishing. The more anglers learn about walleyes the more they realize there are no fixed methods of finding or catching this species.

Despite the unpredictable nature of walleyes, one aspect of this species does appear to hold true. These efficient predators are adaptable enough to live and thrive in a wealth of environments. Beyond this statement, making matter-of-fact claims about how to find or catch walleyes can lead anglers down a potentially rocky path.

Those who try to approach the sport of fishing for walleyes with preconceived notions and angling methods will be humbled by this popular and often-frustrating species. The truth is, walleyes are a complex species that can and often do turn up in the logical spots. They also are found in a wealth of locations in which most anglers would never dream of looking.

In the 25 years I've fished for walleyes, I've taken this species in water less than a foot deep and at depths of more than 100 feet. I've caught fish in gin-clear waters at high noon and I've taken others from water so dirty a jig could not be seen one inch below the surface. I've found walleyes living in submerged weeds, sunken timber, scattered on gravel flats, suspended near the surface, hovering over mud basins and using cane beds for cover. I've enjoyed catching walleyes in sluggish creeks and raging rivers, natural lakes and man-made reservoirs. After all these experiences, I must say again that there are no absolutes in walleye fishing.

Misconceptions about walleyes are a major reason why so many anglers struggle to catch this prized species. Myths about any species or topic often are based on a grain of truth. This is especially true of walleyes.

An angler catches a nice mess of fish by jigging slowly along a rocky reef and as a result walleyes are characterized as structure-loving fish that are seldom found far from the bottom. Fishing after dark, an angler casts cranks to a shallow weed line and catches a few nice walleyes. Before long the story goes that walleyes don't bite well during the day. And so it goes.

When I first started fishing for walleyes there were more myths, half-truths and misconceptions perpetuated about these large-eyed predators

There's much we know about the life cycle of walleyes. What we don't know is what makes walleyes tick and why they do the things they do.

Walleyes are creatures of large lakes, rivers and reservoirs. Rarely does this species fare well in small bodies of water.

than there were cold, hard facts. Today the picture is a little more clear, but walleyes are still a fish that are shrouded in mystery.

What we know about walleyes can largely be categorized as life science. It's true that biologists have learned a wealth of information about the life cycle of walleyes. Thanks to some dedicated scientists we know that walleyes spawn in the spring. They prefer to spawn on a mixture of rock, gravel and sand. We also know that some form of current or wave action is important to the survival of the eggs. Walleyes deposit their eggs in water from 39-45 degrees and we know the parents provide no care for the young.

In general, walleyes are creatures of large natural lakes, reservoirs and rivers. Rarely are significant populations of walleyes found in small bodies of water.

Both walleyes and saugers, a close relative of the walleye, often live in the same bodies of water. Walleyes are more wide spread than saugers which tend to be most numerous in the major river impoundment systems of the Dakotas, Montana, Wyoming and Kansas. Saugers are also abundant in major rivers such as the Mississippi, Illinois, Ohio and Tennessee.

Walleyes grow larger than saugers and saugers tend to show a preference for deeper water. Scientists have also learned that walleyes and saugers

Saugers are a close relative of walleyes. Walleyes and saugers sometime cross to form a natural hybrid known as the saugeye.

will sometimes spawn in the same areas, producing a natural hybrid known as a saugeye. Saugeye have the physical markings of a sauger, but they grow nearly as large as walleyes.

We know the preferred forage for walleyes include a wealth of minnows and smaller fishes. Walleyes also readily feed on aquatic insects or crayfish if these food supplies are abundant.

We can say with certainty that several distinctive strains of walleyes occur, including one group that prefers to spawn on reefs in natural lakes and reservoirs and another that prefers to spawn in tributary streams. Walleyes of the Wolf River system in central Wisconsin actually spawn in marshlands similar to the habitat preferred by northern pike.

Biologists have determined that, compared to other fish species, walleyes are fast-growing. In waters with abundant forage walleyes grow to sexual maturity in just three years. Walleyes sometimes grow larger than 20 pounds, but rarely are specimens larger than 10 pounds taken by sport anglers.

Walleyes are a biologist's dream come true when it comes to raising fish for stocking purposes. Hundreds of thousands of fingerlings can be produced from small ponds managed especially for raising walleyes.

Tagging studies conducted in Michigan have indicated that walleyes will travel hundreds of miles to reach natal spawning areas. In addition to traveling to spawn, walleyes sometimes travel for reasons no one can understand.

In Michigan, biologists report that a number of fish tagged in the Tittabawassee River, a tributary of Saginaw Bay, later turned up in Lake Erie. In order to make this journey these fish would have to swim out of Saginaw Bay and into Lake Huron, south through Lake Huron to the St. Clair River, through the St. Clair River to Lake St. Clair, through Lake St. Clair to the Detroit River and then finally into Lake Erie. This is a trip of several hundred miles!

Even more strange, in the same region, walleyes from Lake St. Clair have been documented moving to Lake Erie to spawn, while at the same time walleyes from Lake Erie move to Lake St. Clair to spawn! No one can explain why these migrations occur.

Walleyes aren't just nomadic in the Great Lakes region. Fish living in the Missouri River impoundment system often move from South Dakota to North Dakota or from North Dakota to Montana to spawn or in search of food.

On the Mississippi River, walleyes migrate through lock and dam systems to get from one pool to another. Amazingly, fish tagged and released in Iowa have turned up in Minnesota!

We know a lot about the life cycle of walleyes, but as anglers we still struggle with the basic questions of how to locate these fish consistently, what lures or baits will produce the most consistent angling action and why.

Because anglers for generations have struggled to find and catch this popular species consistently, a seemingly endless list of excuses have spawned

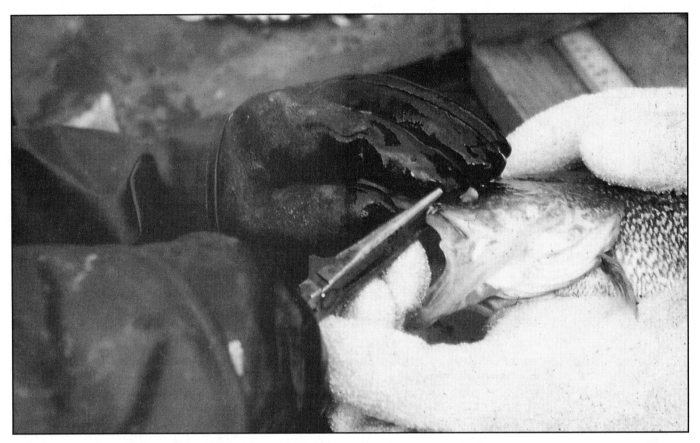

Tagging studies have determined that walleyes often migrate many miles to reach suitable spawning grounds or abundant food sources.

Minnows and small fishes are the mainstay of the walleye's diet. This versatile species will feed on just about any fish species smaller than they are.

many myths about fishing for walleyes and why this species is seemingly fickle and tough to catch.

The truth is walleyes are often hard to find because they are always on the move. Like any predator, their survival depends on finding enough to eat. From the moment walleyes are hatched, they are persistent predators. At first the target species of these predators are small zooplankton, but within weeks young walleyes are eating a wealth of small fishes.

So aggressive are these young walleyes that fish raised in stocking ponds begin to feed on one another if they are left in the ponds too long. In a matter of days an entire year class of walleyes can be wiped out except for a handful of well-fed survivors.

In the wild, walleyes survive in much the same way as a pack of wolves. Wolves have been reported to follow caribou herds hundreds of miles from the spring calving grounds to their winter haunts. Along the way the young, sick and injured are picked off by the wolves.

Walleyes feed in much the same way. Hungry packs of walleyes follow schools of baitfish relentlessly waiting for the right moment to pick off an easy meal.

The way walleyes hunt gives an insight into why this species is notorious for being here today and gone tomorrow. Bass are an ambush-style predator that lays in wait for prey to pass within striking distance.

Cover such as submerged weeds or wood plays an important role in providing bass a place to lay in ambush. The thicker the cover the better bass seem to like it. This close interaction with cover is the reason bass are often found in the same areas time and again.

Walleyes, like bass, will sometimes ambush prey, but this species hunts more like a shark than a bass. Walleyes locate prey species by constantly cruising the edges of cover, bottom structure or open water.

Anyone who has ever been ice fishing in a dark shanty and watched schools of yellow perch come and go, has witnessed a behavior that's typical of walleyes. Walleyes, sauger, saugeye and yellow perch are all members of the same family and are seemingly always on the move.

Open cover types such as scattered weeds or submerged stumps represent the perfect combination of cover and open water. Walleyes thrive in an environment where they can slowly cruise within or near a cover type that helps to hide them from their next meal.

Dense cover such as mats of coontail or other weeds that grow up to the surface are a less desirable habitat for walleyes. In this situation walleyes are forced to hunt the edges enabling forage species the option of easily escaping into the dense cover.

Forage types and the habitat requirements of these species largely determines where walleyes spend their time. For example, if a lake has an abundance of spottail shiners, these minnows tend to favor shallow shoreline cover and structure. Places where deep water and shallow water meet such as the edges of weed lines, points and sloping bottom contours, are logical places for walleyes and shiners to come in contact with one another.

Fisheries that support pelagic or open-water forage species such as smelt, alewives, emerald shiners, gizzard shad or young-of-the-year drum tend to lure walleyes into the open water. Walleyes tend to suspend below the forage fish, often forcing them to the surface where they can block any escape route and feed at will.

What's even more perplexing is that in any given body of water walleyes are likely to be located at any number of locations. Some walleyes seem to favor weed cover, while other fish in the same body of water find hunting for suspended forage more to their liking. Complex bodies of water that have a wide variety of forage and habitat types create the frustrating situation where walleyes can be just about anywhere at any time.

We know that forage species play a big role in the location of walleyes. It's also common knowledge that natural features such as points, reefs, islands or other "structure" are likely places to find both forage fish and walleyes.

Unfortunately, many of the obvious places to look for walleyes are too small to hold significant numbers of fish. Think of spots like the tips of points, small sunken islands or fast sloping breaks as a dinner table that provides a limited amount of seating. Larger features such as flats or large reefs are more likely to support impressive numbers of fish.

Large features attract more walleyes, but the fish are normally scattered and difficult to contact without covering lots of water. Hence, the ways we fish for walleyes has a lot to do with the types of areas where they are found.

Isolated or small spots can be fished efficiently and quickly with presentations such as jigging or casting slip bobbers. Larger spots such as flats are better tackled using a presentation that covers water. Drifting spinner rigs or trolling crankbaits are presentations that work well in such areas.

In order to fish walleyes successfully, anglers must be prepared to use any number of presentations including, but not limited to, trolling crankbaits, casting cranks, casting jigs, vertical jigging, dragging slip sinker rigs, pitching slip bobbers, drifting bottom bouncers and slow trolling spinner rigs. Sadly, very few anglers master all these presentations. Most anglers tend to fish using one or two favorite methods.

The primary reason so many anglers struggle at walleye fishing is because they are unwilling or unable to identify the presentation that is best suited at a particular time and place. Where walleyes are located dictates the best fishing presentation.

Some situations are more obvious than others. For example, if walleyes are found hovering around a sunken island in 30 feet of water, casting a slip bobber rig isn't going to be the most productive way to contact fish. A bottom bouncer with one of several different snell options is probably going to be a good way to start fishing.

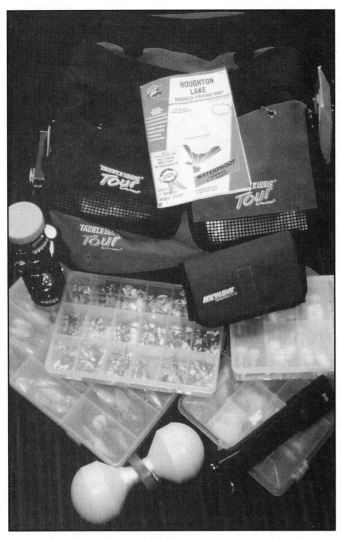

In order to catch walleyes consistently anglers must be skilled at using a wealth of tackle and presentations.

If walleyes are found feeding on river flats in 3 or 4 feet of water, it's going to be tough to position the boat directly over the top of the fish to jig vertically. Backing up and casting to the fish makes the most sense.

When walleyes are suspended in the water column it's not practical to use jigs. Trolling crankbaits, spinners or spoons is the best way to attack this situation.

The list of examples could go on and on. Walleye fishing boils down to a handful of presentation options that are dictated at least in part by fish location. Anglers routinely try to force feed walleyes with presentations that worked in the past, falling back on methods they have faith in rather than ones best suited to the situation. The result: frustrated

anglers that figure because their chosen angling methods aren't working that the fish aren't biting.

I've witnessed this happening more times than I can count. Even experienced walleye anglers often do poorly because they make the mistake of sticking with a presentation they are comfortable with, rather than trying different methods to see if others produce more or bigger fish.

Often this situation develops because an individual is especially skillful at one method of fishing. Usually the technique this angler masters is one that works well on a favorite or frequently fished body of water. When traveling from one body of water to the next, I often encounter anglers who are excellent jig fishermen on one lake, but put them on a different body of water with a crankbait and they don't know where to start.

So common is this problem that some of the leading names in fishing often are guilty of being near-sighted. The desire to fish using methods that are familiar and comfortable can be overwhelming. Yet it's clear to see the most consistently successful anglers are those who master all the common walleye fishing presentations. Good anglers use fishing presentations like tools to complete a job effectively and efficiently.

Even once an angler gains experience and faith in several different walleye fishing presentations, there is always the risk of falling victim to another common mistake. Once an angler has had success in a particular body of water with a specific presentation, it's common to apply this information as a blanket solution to catching fish.

No single fishing presentation always works in a given situation. Just the way walleyes shuffle the deck by moving from location to location, they also respond to angling presentations differently on different days.

Expecting walleyes that responded in one way today to respond exactly the same way tomorrow is a situation professional anglers jokingly refer to as fishing memories. Rather than experimenting with suitable presentations to see if the fish are more responsive to one over another, many anglers get tunnel vision based on what was working recently or what other anglers told them to use.

When walleyes don't jump on a method of fishing that was working recently, it's logical to figure they just aren't biting. This way of thinking gets walleye anglers into trouble time and again.

Forming pre-conceived notions of how walleyes will respond to various presentations is no different than force feeding walleyes. Don't hit the water convinced you have the answers.

Where walleyes are located dictates the types of presentations that are most suitable. This angler is casting jigs to walleyes in shallow water. Casting is a good way to reach out to fish that may easily be spooked by the boat.

Treat each new day on the water as a fresh beginning. If a particular presentation has been working well in a given spot, don't fix what isn't broken. However, if the fish are present and not responding, it's time to try other presentations.

Walleyes often ignore one presentation and attack another for no apparent reason. This trait is part of what makes fishing for walleyes so fun and challenging. Sometimes even a subtle change can make the difference.

Not long ago I was fishing walleyes on Lake Erie using bottom bouncer weights armed with snelled spinners and nightcrawlers. Fish were snapping up harnesses featuring No. 5 Colorado blades. The best colors were firetiger and green, but a number of other colors also produced fish. The following day, the graph indicated fish were still at home, but there were few volunteers interested in the identical rigs they hammered 24 hours earlier.

I started experimenting with blade colors and sizes. Eventually I discovered that what they wanted was a smaller blade with less vibration and flash. I dropped down to a No. 2 blade and the action picked up immediately.

The point of this whole chapter is to instill flexibility and creative thinking among anglers.

Approaching walleye fishing with a rigid set of standards and pre-conceived angling methods may produce results today and even tomorrow, but in the long run the unpredictable nature of this species always levels the playing field.

Walleyes are a species that we may never fully understand. A little information can be a dangerous thing and such is the case with walleyes and walleye fishing.

There are no absolutes in the walleye game. The standards for finding and catching these fish are constantly changing as our knowledge and understanding of the species grows. Becoming a more successful walleye angler is about approaching each new day on the water armed with the knowledge of yesterday, yet prepared to learn more for tomorrow.

Anglers who approach this species with an open mind, willingness to learn and desire to experiment are well on their way to catching more walleyes.

In the next chapter we'll focus on the ongoing chore of finding fish. The more skillful anglers become at locating walleyes, the more time they can dedicate to catching them.

CHAPTER 2
FINDING WALLEYES FAST

Time is the enemy of everyone who fishes for walleyes. Tournament anglers have a set amount of time to find and catch walleyes. Recreational anglers only have so much vacation time or so many days off work to dedicate to fishing.

Mike McClelland is a famous tournament angler who coined the phrase, "Walleyes are easy to catch, just hard to find." The truth is consistently finding walleyes is the challenging part of fishing for this species.

The time we can allow for fishing is limited and unfortunately the most time-consuming part of walleye fishing boils down to finding fish! The wandering nature of walleyes makes predicting their whereabouts a constant challenge. While I'm not opposed to a challenge, the process of finding fish takes precious time away from the fish-catching part.

I wish I had a quarter for every time I've spent several days looking for walleyes, only to locate a group of fish as the trip draws to a close. As my buddy Mike McClelland is so fond of saying, "Walleyes are easy to catch, just hard to find."

Mike suggests that the real challenge in walleye fishing is in the finding, not the catching. Of this there is no doubt, yet waxing philosophical doesn't make finding these popular fish any easier nor does it make the process any less frustrating.

Walleyes have the uncanny ability to survive and thrive in a wide range of environments. The adaptable characteristics of these fish is what makes them both a capable and resourceful predator.

For example, walleyes are frequent visitors to hard bottom areas holding perch, suckers and other bottom-dwellers. In the same lake, you could easily find walleyes using weed edges both to hunt for food and find cover from predators. If the same lake has a significant amount of submerged wood along the shoreline, walleyes will take advantage of this cover type as well. Should the lake support a suspended forage species such as emerald shiners, don't count out an open water bite.

Frankly, walleyes can be just about anywhere they find suitable supplies of food and cover. In the case of suspended, open-water fish, walleyes will even give up cover in favor of a readily available food source!

All this talk about the here-today, gone-tomorrow nature of walleyes isn't intended to scare anglers, but rather to prepare them for reality. Walleyes are not easy to locate because they are seemingly always on the move. It's interesting to note that the most useful information for consistently locating walleyes isn't gained by being the first one on the water.

THE INFORMATION GAME

How many times have you visited a new body of water, stopped at a bait shop, asked a few questions about where to find good fishing and headed directly for the boat ramp? Most anglers are cut from the same cloth. In short we are all in a hurry to go fishing.

When it comes to walleyes, time is usually better spent on shore collecting information than wasted blindly checking spots on the water. Recently I fished a tournament in Northern Michigan on a chain of lakes I had never fished before. Before leaving I purchased a map of the lakes and

Visiting with bait shop owners, conservation officers and other fishermen is the fastest way to get a "feel" for where walleyes are most likely to be.

spent a little time looking over the major features such as points, flats and weed beds.

Next, I called a conservation officer stationed in the region and asked some basic questions about walleye fishing on these lakes. I was interested in knowing if the lakes contained lots of fish or if walleyes were less numerous than other species. I also wanted to know which of the lakes he felt offered the best fishing. In addition, I was curious about the average size of the fish taken and if early summer, when we would be fishing, was a productive period.

Before I ended the conversation, I asked if he could recommend any local anglers or guides who might be able to provide some fresh fishing information. I called the contacts he suggested and asked them the same questions directed at the conservation officer. I also asked how they normally catch their fish, what depths produce the most or biggest fish, the types of cover or structure fish are most often found near and if there are obvious spots I should be checking out.

The day we arrived at the lake I stopped in at each of the three bait shops in town. At each I purchased some bait and asked the same set of questions. I showed them my map and asked if there were locations they would recommend trying for walleyes.

After visiting all the bait shops, talking with a conservation officer and several local anglers I started making note of the answers they gave. It became obvious that everyone agreed that one of the lakes in the chain held more fish, but that a different lake contained larger fish. I also learned that most of the local anglers prefer to fish spinners near the bottom, but that a suspended crankbait bite can be productive at times.

Based on the information obtained for these sources it was time to launch the boat and begin the on-the-water search. I convinced a friend who's interested in learning more about walleye fishing to spend a couple days on the water with me.

We launched the boat and motored directly to several key spots other anglers had recommended. A couple groups of boats were fishing in areas where we expected to see angling pressure. Figuring I could come back and check these obvious spots later, I decided to continue getting familiar with the lake by running the shoreline and checking out major features.

Several of the anglers I talked with indicated that 19 to 21 feet was a good depth at which to find fish and many of the spots anglers recommended trying were flats. At the north end of the

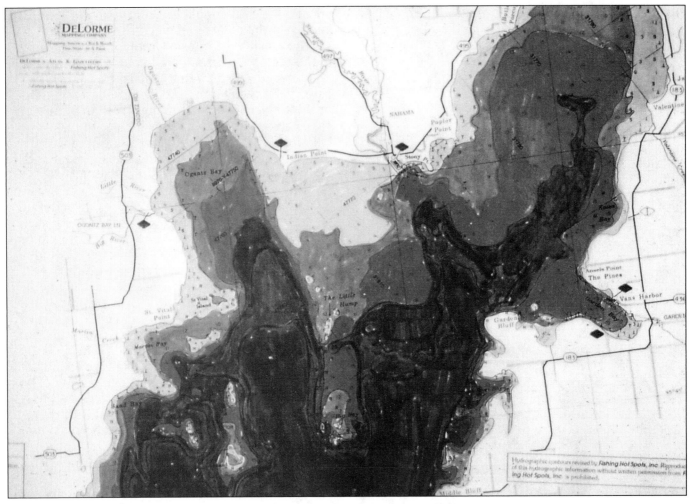

Maps are an invaluable aid to finding walleyes. Before each fishing trip, lay out the map and study the major features such as points, inflowing rivers, weed edges, reefs and open water basins.

lake the map showed a large flat stretching for miles, interrupted only by a major point. The flat gradually sloped from 18 to 23 feet of water.

When we arrived at the spot, no one was fishing the area. Slowly cruising the flat and watching the sonar turned up a good number of fish near the bottom and lots of baitfish both suspended and near the bottom.

This spot looked too good not to drop lines for a few minutes. Moments after breaking out bottom bouncers and spinner rigs we slipped a landing net under our first walleye. A few minutes later another fish came to net and during the course of the afternoon, several more fell victim to the same presentation.

Trolling as fast as I could and still keep contact with the bottom, I picked apart the flat, finding several spots-on-the-spot that seemed to hold more fish for some reason.

It was obvious my friend was impressed with how quickly we located and caught fish, but what he didn't know was how much time I devoted to finding fish before hitting the water. Had I not discovered from several sources that flats were producing fish, I might not have even given this particular spot a chance. Also, because the spot wasn't being pounded by local anglers, it produced more consistently than similar areas where boat pressure was heavy.

The most successful tournament anglers on the professional tours often arrive at a fishing site two or more days before the pre-fishing period begins. This extra time is spent not on the water, but talking to local anglers and bait shop owners. The pros will also visit boat landings, study maps and collect every bit of fishing information possible.

Some anglers even go so far as to color in the contour lines of their maps so they can more easily

Groups of boats make it easy to locate popular fishing sites or what are sometimes called community spots. Usually these sites are picked over and the fishing is spotty.

spot features of interest. Any GPS coordinates collected are written on the map for quick reference.

When fishing large bodies of water such as Lake Erie, it's common for two or three anglers to split the price of a small charter plane. By flying over the water it's easy to spot packs of boats that tend to form on the major schools of fish. The locations are then marked on a map for future reference.

Once all this information is collected, locating fish becomes a matter of checking potential spots. If the water is 15 feet deep or deeper, spend a lot of time cruising over the area watching the sonar unit closely. In most situations if fish are home, the sonar will confirm it.

Sometimes, fish holding very tight to bottom will not appear on the sonar screen. This is especially true if the bottom is irregular or has lots of rocks or boulders that fish can hide among.

This is the very reason I purchase the best quality sonar equipment I can get. A sonar unit that features 3,000 watts of power is going to mark fish holding tight to bottom better than ordinary units that feature 500 or 600 watts.

If the water is shallow, you'll need a crystal ball not a sonar unit to locate fish. In shallow water fish normally move out of the way of the boat before the sonar can mark them. Also, the-transducer coverage is so small that it's unlikely fish will be marked.

The only practical way to determine if fish are in shallow water is to fish for them. This is precisely why shallow water walleyes are so often overlooked, because anglers don't dedicate enough time to fishing shallow water thoroughly.

FINDING FISH ON UNCHARTED WATERS

All these tips for finding fish before launching the boat are helpful when maps and information can be readily collected. In some situations, anglers are faced with little or no advance information to go on.

This situation is common on fly-in fishing trips where a pilot drops a group of anglers on a remote lake, then comes back and picks them up a few days later. If you expect the outfitter or pilot to know where to fish, you're in trouble. Most of the time these guys are so busy they barely have time to sleep, let alone fish.

Another strike is the fact that most of these lakes aren't mapped. Anglers are forced to hunt for fish using nothing more than a sonar unit, intuition and hard work.

When on fly-in fishing trips I ask the pilot to circle the lake once or twice before he lands the plane. From the air a lot of features are easily noted such as major points that drop off into deep

Sonar is a valuable tool for locating walleyes in water more than 15 feet deep. Anglers are wise to purchase the best quality sonar equipment they can afford. Higher quality units feature more power and are better able to mark fish near bottom or among cover.

water, weed beds, islands, submerged islands that top out in shallow water and in-flowing rivers.

Make a mental map of the primary features. If nothing else you'll have a lay of the land that will be helpful in navigating the lake.

If a party of anglers are being flown out as you arrive, spend a few minutes visiting to find out how the fishing has been and the primary spots and techniques that produced.

I remember one fly-in trip where the fellas flying out passed on some information that turned out to be the key to our whole trip. The walleyes were biting best on jigs tipped with minnows. Having fished the lake before, these guys came prepared with minnow traps. Each day they emptied the traps of small minnows that provided countless walleyes.

When I heard that minnows were the trick, I talked them into selling me their minnow traps. I'm glad I did, because without minnows we would have struggled to catch fish. During our stay almost every fish we caught came on a jig and minnow.

Sometimes knowing where to fish isn't enough information. In this case you had to have minnows or you simply weren't going to catch many fish.

Should you arrive at the lake cold turkey with absolutely no information on where to find fish or what they are most likely to hit, spend the first day on the water looking over the lake with the help of a portable sonar unit. I'd sooner leave my fishing rods at home than my sonar. Without this fish-finding tool, you'll have little choice but to fish the points, shorelines and visible cover such as weeds or downed tree tops.

Most portable sonar units are powered using a couple of lantern batteries. Gel type batteries are a much better option. Not only do gel batteries hold a charge longer, they can be recharged and used over and over again. A rechargeable gel battery will pay for itself after only a few uses.

One gel battery will usually run a liquid crystal type sonar unit for several days. If no electricity is available to recharge batteries, be sure to take along a spare to insure power doesn't run short.

You'll also need something to hold the transducer in place on the transom of the boat. A handy bracket made especially for this purpose is produced by the Tite Lok company.

When fishing fly-in lakes have the pilot circle the lake a time or two before landing. From the air major features of the lake such as points, breaklines, weed beds and in-flowing streams can be readily spotted.

I enjoy the challenge of finding walleyes with nothing more to go by than a sonar unit and experience. It may take a while to locate fish, but once a location and pattern falls together the feeling of satisfaction is worth all the effort.

The time of year makes a big difference as to the whereabouts of walleyes in most waters. Remote fly-in trips are usually scheduled in May, June, July or August. Early in the spring, expect to find walleyes in or near areas suitable for spawning. If the lake has a major river flowing in, chances are walleyes will use this river for spawning. Expect to find walleyes in the river or at the point where the river dumps into the lake during May.

If a waterfall or rapids prevents fish from migrating upstream, you may have located a bonanza. Numerous times I've found hundreds and hundreds of walleyes packed up below a waterfall. In many cases you can hook a fish almost every cast!

If a body of water doesn't have a spawning stream, walleyes will lay their eggs on rock, gravel or sometimes sand bottoms where wave action provides a constant supply of oxygen-rich water. Spawning can take place in a foot or 2 of water all the way out to 20 foot or more.

When females lay their eggs they tend to spawn and then leave the area immediately. A number of males will normally fertilize the eggs. Perhaps waiting for more females to arrive, male walleyes tend to stay in the spawning grounds for weeks after the females have spawned and left.

Eventually even the spawn-crazy male walleyes return to the lake where they spread out to look for forage. Emerging weed beds that pop up in water from 4 to 10 feet deep can be one of the best places to locate these fish during June. It's here that perch collect to spawn, providing walleyes with a ready-made meal ticket.

As June flows into July, walleyes spread out in the lake and begin to take up residence on the deeper weed edges, points that drop into deep water and mid-lake structures such as sunken islands or the saddles between islands. Some fish may be shallow throughout the summer, especially if quality weeds such as cabbage or common pond weed are present. Large flats that support good weed growth can hold walleyes all summer long.

If weeds are a limited commodity, walleyes will begin showing up in much deeper water during July and August. Now the location of fish becomes much more difficult to predict. Walleyes can be found on sunken islands and reefs, saddles between islands, off the tips of major points or the mud basins in the middle of the lake.

If the lake has a forage species that often suspends in the water column, such as whitefish or ciscoes, an open water trolling bite can take place during the heat of summer. Trolling crankbaits or

A portable sonar unit is must-have equipment for fishing fly-in or other remote waters. A number of manufactures produce portable sonar units that come complete with sonar, battery, transducer and carrying case.

spinners with planer boards is going to be the most productive way to fish open water.

Sunken islands and mid-lake reefs are prime spots to check using bottom bouncers and spinner rigs or slip sinker rigs tipped with leeches or crawlers. It may be necessary to fish early in the morning, during the evenings and after dark to catch fish during the middle of summer.

The guys I fish with hit the water before first light, settling for coffee, a donut or a piece of toast instead of a full breakfast. By late morning the crew is back at camp and hungry as a bunch of lumberjacks. After eating it's time for a nap. Later in the day everyone heads for a boat and fishes until dark.

Late in the summer most of the walleyes caught are taken within an a couple hours either way of sunset and sunrise. This pattern holds

especially true in clear, natural lakes. The more "color" the water has the more likely walleyes will bite throughout the day.

The middle of the day is a good time to cruise the lake watching the sonar for significant pieces of bottom structure. To actually mark fish it will be necessary to slow the boat down to less than 10 mph. At higher speeds turbulence from the outboard prop and the boat hull make it difficult to mark fish.

PRESENTATIONS FOR HUNTING WALLEYES

We've touched briefly on some presentations to try in certain situations, but we haven't discussed how important it is to keep moving when hunting for walleyes. Cruising the lake and hunting for fish using the sonar unit is a good way to identify specific spots to fish. However, sooner or later it's going to be necessary to drop a line in the water and see if the marks your graph indicates are walleyes. For the record, there's no way to determine species by simply looking at fish marks on a sonar unit.

When walleyes are in shallow water, sonar is of little value in locating them. The only practical way to find walleyes in this situation is to break out a rod and fish for them.

When it comes to eliminating water, some presentations are more efficient than others. Jigging for example is a great way to catch walleyes, but a jig casted, dragged or drifted into position can take a lot of time to thoroughly fish potential water.

Faster presentations such as trolling crankbaits, dragging bottom bouncers or casting crankbaits rank as better choices when a lack of information forces anglers to move quickly until fish are found. Use these fast-paced presentations to sweep as much water as possible. Keep in mind the object is to locate an active fish or two that gives away the presence of others. Once fish are located chances are a slower presentation is going to produce more bites.

Locating a fish or two is a giant step in the right direction. Not only is this area likely to produce more fish, the door is now open to look for similar areas that may also be holding fish. If a map is handy for reference, note the physical characteristics of the area that's producing fish and look to see where other spots with similar features occur.

Without a map to guide you, it can be difficult finding areas similar to those that produced fish. A

Walleyes show up in patches of aquatic weeds soon after the spawning season is complete. Depending on the amount of weed cover and forage, some walleyes may spend the entire summer in the weeds.

trick that might help is to pay attention to the lay of the land. For instance, a cliff that drops off sharply to the water edge, most likely tapers sharply into the water. A shoreline as flat as a prairie probably continues in the water as a large slowly tapering flat.

MORE FISH-FINDING TIPS

It never hurts to check out any place where deep water and the shoreline meet. Walleyes are fond of forcing their prey into areas where a potential meal has a hard time escaping. Cliffs that dip into the water can be excellent places to find walleyes.

Narrow places where points jut out into the lake or the lake simply funnels down are also good places to look closely for walleyes. A natural current seems to form in these areas attracting walleyes during the spring, summer and fall seasons.

If your fishing trip occurs during a major insect hatch such as the giant mayflies common throughout the north, you can expect that walleyes will be stacked into the mud flats where these insect larva lay dormant in the mud waiting for the precise moment to hatch into a flying insect. In some lakes walleyes feed so heavily on mayflies that most of the fish in a given body of water will migrate to the primary areas where these flies hatch.

Lakes with weed cover and heavy boat traffic sometimes see a unique weed bite that occurs not on the deep water side of the weeds, but rather on the shallow water side. Wave action from boats and personal watercraft stir up the bottom creating an ideal situation for walleyes to slip into shallow water to feed.

The best fishing corresponds with the times boat traffic is heavy and the water clouds up. Plan on fishing this pattern from noon to 4 p.m. Boats tend to stay out of shallow water areas, setting the stage for bite that goes unnoticed on most bodies of water.

SUMMING IT UP

Compared to other species, walleyes are harder to locate on a day to day basis. No guarantees or absolutes can be provided as to the whereabouts of this elusive species. The fact is, finding walleyes is an on going chore that never ends. Every new day on the water begins with the task of finding fish that aren't where they are supposed to be or where they were yesterday.

Anglers who understand walleyes often joke that if these fish aren't shallow they're probably deep and if they aren't deep they're probably somewhere in between. The truth is walleyes can be almost anywhere. Finding fish fast is a chore that can only be accomplished by gaining as much information as possible, eliminating the unproductive or unlikely water and concentrating on presentations that make the best use of time.

Time is the enemy of walleye anglers. No matter how it's sliced, every minute spent looking for fish is another minute of lost fishing time.

In the next chapter we'll talk about the weather and how it impacts on walleye fishing.

CHAPTER 3

WEATHER AND WALLEYE

Weather is as important to fishermen as it is to farmers. Like the seeds sown by the farmer, walleyes are influenced by daily changes in weather conditions. In the case of fishing, some weather conditions are favorable and others seemingly cause walleyes to turn off like a switch.

There's hardly an angler who wouldn't agree that weather influences fish behavior, yet few understand how weather works or the specific impact it has on fish and wildlife. Planning your fishing trips to coincide with favorable weather and fishing conditions is every anglers dream wish. Unfortunately even weather forecasts from the best sources are wrong about 50 percent of the time. Ultimately, anglers are usually forced to tolerate whatever weather conditions and resulting fish moods occur.

Since we can't control the weather and in many cases we can't pick our fishing days, the only alternative anglers have is to develop angling strategies based on the mood and or feeding activity of the fish. Weather clearly plays a role in how walleyes react to various fishing presentations. Common sense also plays a role in how anglers approach various fishing conditions.

For example, during a major cold front walleyes become lethargic, less active and prone to ignore fast-moving lures. Common sense dictates that speed trolling crankbaits isn't going to be as effective as a slower presentation such as jigging or rigging that teases walleyes with an easy meal that's tough to resist.

On the flip side, when walleyes are biting readily, slow presentations waste valuable fishing time. It makes more sense to move quickly and cover as much water as possible in an effort to contact as many fish as possible.

HOW WEATHER WORKS

Before getting into tactics for catching walleyes in various weather conditions, it's important to understand how weather patterns occur.

"Heat is the mechanism that causes weather," says Dave Barrons an avid fisherman and TV weather specialist from Michigan. "Warm or cold air masses moving across the continent form

Not every day ends with calm weather and a beautiful sunset like this. Weather has a dramatic impact on walleye fishing and anglers are often forced to deal with less than ideal conditions.

Weather has a strong influence in both the activity level of fish and the presentations they are most likely to hit. This angler was faced with fishing in a stubborn cold front. He wisely selected a jig fished slowly along the bottom.

fronts that influence our daily weather patterns. A weather front is simply the boundary formed when one air mass pushes against another. A cold front is cold air pushing against relatively warm air and a warm front is relatively warm air pushing against a cool air mass."

Cold fronts often follow storms and are normally made up of air that's somewhat cooler than the surrounding air. Cold fronts also tend to be associated with clear skies and air temperatures that are several degrees cooler than the preceding air mass. The air in a cold front is also somewhat heavier than the air around it. Weather forecasters refer to this condi-

tion as a high pressure ridge and these masses of air tend to settle towards the ground.

Warm fronts are made up of air that's warmer and lighter than surrounding air. Because the air is warmer and lighter it rises into the atmosphere. Typically the barometric pressure is lower than that experienced with a cold front. Unlike cold fronts, warm fronts often form a vortex or spinning of air. In extreme cases when the barometric pressure drops sharply a tornado can result.

Low pressure air centers are storms waiting to happen. When a cold front collides with a warm front, the mixing of air can generate threatening weather.

The old joke; if you don't like the weather, wait a few minutes and it will change, rings true in the Midwest where walleye fishing has its strongest following. "The Midwest is located in what is sometimes called the 'Mixing Zone.' Cool air masses coming from the west and north mix with warmer air pushed up from the gulf states. The result is an unstable air mass that can generate a wealth of weather conditions including but not limited to rain, sleet, fog, drizzle, wind and snow."

The north and south fluctuations of the jet stream also have a profound impact on the weather. If the jet stream dips far to the south, residents of the north experience unseasonably cool conditions from cold northern air masses. The reverse holds true when the jet stream passes north into Canada, blocking cold arctic air and allowing warm moist air from the south to flood the region.

"The Midwest region is also prone to storms," says Barrons. "Many weather fronts that get started out west build momentum until they reach the Great Lakes region and mix with air masses coming in from the south. Different air masses coming together often causes storms to develop in this region."

During the spring and fall months weather is exceptionally unstable. Front after front passes through the nation from west to east making for unstable weather and fishing conditions just about everywhere. "Most states in the northern part of the nation only enjoy about three to five weeks of stable weather each summer and another three to five weeks of stable or predicable winter weather each year," explains Barrons. "The rest of the time we're open to a variety of unpredictable and often unpleasant weather conditions."

HOW WEATHER INFLUENCES WALLEYE ACTIVITY

Like all fish, walleye activity is influenced, in part, by weather conditions. The very best conditions for walleye fishing are periods of extended stable fair weather. Any time the weather stays the same for several days the fishing is likely to improve each day. Ideally these conditions would include warm or seasonally mild temperatures and some sunshine, but several days of cloud cover can also yield good fishing so long as the

Dr. Steven Holt caught this walleye on a hot and humid day with little or no wind. Weather like this is rarely associated with good fishing conditions, but the fact is walleyes often bite best in hot, stable weather.

daily temperature and wind conditions remain about the same.

Extended periods of hot and calm weather often cause walleyes to bite like there will be no tomorrow. Sometimes called the Dog Days of Summer, most anglers associate hot and sticky days as poor fishing conditions. While the warm weather is uncomfortable for anglers, the fishing action can be outstanding.

The worst conditions for finding cooperative walleyes are severe cold fronts that follow low pressure storms. Fishing success just prior to the storm front can often be excellent. Those folks who have bird feeders understand that just before a storm front arrives, feeding activity at the feeders is brisk. Wildlife can sense foul weather is approaching and will often feed heavily just prior to the storm. Walleyes are no exception to this rule.

However, once the storm passes the cold front that follows can spell lousy fishing conditions for several days. Typically these cold fronts arrive featuring bright clear skies and a dramatic temperature drop that not only impacts on air temperature, but can cause water temperatures to plunge as well. High barometric pressure takes over the scene and walleyes that were active just a day or two prior seemingly disappear.

While no one knows for sure why walleyes and other fish often "turn off" in cold front conditions, it's logical that groups of active fish may disperse or simply head for cover and lay low for a day or two. Perhaps the increased light penetration triggers this or maybe its the high barometric pressure. Whatever the cause, the day a cold front arrives and the next couple days are usually associated with poor fishing success.

Each day that passes after a cold front, anglers can expect the fishing to improve until eventually fishing success completely recovers. Unfortunately within days or sometimes hours a new cold front approaches threatening to repeat the whole process. And so it goes.

Cold front conditions seem to have the most dramatic impact on natural lakes and other clear-water fisheries. On numerous occasions I've witnessed fishing conditions on clear-water fisheries go from boom to bust overnight. In each case, a dramatic high pressure center and cold front could be blamed for the poor fishing conditions.

Rivers seem to be impacted least by cold fronts. I've often experienced good to excellent river fishing during a cold front. The answer to this phenomenon could be as simple as light pene-

Increased activity at a bird feeder can be an indication of an approaching storm and low pressure cell. Fish and other wildlife have an uncanny ability to sense these changes in weather.

tration. Rivers tend to be more turbid while natural lakes are often clear and allow maximum light penetration. Perhaps barometric or air pressure doesn't impact as strongly on flowing water as still water. The fact is no one knows for sure how or why walleyes react to cold fronts.

A few clear-water fisheries are known for producing fair to good fishing in cold fronts. Lake Erie is a classic example. The sheer number of fish in this system seems to offset the negative effects of cold fronts. Apparently, with so many fish available, some that are interested in feeding can be located despite weather conditions. To a lesser degree the same could be said of other large walleye fisheries with abundant populations of fish.

WEATHER-BASED FISHING STRATEGIES

Just about everyone who fishes knows that sooner or later the weather is going to throw a monkey wrench into the fish batter. Despite the fact that weather can often make for poor fishing conditions, that's no reason to stay home. Even when faced with the worst cold fronts, walleyes can be located and caught when anglers approach the situation with some common sense rules.

Locating feeding walleyes after a cold front presents a problem. Not only are fish less likely to bite, schools tend to disperse making it tougher to locate concentrations of fish. What's worse, the fast-paced fishing presentations anglers often depend on to find fish are less likely to produce strikes during a harsh cold front.

During a cold front anglers have little recourse but to slow down and use presentations that cover water slowly and thoroughly. It's also important to focus on known fish-holding structure or cover when fishing in frontal conditions.

If you're new to a body of water, consult with local bait and tackle shops, resort owners, conservation officers or anyone who knows the fishery and is willing to help. Fishing maps, especially those produced by Fishing Hot Spots, Inc., often show popular fishing sites as shaded areas on the map.

Once some sites that routinely hold fish are identified, visit these areas and, using your sonar, get a feel for the size of the structure and cover type. Large complex features are more likely to hold numbers of fish than small isolated sites.

If you can get recent fishing reports that identify where walleyes were caught in the last day or two, these spots are going to be prime locations to search for walleyes during cold fronts. Dependable, fresh information can help eliminate a lot of time spent trying spots that may or may not hold fish.

Concentrate fishing efforts during the prime morning and evening hours and be patient. Fishing after dark can be a good way to scrape up a few fish that otherwise would not have been caught.

When faced with brutal cold fronts a slow and accurate presentation that literally teases walleyes into biting is usually the best. Live bait is going to be better than artificial baits most of the time. Angling methods such as slip sinker rigging, jigging or slip bobbers are a few popular ways to fish live bait slowly and precisely.

If artificial lures are used, try trolling more slowly than normal or using baits with a more subtle or subdued action. For example, stickbaits feature a more subtle wobble than lipped crankbaits. Slow trolling stickbaits weighted with in-line sinkers is one way anglers on Lake Erie and other large bodies of water hunt for open-water fish during cold fronts.

It's not a bad idea to concentrate fishing efforts on rivers during cold front periods. It's not known for sure why river fish seem to be less impacted by cold fronts than walleyes living in natural lakes, but this fact is obvious to anyone who has spent a fair amount of time fishing both types of water.

Gradually, the negative effect of cold fronts diminish and stable weather begins to take control. When fishing conditions improve, switch to techniques that cover more water and speed up the search for walleyes a little. Depending on the situation, a bottom bouncer armed with a snelled spinner and juicy nightcrawler may be the best choice when drifted or slow trolled along the bottom. Another good choice would be a crankbait cast or slow trolled into position. Each of these methods are faster presentations that are useful for covering water quickly and efficiently.

Covering water quickly enables anglers to search for active pods of walleyes that could be difficult to locate with slower presentations such as jigs or slip sinker rigs. Once fish are found the

Rick LaCourse of Oregon, Ohio used stickbaits to troll up this Lake Erie walleye during a nasty cold front. The key to success in frontal conditions is to slow down and use baits with a more subdued action.

angler will be faced with the decision of sticking with the presentation that located and caught fish, or changing presentations to match the conditions.

When faced with this problem remember that fish location dictates presentation. If fish are located in loose groups or scattered along flats, trolling, casting or drifting crankbaits or spinners generally is the best way to catch walleyes. If a concentration of fish are located on an isolated point, hump or particular piece of bottom structure or cover, precise presentations such as casting jigs, jigging spoons or slip bobber rigs are going to be the most efficient ways of catching more walleyes.

in windy conditions and switch instead to jig dragging or another presentation.

Wind can help or hurt your chosen presentation, but one thing always remains constant. Successful anglers work with the wind instead of trying to fight it. When drifting, if the wind becomes too strong, use a sea anchor to slow down the boat's drifting speed.

When trolling with the wind the boat's forward speed is influenced both by the wind and the motor thrust. Throttle down to maintain the ideal speed. In exceptionally windy weather it may be

A sea anchor is a useful tool for controlling boat speed while drifting. The most successful walleye anglers learn to work with the wind instead of against it.

MANAGING THE WIND

In walleye fishing the wind can be an angler's friend or foe. A little wind helps many presentations such as drifting, trolling or casting slip bobbers by moving the boat or bait, breaking up the surface of the water and reducing light penetration.

By the same token, wind can make some presentations more difficult to use. It's tough to feel bites while casting jigs when the wind puts a bow in the fishing line. Avoid jig casting presentations

Walleyes living in rivers seem to be less impacted by cold fronts than those living in natural lakes or reservoirs.

Monitoring weather broadcasts on a VHF marine radio is a good way to stay on top of changing weather conditions.

necessary to put the boat in and out of gear periodically to slow down the trolling speed.

Troll with the waves and make short and precise downwind passes through the school of fish, then pick up lines, run back up wind, set up again and make another pass. While this might seem like a lot of work, turning the boat into the wind and trying to troll against the waves causes a number of problems.

Trolling against the wind makes it tough to control the boat and trolling speed. If a fish is hooked, the boat must be kept moving forward at a steady speed to avoid giving the fish slack line. Fighting the wind requires someone to be steering the boat constantly and rarely produces better results than trolling with the wind.

When anchoring in the wind to cast slip bobbers, always anchor with the bow into the wind and have enough anchor rope available to insure the anchor holds securely. It's a good rule of

thumb to have at least three to four times as much anchor rope as the water is deep. In other words, to anchor in 25 feet of water, plan on having up to 100 feet of anchor line.

A little wind is often a good thing in walleye fishing, but too much wind can turn a fun fishing adventure into a dangerous situation. Walleyes are often taken on large bodies of water that can become unsafe for small boats at a moment's notice.

"Anglers who venture onto large bodies of water need to pay especially close attention to weather reports," says Dave Barrons. "Your local weather report on the TV or radio isn't enough information. I recommend watching reports on the Weather Channel, contacting the National Weather Bureau, monitoring weather broadcasts on marine radios and visiting with local Coast Guard stations. To insure you don't get caught on big water in heavy winds, monitor every weather source you can and keep tabs of weather trends over the past couple of days."

Wind is represented on a weather map by isobars or parallel lines. When the lines are close together windy conditions will occur. When the isobars are spaced out, calm conditions will prevail.

Knowing what wind conditions to expect on the water is a major part of monitoring the weather. Every fisherman should consider investing in a VHF marine radio that also has a weather band. Monitoring these weather broadcasts can warn anglers of threatening weather and should the need arise, allow anglers to call for help.

VHF marine radios operate using line of sight transmission. In other words, the taller your antenna the further you'll be able to broadcast or receive messages. Hand-held style radios typically offer ranges varying from a mile to 5 miles. Base units with a 3-foot antenna normally reach out to about 5 miles and radios with 8-foot antennas can broadcast up to 10 or 15 miles.

Weather is a walleye fishing variable that no one can control. The key to having success is understanding how different weather patterns are likely to impact on fishing conditions and adjusting fishing strategies accordingly.

Having a barometer handy is a good idea for any serious fisherman. While we don't know exactly how weather patterns influence fishing success, we do know that barometric pressure does seem to have a measurable impact.

Dave Barrons suggests purchasing a fisherman's barometer and taking note that the best times to fish will normally be with barometric pressure readings between 29.85 and 30.1 inches. Straight up on a barometer is 29.95 and usually fishing is best in stable weather or during a slowly falling or rising barometer.

In other words when the needle is straight up or slightly left or right of center fishing is potentially going to be at its best. When the needle drops quickly, a storm is likely on the way and anglers should stay off the water.

So many variables are associated with weather that a multitude of fishing problems result. There are no easy answers to these problems. Unfortunately the way weather impacts on walleyes is still mostly a mystery.

Despite all we know about what causes weather and how to predict it, finding and catching walleyes in tough weather conditions is one of those challenges we may never fully conquer. When it comes to weather and walleyes, anglers are forced to play it conservative. Use common sense, fish slowly and make the best of what may simply be lousy fishing conditions. If this advice sounds a lot like biting the bullet, remember that a bad day of fishing is better than a good day at work!

In the next chapter the topic turns to caring for live bait. Healthy live bait is a critical part of many walleye fishing presentations.

CHAPTER 4
SELECTING AND CARING FOR LIVE BAIT

I'm often asked, will walleye tournaments ever ban the use of live bait? My answer is always the same: I hope not! To me live bait is as much a part of walleye fishing as the spinner bait is to bass angling. While I often catch walleyes on artificial lures, I simply can't imagine not enjoying the angling edge that live bait provides.

All too often I've witnessed angling situations where live bait out produced artificial lures. In

keeping, I've also seen when one type of live bait was more productive than another.

One situation in particular still haunts me, although it happened more than 10 years ago. I was fishing a popular lake in Ontario around the season opener in mid-May. The lake is noted for producing excellent numbers and good-sized walleyes. I showed up at the local bait shop prepared to purchase minnows, but I got sticker shock

Nightcrawlers, minnows and leeches are the three most popular live baits. Care for them and they will catch fish.

when I realized the owner was charging $5.00 per dozen and each dozen was carefully counted out!

I elected to purchase a couple dozen nightcrawlers instead of the minnows, even though the owner provided a friendly reminder that minnows were producing better. Once on the water I quickly realized the error of my ways. Boats all around us were catching walleyes at will, and you guessed it, they were using minnows. I couldn't buy a bite on nightcrawlers or jigs dressed with plastic grubs or crankbaits or anything else for that matter.

After several hours of frustration I couldn't stand the humiliation any longer. I turned the boat towards the launch site and headed directly to the bait store. The smirk on the owners face said it all when I asked for a couple dozen walleye minnows.

Convinced that I had the tools to make short work of a limit of walleyes, I rushed back to the lake and motored directly to the spot where, moments ago, fish appeared to be lining up to be caught. My first cast produced a nice fish. Moments later I caught another, but as if a light switch was turned off, the bite soon died. A storm front moved in and cold rain and wind ruined the fishing for the next few days.

After spending several hundred dollars in lodging, gas, food and tackle, I let $10 worth of minnows ruin what could have been a memorable day on the water. That bitter lesson taught me the basic facts about live-bait fishing. It's impossible to predict exactly which type of live bait will be the most productive on any given day. I also learned you can't force feed walleyes no matter how hard you try.

These days if I expect to fish live bait, I take along a good supply of minnows, leeches and nightcrawlers just to be sure I have what the fish want. I experiment with all three baits and let the fish tell me which one they prefer.

Keeping all these baits alive and frisky can be a tricky undertaking, especially during the summer when the weather is hot. Some species such as minnows are especially hard to keep alive without some special equipment and care.

MINNOWS

The term minnows is used to describe a wealth of fish species that commonly end up at the point of a hook. Some species are more hardy and easier to keep healthy than others. For example, emerald shiners are one of the most common

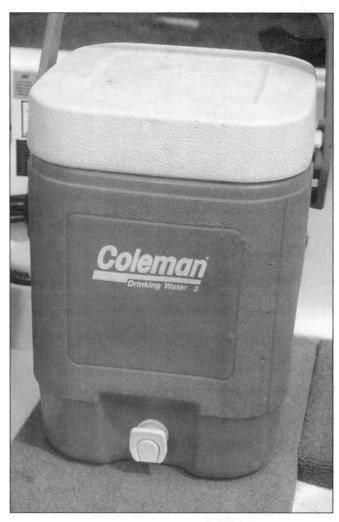

Coolers with snap-down lids make excellent bait containers for minnows. The insulation value provided by a cooler helps to keep the water cool and the oxygen level high.

minnow species. A beautiful little fish, emerald shiners feature a silvery coloration mixed with iridescent blues, greens and pinks. If these bait fish weren't so popular with fishermen, you might expect to see them sold in tropical fish stores.

As attractive as emerald shiners are, they are just as delicate and difficult to keep alive. The oxygen requirements of these minnows is much higher than other species. Over crowding them in a bait bucket is the fastest way to turn them all belly up. Delicate species such as emerald shiners need to be stored in a container that features an aeration or oxygen circulation system. A number of bait buckets come with battery-powered aerators that keep the dissolved oxygen content in the water high and minnows healthy. These buckets range in size from models that hold 3 gallons to oversized models that hold 20 gallons of water.

A cooler with a snap-down lid can also be easily converted to an aerated bait tank by rigging a bilge pump or other aerator style pump in the cooler. Insulated coolers also have the benefit of keeping the water temperature down so that a higher percentage of dissolved oxygen can be maintained in the water.

Some fishing boats feature aerated bait wells that do an excellent job of keeping minnows or leeches healthy. If the bait well in your boat is located in front of the steering console, check the water level each time you motor from one spot to the next. The sloshing motion can cause much of the water to drain out the overflow while the boat is moving from spot to spot.

I frequently store minnows in a small bucket that fits nicely in my live well located at the rear of the boat. The bucket confines the minnows so they are easy to catch, yet there's plenty of oxygen because the live well features both an aeration and re-circulation system. My boat features timers on the aeration and re-circulation system that allows me to control how often these systems kick on. Leaving the aeration system in the live wells running all the time can drain the boat's cranking battery in short order.

Selecting minnow species that are more hardy is an easy way to insure your bait will be frisky when needed. Fathead minnows are not only one of the more common species, they also require very little care. Small sucker minnows are hardy and a good choice. Other top minnow choices include spottail shiners, dace and chubs.

LEECHES

One man's bait is another man's nightmare. Ribbon leeches are a popular fishing bait, but not every angler considers these creatures to be user friendly. While they are perfectly harmless, leeches won't win any beauty contests.

What leeches lack in beauty they make up for in wiggle, fish catching ability and hardiness. So long as they are provided a constant supply of cool fresh water, leeches will thrive for several weeks. The first step in caring for leeches is to remove them from the delicate cottage cheese cartons they are often sold in. A number of durable plastic containers designed for storing leeches are available. I've found that a small plastic drink cup with a lid that snaps down

The author's wife, Mari, rates leeches as her least favorite walleye bait!

securely or a plastic bucket designed for freezing foods makes a great leech container. Punch a few small holes in the lid of the container so there is a flow of fresh water and place the cup in a bait well, live well or bait bucket with a battery-powered aeration system.

Between fishing trips leeches can be stored in this same plastic container in the refrigerator. Those who are not willing to mix fish bait with the family food, can store leeches, crawlers and minnows in an old refrigerator or one of the small campus-sized units purchased especially for this purpose.

NIGHTCRAWLERS

Nightcrawlers may be the most universal fish bait known to man. One thing is for sure, more

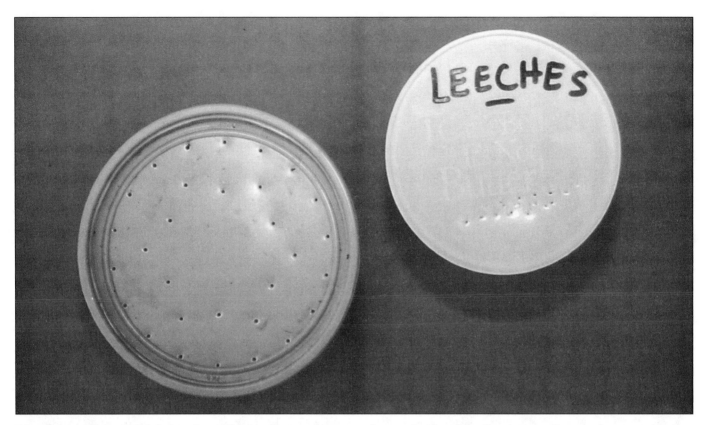

Plastic containers with snap-down lids make good storage boxes for leeches. Be sure to change the water regularly and keep leeches cool.

nightcrawlers are sold to walleye fishermen than minnows and leeches combined.

The popularity of nightcrawlers can certainly be linked to their renowned ability to trigger fish to bite, but the reason nightcrawlers work so well on walleyes is a mystery. Nightcrawlers aren't exactly a natural food for this species, but that doesn't seem to bother the fish.

My buddy and popular walleye fishing pro Mike McClelland likes to say that the first nightcrawler a walleye ever sees is going to have a hook in it! Mike's assessment of the relationship between walleyes and nightcrawlers is accurate, but don't leave for your favorite walleye lake without a good supply of crawlers.

Nightcrawlers can easily be kept for weeks with minimal care. That's why many anglers purchase crawlers not by the dozen, but by the flat. A flat of nightcrawlers contains approximately 500 worms. When large quantities of crawlers are purchased the price per dozen goes down sharply. Often a couple anglers will go in together to share the savings.

Worm flats are normally made from foam that works fine as a home base storage container, but not as a means of traveling with or storing night-crawlers while actually fishing. I use a couple plastic coolers for storing and using crawlers while on the road. A 40-quart cooler is used as the main storage container and a small six-pack style cooler used to haul a daily supply of crawlers in the boat.

When flats come from the bait dealer they are usually filled with rich organic soil, peat moss or commercial worm bedding. Commercial worm bedding is typically paper that's ground up to a fine texture.

All three of these bedding materials work well, but soil is messy. I prefer to use peat moss or commercial paper bedding because it keeps both my hands and boat cleaner.

The most important consideration when buying, using and storing nightcrawlers is temperature. If nightcrawlers are exposed to temperatures above 50 degrees they will quickly die.

A simple photography thermometer is a good investment when it comes to monitoring the temperature of nightcrawler bedding. Drop one in the bedding and check it periodically to be sure the bedding remains below the critical 50-degree mark.

There are lots of ways to keep worms cool, but most anglers depend on ice to keep the worms

Nightcrawlers are usually sold by the dozen, but better prices can be had if crawlers are purchased by the flat. A flat usually holds around 500 crawlers.

and bedding material the ideal temperature. Water is the other enemy of nightcrawlers. Worm bedding should be moist, but not wet. If ice is simply placed on the bedding, when it melts the bedding becomes saturated and the worms can't breathe. Chemical style freezer packs are a popular way of keeping the bedding cool without the worry of melting ice spoiling the bedding. For day trips this method works nicely, but on extended trips where a freezer isn't handy, ice is the only practical way to keep the bedding below 50 degrees.

Fill a plastic container with ice cubes and seal it with a water tight lid. Next place this container of ice in a cooler filled with worms and bedding. As the ice melts inside the container, simply remove it and pour out the water, add more ice cubes and you're good to go.

To condition crawlers into the largest possible specimens, buy some commercial worm food and sprinkle a little on the top of the worm bedding in your main storage container. When all the food has disappeared from the top of the bedding, add a little more.

Here's a trick I learned years ago that helps keep the mess associated with fishing with crawlers to a minimum. Keep a plastic bucket the size they used to sell ice cream stored in your boat. When fishing crawlers, fill the bucket with water and each time you take a crawler out to use it, dip the crawler in the clean water to wash off loose bedding. Hook the worm as desired and then rinse your hands off again in the bucket. Keep a towel handy to dry your hands and you'll be amazed how much cleaner crawler fishing becomes.

When the water gets dirty, simply replace it with clean water. Some anglers go so far as to rinse dirt bedding off their crawlers before putting them in a peat moss or paper bedding material. It all depends on how clean you like to keep your boat, and how much you hate black stuff under your fingernails and how much effort you're willing to put into it.

STORING BAIT WHILE ICE FISHING

When ice fishing minnows are the primary live bait used for walleyes. Keeping the water cool isn't a problem, but keeping the water from freezing can be. A small insulated cooler is the best way to prevent the water from freezing. I use a 3-gallon Coleman drink cooler with a handle that locks the lid down securely. That way if the cooler gets tipped over while I'm traveling from one spot to another, my supply of minnows is safe.

If weight is a concern, try storing a dozen minnows in a gallon-size drink cooler with a screw type lid. These spill proof containers are durable and will do an excellent job of keeping minnows alive and healthy.

WHAT WORKS WHEN

As mentioned earlier, the best strategy for live bait fishing is to have a selection of all three common types handy. Experiment with baits and let the fish decide. However, be advised that there are

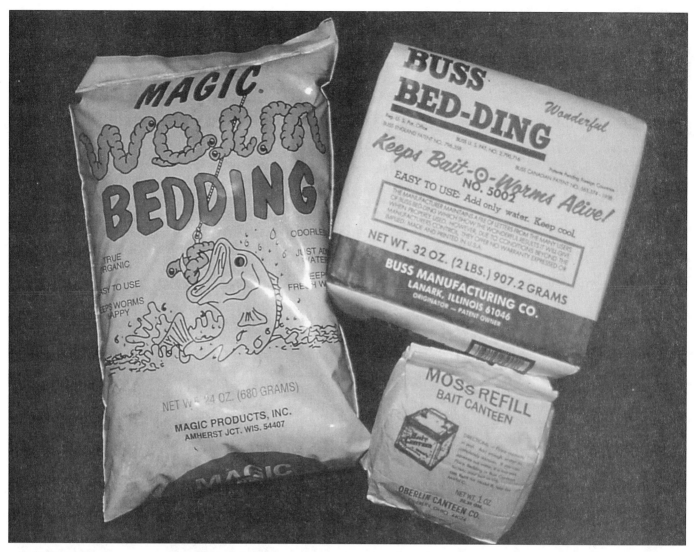

Commercial paper worm bedding is cleaner to work with than the soil worms usually come packed in. When adding water to commercial bedding, make sure to squeeze out excess water and chill the bedding before adding the worms.

times when certain types of bait are likely to be more popular.

A few years back I had an experience while fishing an In-Fisherman/Cabela's tournament on Lake Erie that sticks with me. The local bait stores only had small emerald shiner minnows netted from the lake. Less than ideal bait, the average minnow was the size normally used for perch fishing. Keeping these delicate under-developed minnows on a jig was driving me nuts.

In frustration I contacted a friend of mine who sells bait and had him ship me a gallon of fathead minnows. The minnows arrived in good shape and I transferred them into a wire basket that hung on the end of the dock. On the first day of the tournament the pro angler I was paired with

for the day elected to use the small emerald shiners available locally.

As I recall, his theory was that walleyes wouldn't hit minnows that aren't native to their environment. He was right about one thing, fatheads aren't native to Lake Erie. However, within minutes it was obvious my non-native fatheads were not only welcomed by the walleyes, but they were out-producing the native shiners four-to-one. I caught fish almost at will, meanwhile my competition became more and more frustrated until finally he broke down and asked if he could use some of my fatheads!

My fatheads worked because they were the right size and they wiggled and squirmed like a minnow is supposed to. The small shiners were

A thermometer is a handy item for insuring crawlers stay cool. The temperature of worm bedding should never exceed 50 degrees.

in bad shape the second you put a hook in them. A limp and lifeless shiner just can't compete with a healthy fathead or any other minnow for that matter.

After the tournament, I stopped at the Detroit River for a day of fun fishing on my way home. I told my buddy at the local bait shop about my fathead experience and he smiled. "Those fatheads may have worked on Lake Erie, but don't bother using mud minnows here in the river," was his advice.

Curious how fatheads would compare to healthy 3-inch shiner minnows, I bought some shiners and headed for the river. On one rod I fished shiners all day and on the other I fished the fatheads left over from Lake Erie. The results? A dead tie. Walleyes slurped up both varieties of minnows with equal enthusiasm.

The moral of these stories? Don't worry about the species of minnow you're using, just make

sure you have plenty of healthy bait in the size walleyes are used to feeding on.

When it comes to fishing with live bait, some general rules usually apply.

Early in the spring during the spawning and post-spawn period, it's hard to beat a healthy minnow as bait. Not only are minnows easy to keep and use at this time of year, experience dictates that in most instances walleyes will favor minnows in cold to cool water.

About the time water temperatures rise into the upper 40-degree range, nightcrawlers become a strong candidate for live-bait fishing. Leeches can also be effective when the water temperature nears this magic mark.

During the summer months, crawlers and leeches are hands down the most popular choice

As a general rule minnows are most effective as a walleye bait during the spring, fall and winter months when they can be kept alive easily.

Bigger than normal minnows are an advantage when fishing during the fall.

among live bait fishermen. Part of this choice relates to the fact that keeping minnows alive during the summer is tough and anglers tend to use other easier-to-store bait. That doesn't mean that walleyes won't hit minnows during the summer or that anglers shouldn't try using them. It only means that minnows are a struggle to keep alive during the warm periods of the year.

In the fall, both crawlers and minnows are great choices for live-bait fishing. Leeches work in the fall as well, but supplies of these fish-catchers are often hard to come by during the fall.

In fall, a trend towards larger minnows also develops. The 2- or 3-inch minnows that worked well during the spring and summer may not be the best choice during the fall. Walleyes and saugers show a preference for larger minnows during the fall. Perhaps these fish instinctively know that winter is coming and that eating larger meals helps increase food intake while reducing the amount of energy required to find food. Maybe walleyes are conditioned to feed

on larger prey because most of the minnows in their environment are nearing mature size. Whatever the reason, few anglers who have fished extensively in the fall would disagree that big minnows produce more fish than small minnows.

One of my favorite baits to use in the fall is a 4- to 6-six inch red-tail chub. These delicate minnows require lots of care. Keep them in an aerated cooler or the baitwell of your boat and make sure to check them often for signs that they are stressed.

If you can't find red-tails, creek chubs, golden shiners or small suckers are good choices for fall fishing.

The key to successfully using live bait is finding a healthy supply and taking the steps to keep it that way. Live bait needs care on and off the water. A little care insures that your minnows will have spunk, leeches will have unlimited wiggle and crawlers plenty of squirm.

In the next chapter we'll explore rods, reels and lines that are best suited for walleye fishing.

CHAPTER 5

ESSENTIAL RODS, REELS & LINES

Walleye anglers can learn a lot from bass fishermen. Take a quick peek into an avid bass angler's boat and you're likely to find a different rod and reel combination for every presentation he expects to encounter during his day of fishing. You'll find graphite spinning rods rigged with light line for casting small tube baits and grubs, baitcasting combinations for spinnerbait fishing, fiberglass rods designed with soft actions for throwing crankbaits and flippin' sticks for working weedless jigs into heavy cover.

To the casual angler all these different rod and reel combinations may seem excessive, but the truth is a bass angler who uses a specific rod for a specific fishing presentation is no different than a carpenter who uses a framing hammer to drive spikes and a lighter hammer for finish nails. Imagine the futility of trying to cut trim boards with a chain saw or using a screwdriver as a nail set.

Walleye anglers need to think of rods and reels as tools that help to complete various fishing tasks in a successful and efficient manner. One of the best ways to explore rod, reel and line combinations is to take a detailed look at each of the common methods used to catch walleyes. The good news is that certain rod and reel combinations can be used effectively for several different presentations. The bad news is, some fishing presentations such as trolling will require purchasing matched sets of gear so the maximum number of lines allowed by law can be fished.

JIG CASTING

Jig casting is not only one of the most common ways to catch walleyes, it's also one of the most enjoyable. It's tough to beat the feeling of a walleye slurping up a jig or the sense of satisfaction an angler gets when setting the hook into a stubborn fish.

Effective jig casting calls for a spinning rod that is light in weight, sensitive and rather short. The best jig casting rods are between 5-1/2 feet to 6 feet long. The action of this rod can vary from medium/light to medium.

Rods made from a high percentage of graphite fiber are the only logical choices. Avoid fiberglass or glass/graphite composite rods for jig casting. These rods do not have the lightness and sensitivity characteristics it takes to feel subtle bites.

Graphite is the place to start your search, but don't make a hasty decision when picking out a jig casting rod. The graphite fiber used in fishing rods comes in a number of different grades. Some of the common grades or marketing names used with graphite rods include IM6, IM7, IM8, HM54, HM85. As you might expect, the grades that are the lightest, most sensitive and best able to telegraph vibra-

Walleye anglers can learn a lot from bass fishermen. Bass anglers routinely use rods and reels that are designed for a specific presentation. The same should be true of walleye anglers.

tions are the most expensive. Unfortunately, these rods also tend to be the most fragile.

Graphite rods typically range in price from $50 to $300. For most anglers the brand or model they purchase boils down to how much time is spent fishing and how much money can be invested. Concerns about brands and budgets aside, the best advice I can give you is to purchase the best quality jigging rod you can comfortably afford.

For many years I've conducted most of my jig casting with a 6-foot medium-action spinning rod produced by Quantum known as the Tour Edition IM7. The model I use features a cork, Tennessee-style handle that requires the reel to be taped in place using friction or electrical tape.

I prefer rods with Tennessee-style handles over rods with fixed reel seats for a couple reasons. Taping the reel onto the handle allows me to position the reel at the exact point on the rod handle that causes the combination to balance perfectly in my hand. Not having a reel seat on the rod also makes the overall package a little lighter.

More important than the brand, graphite content or the design is the fact that I've used this rod extensively and become comfortable with it. Once you find a jig casting rod that is comfortable to fish, stick with it.

This style of rod craves a light spinning reel. It would be silly to purchase a high quality graphite rod and arm it with a large, bulky and heavy spinning reel.

Most spinning reels are sized by number, but some are sized by the line capacity. I normally select a size No. 1 reel for jig casting or a reel that's capable of handling 100-150 yards of 6-pound test monofilament. Larger reels aren't necessary and they simply add unwanted weight to the overall rod and reel combination.

Continuous anti-reverse is one of the important features to look for when shopping for spinning reels. Reels with continuous anti-reverse have none of the annoying slop or play in the handle typical of lesser reels. This simple feature enables anglers to maintain better contact with their lure, therefore increasing the overall sensitivity of the rod and reel combination. When a bite occurs, continuous anti-reverse also insures a quick and solid hook set.

The best lines for jig casting are premium quality monofilament. Monofilament has just the right amount of controlled stretch that is ideal for jig casting situations. Many of the co-polymer lines on the market are formulated to come off the reel spool smoothly and without coils that can cause tangles and reduce sensitivity. Stren's popular Easy Cast is a good example of a co-polymer line that performs flawlessly for jig casting. Other good lines for this application include Berkley Trilene Pro Select, Super Silver Thread and Spiderwire Super Mono.

The line properties that are important for jig casting include good knot strength, low diameter, limpness and low memory. When selecting a line

These anglers are casting jigs using a graphite spinning combination. A medium-action rod about 6 feet long is ideal.

The author prefers to use spinning rods with a Tennessee-style handle because the reel can be taped into place at exactly the balance point that feels best.

color, it's important to be able to see the line, but some of the line colors designed to be visible can be overkill in this department. Berkley's Solar and Stren's Golden are two examples of products that are more visible than necessary in most situations.

I've always found that Stren's Clear/Blue High Vis offers just the right combination of visibility above water and stealth underwater. Berkley's Clear/Blue Fluorescent has similar properties.

VERTICAL JIGGING

Vertical jigging is a presentation that calls for a more specific spinning rod action than casting. Normally conducted in rivers early and late in the season when the water is cold and walleyes are lethargic, a vertical jigging rod must provide the ultimate in sensitivity and deliver a little stiffer action than recommended for other applications. For this presentation rods from 5-1/2 feet to 6 feet are pre-

ferred. Longer rods tend to have too much flex in the tip, making them less desirable.

Let's concentrate on the stiffness factor first. The stiffness of a spinning rod is directly related to the sensitivity of the rod. Stiffer rods tend to flex or bend less at the tip than lighter action rods, making them more sensitive to subtle bites.

The stiffness of the rod is apparent when lifting the jig up and down in the water. If the rod flexes significantly from the weight of the jig, the bend in the rod actually becomes a shock absorber that makes it difficult to detect bites or the sensation of weight. When vertical jigging, the only indication that a fish has taken the bait is often a sensation of weight or a mushy feeling as the jig is lifted. A stiff rod simply makes it easier to detect bites.

There are two ways to increase the stiffness of a spinning rod. The first is to select a heavier action rod, such as a medium action over a medium/light or a medium/heavy over a medium. When you go up in action, most rods also become a little larger in diameter and slightly heavier.

The other way to make a spinning rod stiffer is to cut the rod down by removing an inch or two from the tip. Once the rod is shortened to achieve the ideal stiffness, a new tip is installed and the rod is ready for action. If you choose to cut off an existing rod, do so with a high speed cut-off saw like those used for cutting arrows. A high speed saw won't splinter the graphite fibers and ruin the rod.

I've cut my rods down to make them the desired stiffness for years and to me it's no big deal, but for some anglers cutting the tip off a perfectly good graphite rod is like throwing dollars instead of pennies into a wishing well. The choice of cutting down a rod or purchasing one stiff enough is up to each individual angler.

Regardless of how you select a vertical jigging rod, be sure the rod is at least as stiff as a medium-action rod. Match this rod with a spinning reel that includes continuous anti-reverse, similar to that described for use with jig casting.

When vertical jigging both monofilament and the new super braids have a place. For jigging in water less than 20 feet deep, premium 6-pound test monofilament line is tough to beat. Monofilament lines for vertical jigging need to be limp, have good knot strength and low memory. Some excellent choices include Stren Easy Cast, Stren Magnathin, Berkley Trilene Pro Select, Super Silver Thread, Silver Thread Excalibur, Spiderwire Super Mono and Ande Premium.

The new low-stretch monofilaments such as Stren Sensor are excellent choices for vertical jig-

This spinning reel is equipped with a continuous anti-reverse feature that insures there is no play in the reel handle. This feature helps to make the rod and reel combination better able to telegraph light bites.

ging. The reduced stretch (30 percent to 50 percent less than regular monofilament) in this line makes it easier to detect bites, especially in deep water.

When jigging in water deeper than 20 feet, the maximum sensitivity and low stretch characteristics of the super braids offer significant advantages. Not only do these lines feature very low stretch, they are also thinner in diameter than identical break strength monofilaments.

The thin diameter and low stretch characteristics of braided super-lines work together to help anglers stay vertical and detect even the lightest bites. A lot of braided lines are on the market but the most popular choices include Spiderwire Fusion and Berkley Fireline. Select a product that features a diameter similar to or smaller than 6-pound monofilament.

The chief disadvantage to braided lines is they are more expensive and offer less knot strength than monofilament. However, in deep water vertical jigging situations these disadvantages are overshadowed by the advantages of a low-stretch line with more sensitivity.

Braided super-lines are produced in both low- and high-visibility colors. For vertical jigging in rivers where water clarity is often murky or worse, the high-visibility lines are the better choice.

SLIP SINKER RIGGING

Slip sinker fishing, what is often simply called "rigging," is a presentation that doesn't require as rigid a selection of rod length and action as vertical jigging. However, like all the presentations outlined thus far, rigging is best performed using quality graphite spinning tackle.

Rod length can vary from 6 to 7 feet and action ratings can range from medium/light to medium. Personally, I feel a rigging rod should be longer than a jig casting or vertical jigging rod. The extra rod length comes in handy to present the bait out a little farther from the boat. A longer rod also provides more power for a solid hook set when a bite occurs a considerable distance from the boat. A medium-action rod has always served me well while rigging.

Reels used for rigging require a little more line capacity than those for casting or vertical jigging. A Size 2 reel that is rated to holed 150 yards of 8-pound test is ideal. The continuous anti-reverse feature outlined in jig casting and vertical jigging is not critical for rigging. Here's why; while rigging the reel bail is kept open and the line held with the tip of an index finger. When a bite is detected the angler simply drops the line and gives the fish some slack so it can eat the bait without feeling line resistance or the angler.

When it's time to set the hook the angler closes the bail and slowly reels up the slack line until the rod tip is near the water and the weight of the fish can be felt. At this point the angler sweeps the rod upwards in a powerful hook set. A reel with a continuous anti-reverse feature adds no particular advantage to this presentation.

Monofilament fishing line is the best choice for rigging. Because rigging is often used to trigger negative or lethargic walleyes into biting, the controlled stretch of monofilament enables the angler to detect the strike without the fish feeling unnatural pressure. Premium line in the 6- or 8-pound test size works best.

SLIP BOBBER FISHING

For years I've used the same rods and reels for both slip sinker rigging and slip bobber fishing.

Not only do the rod length and actions match up nicely for these presentations, the line sizes used are also universal.

There is, however, a slight advantage in having a 7- or 7-1/2-foot rod for slip bobber fishing. The longer rod makes it easier to mend line (keeping the line out of the water) when drifting floats into position. Such a subtle advantage isn't something that warrants going out and buying all new tackle.

The reels used for slip bobber fishing can be the same as those for rigging. The monofilament line used should be 6- or 8-pound test and, because there is no need to see the line, I'd suggest a clear or green line color that blends into the water nicely.

DRIFTING/TROLLING BOTTOM BOUNCERS

Fishing bottom bouncers is one of the most popular and effective ways of catching walleyes found on sand, clay, gravel or scattered rock flats. Because bottom bouncers are heavier than other walleye fishing presentations, a baitcasting style rod and reel combination is advised.

Rods can range from 6 to 8 feet long with a medium/light to medium action. Shorter rods are handy when it's necessary to hold the rod in your hand while fishing, such as when slipping around the edges of a sunken reef with the help of an elec-

A vertical jigging rod should be a little more stiff than a jig casting rod. The extra stiffness enables the angler to feel the bottom easily and detect even subtle bites. In areas where two rods can be fished, a pair of identical vertical jigging rods will be required.

Super-braid lines such as Fireline are a good choice when vertical jigging in deep water. The thin diameter and low stretch features make it easier for anglers to maintain contact with the bottom and feel bites.

tric motor. For other applications including drifting or trolling, where the rods are often placed in strategically located holders, a longer rod helps to increase the lure coverage.

A 7-foot triggerstick is an excellent compromise that can be used effectively for most bottom bouncer presentations. However, if the rod will be held a considerable amount of the time, a lightweight graphite model is the best choice. Rods that spend most of their time in holders need not be expensive graphite models. In fact, more affordable graphite/fiberglass composites are an excellent choice for drifting or trolling applications.

The reel used on a bottom bouncer rod should be a baitcasting model with a line capacity that accepts a minimum of 125 yards of 12-pound test. I prefer a little bigger reel that accepts 200 yards of 12-pound test. The extra line capacity allows me to get double duty from this reel for fishing lead-core line and some other trolling applications.

I also recommend that anglers look for a reel that offers a flippin' feature. This feature allows the reel bail to be opened and closed by simply pushing a button. Baitcasting reels that don't have a flippin' feature require the angler to turn the reel handle to close the bail after letting out the desired amount of line.

Taking the small step to turn the reel handle and close the bail each time more line is let out may not seem like much of an inconvenience, but it's important to keep in mind that when fishing bottom bouncers many anglers fish a rod in each hand. If the bottom is irregular the angler is constantly adjusting the amount of line required to maintain contact with the bottom. A flippin' feature makes this chore easier, especially if two rods are used at once.

When fishing bottom bouncers in deep water, line-counter reels can be very helpful for monitoring productive lead lengths. Until recently anglers only had one or two line-counter reels to choose

The same rods used for slip sinker rigging make excellent slip bobber rods. A 7-foot medium-action spinning rod is ideal for these presentations.

from. Thanks to competition in the marketplace, a dozen or more choices are currently available. Even better, the price on line-counter reels has dropped sharply as a direct result of this friendly competition.

When shopping for line-counter reels, find the brand, model and size that best suits your needs and purchase enough to supply all the rods you expect to fish with. Because of differences in reel size, spool diameter and gear ratios, all line-counter reels can't be expected to register lead lengths identically. In other words, a Daiwa SG27LC isn't likely to read the same number as a Penn 855LC when exactly the same amount of line is out. While the variance in lead lengths from one brand of reel to the next isn't significant, it makes sense to match your equipment to avoid any confusion.

Smaller and more compact reels such as the Cabela's Depthmaster Tournament, Penn 855LC Marado Compass C 631 or Shimano Bantam 1500LC make the most sense for matching with bottom bouncer rods because they are lighter and easier to hold for long periods of time.

For most bottom bouncer applications premium monofilament in the 10- to 12-pound test range is the best choice. For deep water applications where it becomes more difficult to maintain contact with bottom, braided super-lines offer a distinct advantage. The combination of thin diameter and low stretch enables these lines to perform at a higher level in deep water. All the popular brands are good choices. I prefer to use 10-pound test for bottom bouncer fishing applications.

DEAD RODS

An important rod that few anglers have discovered is one that's simply called a dead rod. The name comes from the way this rod is fished. A dead rod is used to add a second line in the water that the angler doesn't need to tend constantly. Usually placed in a rod holder, this outfit is often equipped with a simple rig such as a split shot and hook or floating jig head baited with a nightcrawler, minnow or leech.

The dead rod is designed to fish while the angler is concentrating on another presentation such as slip sinker rigging or jig casting. A legend in walleye fishing, Bob Propst Sr., popularized the use of dead rods for walleyes. Bob's choice for a dead rod is an inexpensive fiberglass steelhead-style rod with a very soft action. The rod is usually

The extra power of baitcasting tackle is required for fishing bottom bouncers. A 7-foot medium-action triggerstick equipped with a baitcasting reel is ideal for fishing bottom bouncers.

8 to 10 feet long and equipped with a spinning reel loaded with 6- or 8-pound test monofilament.

The length of the rod helps to keep the lure away from the boat and to avoid tangles with other lines. The soft action is critical, so that walleyes don't feel resistance immediately when they bite. Over the years, I've watched Bob catch countless walleyes using a dead rod. On many occasions the dead rod produces more fish than anything else in the boat.

A dead rod may be the most unorthodox rod in a walleye boat, but it can also be one of the most effective.

CRANKBAIT/SPINNER TROLLING

Trolling is about experimenting with lures and lead lengths until a productive combination is discovered. Once the magic mix of lure and lead length is determined, the successful formula is duplicated with other rods and reels in an effort to put more baits in the fish zone.

The need to duplicate lead lengths is the primary reason serious trollers demand matched and balanced rods and reels. Selecting the same rod, reel and even line size insures that information gained while fishing one rod can be transferred identically to other rods as needed.

Anglers who troll for walleyes normally run the maximum number of lines allowed by law. It's not uncommon to find an angler with four or six identical rod and reel combinations ready for action.

On my boat you'll find eight trolling rods most of the time. Four of these rods are armed with monofilament line, two with braided super-line and two with lead-core line. Rigged in this manner I'm ready for just about any trolling situation.

Trolling rods are likely to be the least expensive rods a walleye angler owns. Since most of the time the rod rests in a holder, there's no need to purchase light, sensitive or expensive graphite

A baitcasting reel with a flippin' feature is handy for fishing bottom bouncers. This feature allows line to be let out without having to open the bail and turn the reel handle each time.

rods. In fact, fiberglass or graphite/fiberglass composites are the best choice for several reasons.

Not only are fiberglass or composite rods less expensive, they offer the right properties of flex, power, strength and durability required for trolling. I strongly recommend a downrigger style rod 7 to 8 feet long for all trolling applications. These rods are affordable and designed to take a considerable amount of abuse.

Rods longer than 8 feet are cumbersome to use in the boat and they don't provide any clear advantage. A medium or medium/light-action rod suited for 10-to 20-pound test line is ideal.

All my trolling rods are matched up with identical line-counter reels. It's critical to monitor lead length when trolling and line-counter reels are the only practical way to accomplish this task. I select a line-counter reel that's capable of handling 360 yards of 14-pound test. A reel this size is suitable for walleyes and can also be used on larger species such as trout, salmon, musky or pike. Smaller line-counter reels are good choices for walleyes, but they are a bit small if larger species are also on the menu.

The Daiwa SG27LC is the standard in line-counter reels and retails for around $100. This level-wind style reel has been available for many years and features a silky smooth star drag, gear-driven counter, oversized cranking handle, graphite frame and dependable bait clicker feature. If money is no object, Daiwa also produces a line of electronically controlled line-counter reels that start at about $300 each.

Other electronic line-counter reels include the Penn 855LC and the Cabela's Depthmaster Tournament. Mechanical gear-driven line-counter reels are available from Mitchell, Cabela's, Shimano, South Bend, Marado and Okuma. Line-counter reels range in price from $50 to $300. Most models however are less than $150.

For most trolling applications 10-pound test monofilament is the ideal choice. Because long lead lengths are often used in trolling, lines with controlled stretch make the most sense. Stren's Sensor is a leading candidate for trolling situations because this line features 30 percent to 50 percent less stretch than ordinary nylon monofilament. Other good trolling lines include Silver Thread Excalibur, Berkley Trilene XT, Stren Super Tough, Ande Premium and Maxima. Each of these products feature good knot strength, controlled stretch and high abrasion resistance.

The braided super lines also have a place in trolling. Any time it's necessary to achieve maximum lure depth or use exceptionally long trolling leads, the super lines are a good choice. The thin diameter and low stretch are a winning combination for many trolling situations, including long-lining.

It's important to note that because these lines have little or no stretch, it's very easy to overpower fish during the fight. If too much pressure is exerted, the hooks can easily tear free of the fish. When using super lines it's important to set the drag lighter than normal and to use a softer action

Downrigger rods make excellent general purpose walleye trolling rods. These rods should be matched with identical line-counter trolling reels loaded with exactly the same amount of line.

Bob Propst Sr., is credited with making dead rod fishing a popular walleye fishing method. A lifelong guide and tournament pro, Bob favors a long and soft action fiberglass model as a dead rod.

rod than is typically recommended. Also, take your time fighting fish to avoid losing walleyes needlessly.

Obviously, bass fishermen have nothing over a well-equipped walleye angler when it comes to selecting rods, reels and lines. Think of these items as tools for specific jobs and you'll quickly understand why technique-specific rod and reel combinations have become popular with bass and walleye anglers.

In the next chapter our focus switches to electronics and methods for locating walleyes using the latest advancements in sonar technology.

CHAPTER 6
WALLEYE FISHING WITH SOUND

In the past 20 years a wealth of technological advancements have made fishing more productive and enjoyable. Walleye anglers have benefited from high-tech fishing lines, more sensitive graphite rods, smooth continuous anti-reverse reels, quiet four-stroke outboards and high-performance fishing boat hulls. However, none of these items has had as profound an impact on fishing success as sonar. Like everything else in the world of sport fishing, sonar has improved dramatically in recent years.

My first sonar was a flasher unit that started me down the path of serious fishing. I started out without a clue of how to use this product. At first I could identify bottom, but little else. The varying bands of light that appeared on the screen were a mystery until a fellow angler took me aside and helped me understand how sonar works. Unfortunately, even today most anglers still can't read their flashers as well as they should.

From the earliest flasher units to the most sophisticated liquid crystal readout (LCR) or video displays of today, all sonar functions the same way. Sonar consists of three parts including a transmitter, transducer and receiver.

The transmitter sends an electrical pulse to the transducer, which in turn converts the electrical signals to sound energy. This transmission of sound is directed into the water. Sound waves strike and reflect off objects more dense than water and return to the transducer. The transducer converts

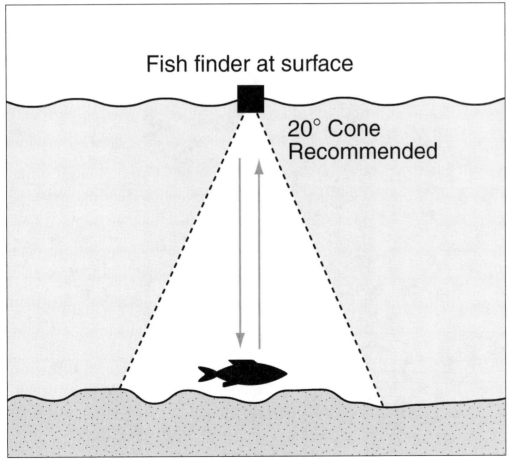

Fish finder at surface

20° Cone Recommended

Sonar bounces sound waves off the bottom. When the waves hit something between the bottom and the transducer they return at a different speed and angle. That shows up as a mark on the readout. In deeper water sonar covers a larger area on the bottom. In shallow water the coverage area is very narrow.

the sound waves back into electrical energy that is forwarded to the receiver. The receiver amplifies and displays the information on a screen.

The transducer is a critical part of any sonar unit. The transducer is a crystal made from two plates of silver, one on top of the other. When an electrical charge strikes the crystal, the plates expand and contract producing a clicking sound. This is how electrical energy is converted into sound energy.

A housing around the crystal forces the sound waves to travel only out the bottom of the transducer. As the sound waves travel through the water the waves expand into a cone shape. The deeper the water the larger this cone angle becomes and the more surface area that is contacted with the sound waves.

This simple principle is why sonar is of little use in marking fish in shallow water. The cone angle is so small, only a tiny portion of the water column is covered by the sound waves. In deeper water the cone angle becomes larger and the sonar coverage is greatly increased.

Since sound travels through water at a constant speed of 4,800 feet per second, the time that lapses between the sound wave striking an underwater item and returning to the transducer is used to calculate how far away the object is. Items between the transducer and bottom (such as fish,

weeds, wood or other items) appear as separate marks at the distance they are from the transducer.

The basic principle of sonar is the same no matter how a sonar unit displays the information. However, the ways this information is displayed can make a big difference in how anglers interpret the data.

Flashers were the first sonar units invented and most of the major manufacturers still produce flasher units. Many anglers prefer to use flashers for a variety of reasons. The truth is, a flasher unit can display depth, fish, weeds, bottom hardness and bottom contour as accurately as an LCR or video unit. The problem is this information isn't in a form that most anglers can readily understand and benefit from.

A flasher operates using two simple knobs. The unit is turned on using one knob. Turning the knob clockwise increases the power the unit puts out. Turn the dial clockwise slowly until a band of light indicates the bottom, then keep turning the knob a little more until a second echo appears below the bottom. When the second echo appears the power has been turned up enough to insure that fish, baitfish, weeds and other small items will be marked.

The power knob will need to be adjusted up and down depending on how deep the water is, the hardness of the bottom and how fast the boat

Flashers were the first sonar units and are still widely used today. Many boat manufacturers install flasher units in the console as a safety feature for high-speed running.

is moving. The second knob is a suppression adjustment. Suppression helps to reduce the number of false signals created from interference such as water turbulence. Suppression is used most often when under power at high speeds.

Some of the displays that appear on a flasher are easy to interpret and others are more complex. A hard bottom returns a wide, bright band of light. Softer bottoms return a more narrow and weaker signal. Fish mark as bands of light, separated from the bottom. Very thin bands indicate small fish, while thicker bands indicate larger fish.

Weeds or sunken wood that sticks up off the bottom read as a series of thin bands of light starting at the top of the weeds and stretching to the bottom signal. This signal is confusing and tough for the average angler to interpret.

Tapering bottom contours also show a complex band of light on a flasher. Because the transducer cone strikes the bottom at several different depths at the same time, a much wider band of light than normal is displayed.

Baitfish appear on the flasher as a series of thin lines of light. In some instances bait can look a lot like weeds and weeds can be mistaken for bait. It takes a considerable amount of time using a flasher to readily interpret all the data this machine can provide. Frankly, most anglers are better off using an LCR or video sonar that provides an easier-to-understand picture of the underwater world.

There are, however, a couple situations when a flasher unit is more useful than video or liquid crystal technology. Ice fishing is the ideal situation for flasher units. Because the sonar is sitting still instead of moving slowly over objects, LCR or video units cannot display the typical fish mark as a hook or arch. Instead, a solid line appears on the screen as long as the fish remains in the transducer cone angle.

With a flasher, a thin bleep of light indicates the presence of fish much the same as when using these units in open water. Also, some LCR units can shut down when exposed to extremely cold weather.

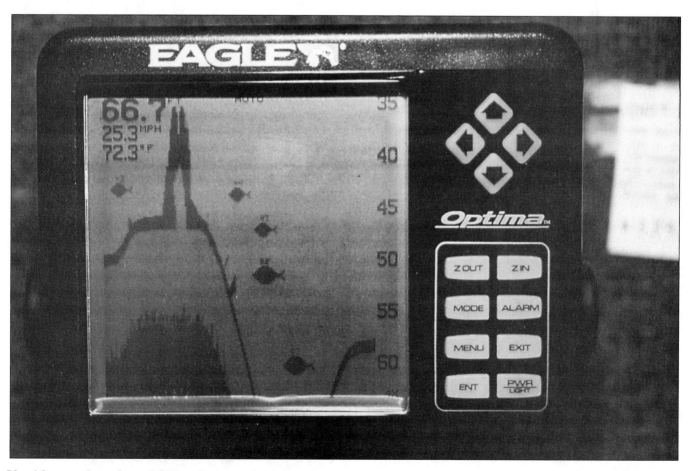

Liquid crystal readout (LCR) style sonar is easy to interpret and use. Most units have a simple menu function that makes it easy to perform basic functions.

Flashers function no matter how cold it gets, so long as there is plenty of juice in the battery.

Flashers also interpret data such as bottom depth more quickly than most LCR or video units. A flasher is generally preferred as a safety aid for operating a boat at high speed. Most boat manufacturers include an in-dash style flasher as standard equipment with their boats.

LIQUID CRYSTAL CRAZY

In the past dozen years the fishing world has gone crazy for LCR style sonar units. As the most popular sonar type sold, LCR units are also available in the widest selection of price ranges and features.

The screen of an LCR unit is as simple to understand as the screen of an Etch-A-Sketch. The bottom is shown as a continuous line with the contour or slope clearly shown. Objects connected to the bottom, such as submerged stumps, rocks or weeds, are outlined clearly, making them easy to interpret. Fish marked in deep water appear as a hook or arch on the screen while fish marked in shallow water appear as small blobs on the screen.

The hardness of the bottom is indicated by a feature known as grayline. This shaded band appears below the bottom and varies in thickness depending on the hardness or composition of the bottom. Good-sized fish also tend to grayline, helping to indicate the relative size of fish marks.

An LCR is also easy to use. Most are programmed using a menu system that takes the angler step by step through basic functions. In addition to the full-screen sonar mode, most LCR graphs offer split screen and zoom functions. Some units allow two transducer frequencies to be used at the same time. Others even use windows within the screen that provide sonar, speed and water temperature at the same time.

Most LCR units use a one-dimensional screen display, but units with multi-dimensional displays are also offered. More of a sales gizmo than a practical fishing tool, some anglers enjoy this unique function in a graph.

The most important features to look for when purchasing LCR equipment is the pixel count and the power or watts the unit generates. The screen of an LCR graph is made up of lots of small pixels or dots. The smaller the dot size the more dots can fit on the screen and thus detailed picture the unit can draw. The most detailed LCR screens

offer up to 300 vertical pixels of resolution or picture clarity. I recommend selecting a model that offers between 200 and 300 vertical pixels.

The power an LCR produces can also be an important feature. More power means the unit will have a greater ability to separate targets that are close to bottom or mixed in some type of cover. Extra power is also useful for marking fish in deep water. Both of these situations occur frequently when fishing for walleyes.

Most LCR units produce 300 to 500 watts. A handful generate up to 3000 watts of power.

I've had the opportunity to examine high-and-moderate-watt sonar units side by side. Frankly, there is no comparison. High-watt units perform far better in deep water or when searching for fish near the bottom.

FINE TUNING LCR GRAPHS

Most LCR units feature an automatic or manual mode. For maximum efficiency these units should be operated on the manual setting.

Every major brand of LCR on the market comes with an automatic mode designed to make these units easy for the average person to use. Unfortunately, these automatic functions compromise some important sonar features anglers pay big bucks for.

I've found that most LCR units function best when operated on the manual mode. Of course, turning off the automatic mode means the operator must set specific functions such as sensitivity, depth level and grayline manually.

Find the menu function that turns the unit from automatic to manual. Once the unit is in manual, set the depth range to match the depth where you're fishing. As you move into deeper or shallower water it will be necessary to adjust this setting.

Next, locate the sensitivity setting in the menu and turn up the sensitivity until the screen on the unit starts to black out from clutter. Back off the sensitivity until just a few dots of interference show on the screen. Turning up the sensitivity helps in showing important details such as schools of baitfish or emerging weeds along the bottom.

Like the depth scale, the sensitivity will also need to be adjusted as the boat moves into deeper or shallower water. I also make adjustments to the grayline feature. The grayline should be set high

enough so a true picture of the bottom composition prints out. If the grayline is turned up good-sized fish will also grayline, helping to differentiate between the size of fish being marked.

Set in this manner, an LCR unit will mark everything and show excellent detail. To maximize detail, put the unit into the zoom mode and select the 2X or 4X zoom option. Zoom essentially makes the picture larger and more detailed. This function is especially useful when trying to mark fish that have their belly to the bottom.

VIDEO SONAR AHEAD OF ITS TIME

Video-style sonar units are great products. Many of these units use color monitors to separate fish marks from other objects. The resolution is great, the power output is exceptional and the overall functions are outstanding. The problem with video sonar is the units are too big and bulky to be practical in boats the size walleye anglers commonly use.

Most video sonar units are the size of a portable TV set. A video unit is at home in a big boat with unlimited cockpit space. Open-bow walleye boats are not practical homes for these units.

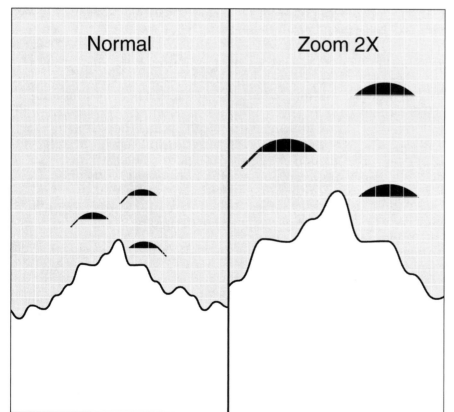

Zoom features vs a regular sonar screen

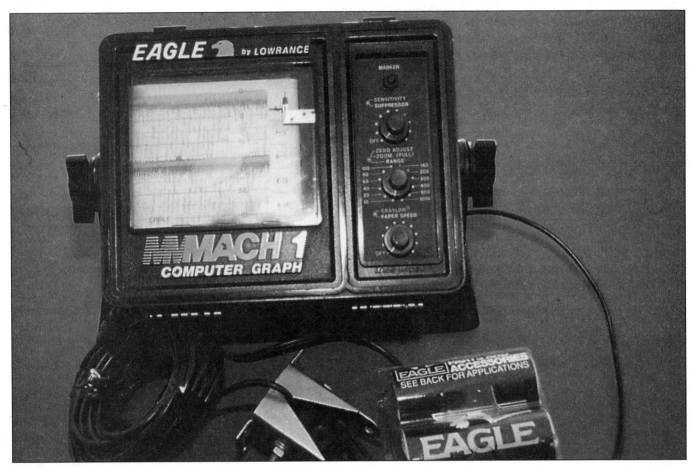

Paper graphs are sadly a thing of the past. Although paper graphs produced a more detailed picture and higher resolution than most LCR units, they require expensive graph paper to operate.

Some day video units will be more practical in a small fishing boat. A number of LCR units have already made this move. Many LCR units can now be mounted into a dashboard or deck making for a clean and functional look.

WHAT ABOUT PAPER GRAPHS?

Sadly, it appears that paper graphs are a thing of the past. The paper graph enjoyed a leading role in the world of sonar for many years. Ironically, the highest quality paper graphs produced a decade ago featured more power, more sensitivity and better target separation than most of the units being sold today. Many of the major brands produced an amazing 1-inch target separation. Most LCR and video units today feature a 6-inch target separation.

Despite the flawless function of paper graphs, they suffered from a couple major problems. Because these graphs use rolls of paper, it's not practical to let the graph run all the time. The paper required to use these sonar units is expensive and the stylus used to burn images into the paper gives off a strong odor. The carbon produced is messy to clean up and the rest is history.

Rolls of paper and the replacement stylus needed are getting tough to come by. Those anglers who own and use paper graphs often swear by the detailed underwater pictures these units generate. Still, the trend towards LCR and video technology is undeniable.

GETTING THE MOST FROM SONAR

Despite the fact that sonar units have become refined and sophisticated in their ability to mark fish and show important under water details, not all anglers are able to accurately interpret the information provided.

Some of the confusion is caused because anglers don't understand the basic principles of

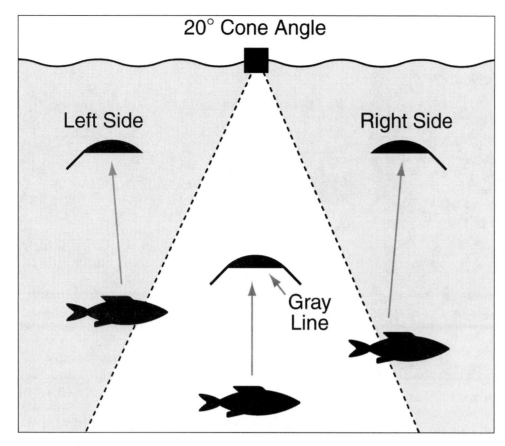

20° Cone Angle

Left Side

Right Side

Gray Line

The arch on a graph forms in relation to where a fish appears in the cone. Fish on the sides of the cone appear as shown. Fish directly beneath the transducer produce the best signal.

sonar and how it works. For example, not long ago I was fishing with a friend who doesn't own a boat or sonar unit. We were trolling and marking fish regularly on the graph. When we hooked a fish, I put the boat in neutral so my buddy could enjoy the fight to the fullest. When we landed the fish, my friend looked at the graph and excitedly announced that we were into a school of huge fish because the graph was covered with fish marks that stretched well across the screen.

The marks that appear on a graph are relative in size to the size of the fish, but also to how long the fish remains in the transducer cone. When we were trolling along at a good clip, marks about 1/4-inch long appeared on the screen. When we slowed down to fight a fish, the marks suddenly grew to 1 inch long because the boat moved more slowly and the fish remained in the transducer cone longer.

Fish marked in deep water appear larger on the screen than those marked closer to the surface. The larger size of the transducer cone angle in deep water explains this phenomenon.

For all practical purposes it is not possible to determine the size of fish by looking at the readout. It is possible to detect bigger fish mixed in

among smaller fish, but the only way to confirm the size is to catch some and compare them.

Not too many years ago a sonar unit was marketed with a feature known as "Species Select." This function claimed to be able to indicate the species of fish the sonar was marking.

Wrong! It is essentially impossible to determine species by looking at marks on a graph. Of course some educated guesses can be made, but once again the only way to confirm this information is to catch a fish or two and see the species they are.

This type of marketing hype only serves to make anglers more confused. As long as manufacturers are more interested in selling products than helping anglers become knowledgeable and skillful, these types of gimmicks will continue to surface.

Another common situation that causes confusion involves baitfish. Baitfish often mark as a blob on the screen that can stretch out in either a vertical or horizontal orientation. I'm amazed how often anglers mistake these dense schools of bait for individual game fish. Because the individual members of a school of bait are so close together the sonar unit interprets them as one large mass.

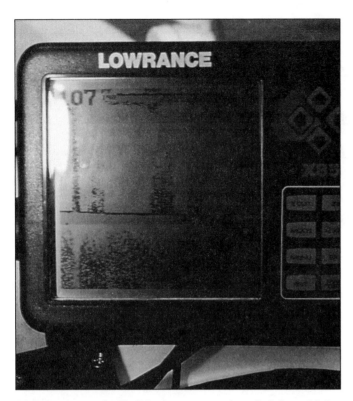

It's a common belief that sonar can mark fish at high speed. Turbulence caused from the motor and hull make it difficult to see fish marks at high speeds. Normally sonar is most useful for locating fish when used at 10 mph or slower.

When the screen is all but covered with bait most anglers recognize what's happening, but when small schools of bait are recorded, these marks are often mistaken for game fish.

It is possible to determine if a fish marked is directly under the boat or to one side or another. A uniform hook on the graph indicates the fish is directly beneath the boat.

The reason a hook shape prints out is because when the fish is first recorded it's at the outside edge of the transducer cone. The sound wave has to travel a little farther to reach the fish and return to the transducer than if the fish were straight down. The beginning of the mark is recorded based on this distance. As the boat moves over the fish, the fish enters the center of the transducer cone. The resulting mark on the graph angles upwards because the distance from the fish to the transducer is slightly shorter. As the boat moves forward the fish is again recorded going out of the transducer cone. As before the distance from the fish to the edge of the cone angle is longer, causing the mark to record a little deeper on the graph's scale.

If a fish is located on the outside edge of the transducer cone and to the side of the boat the mark will not appear as a hook. Because the fish is at relatively the same distance from the transducer the entire time the fish is within the cone, the mark appears as a straight line. It's not practical to determine which side of the boat the fish is on, only that the fish is at the outside edge of the transducer cone.

It's also a common belief that sonar units can be used to mark fish at high speed. Turbulence from the prop and boat passing through the water create too much interference to effectively mark fish at speeds much above 10 miles per hour.

While bottom readings can be recorded at high speed, it's best to slow down when getting serious about looking for fish.

So dependable are modern sonar units that in many fishing situations there's no need to wet a line until fish are located on the graph. This is especially true when fishing in deep water or hunting for suspended fish. In large bodies of water where walleyes often scatter to the winds and suspend near schools of baitfish, the way walleyes are located is by running at high speed for a short distance then slowing down and watching the graph for awhile. If no fish are marked, repeat this run-and-look process until fish are located.

Sonar accessories such as speed and temperature probes are good investments for the walleye angler. The spinner wheels used to determine speed are among the most accurate way to judge trolling speeds. To insure these wheels function accurately, be sure to give them a shot of aerosol lubricant frequently. This spray lubrication treatment insures that road grime, sand and dirt are flushed away from the axle these wheels spin on.

Water temperature is another important bit of knowledge for walleye fishing. While anglers can't use water temperature to determine exactly where walleyes will be or what they will be doing, water temperature does provide some indication to the activity level of the fish. In water temperatures ranging from the high 30s to high 40s walleyes are most likely to strike slow moving presentations. Once the water warms beyond 50 degrees walleyes are much more likely to hit baits that are moving fast or aggressively.

SUMMING UP THE HIGH POINTS

A walleye fisherman depends heavily on a sonar unit. In addition to using this equipment to study bottom details such as depth, bottom com-

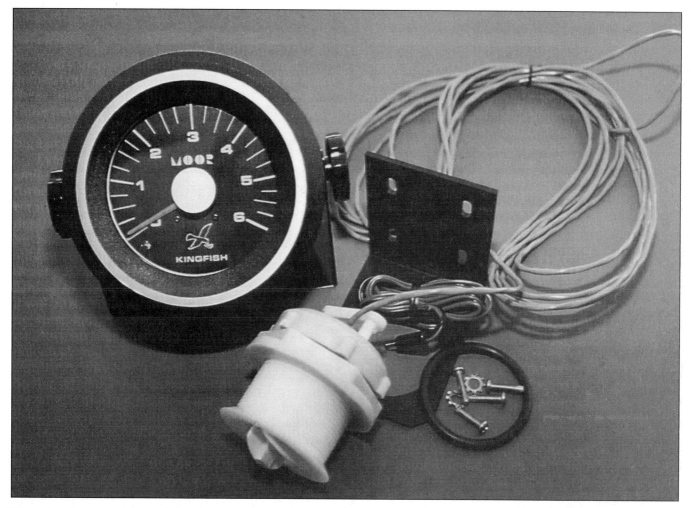

This spinning wheel speed indicator is sensitive enough to give accurate trolling speed readings. This speed indicator is a Kingfish produced by Moor Electronics.

position, the presence of baitfish, weeds and other cover, sonar can show the location of walleyes.

Serious walleye anglers are best equipped with an LCR type sonar unit that offers high resolution. Look for units featuring 200-300 vertical pixels.

A good LCR unit should also produce up to 3,000 watts of power. High powered units do a better job of marking fish in deep water, fish holding tight to cover or the bottom and fish feeding within schools of bait.

All LCR units have automatic modes, but for maximum effectiveness these units should be operated on the manual setting. When the machine is set in the manual mode the angler must set the sensitivity, bottom depth chart, grayline and zoom features as required.

It's a fact that all sonar types function using the same principles, but all sonar units are not created equal. Avoid marketing gizmos and gadgets aimed at product sales and concentrate on models that are both practical and functional.

Walleye anglers are advised to invest in the best quality sonar equipment they can afford. A fishing graph is the most valuable tool a walleye angler has at his or her disposal. Don't cut corners with this vital piece of fishing equipment.

In the next chapter we will focus on another useful piece of marine electronics, the Global Positioning Systems. GPS units are valuable tools for safe and dependable navigation. GPS units are also a useful tool for storing a wealth of fishing information that can be recalled and used as needed.

Quality sonar is a valuable tool for locating walleyes. Anglers are advised to purchase the best quality equipment they can afford. Lesser units may not indicate fish near the bottom like this walleye was.

The book *A Comprehensive Guide to Fish Locators* by Babe Winkelman is an excellent guide to using all the major types of sonar. Copies can be obtained from Babe Winkelman Productions, Inc., PO Box 407, Brainerd, MN 56401.

CHAPTER 7

GPS AND WALLEYE FISHING

Global Positioning Systems (GPS) are the buzz words of the fishing industry. The term GPS frequently rolls off the lips of tournament professionals, outdoor writers, and tackle retailers, but the average angler has yet to appreciate the practical fishing applications GPS technology brings to walleye fishing.

An accurate and dependable marine navigation system, GPS units function using signals transmitted from a series of satellites that orbit the Earth. Essentially GPS works in much the same way as its predecessor Loran-C.

The primary difference is that Loran-C functions using signals that are broadcast from ground-based stations. Because Loran-C signals are ground based they are susceptible to electrical interference from storms. Satellite-based GPS systems are far less susceptible to localized storms, providing more dependable navigation information.

The GPS receiver monitors signals broadcast from a series of satellites. Through triangulation the exact location of the receiver on Earth is determined. With some GPS units up to 12 different satellites are used to provide the most accurate triangulation possible.

GPS navigation systems simply determine your location on Earth. To make this information easier to visualize, graphic plotters are used to show the location of the GPS receiver and the direction of travel. A graphic plotter is like a TV screen that shows the receiver as a blinking cursor and the movement of the boat as a dotted line or plot trail.

Other valuable information also appears on the graphic screen. Waypoints that indicate specific latitude and longitude coordinates can be permanently saved along with icons or electronic marker buoys that are used to mark the location of important data such as landed fish. A number of different icons can be selected to help differentiate from various features of importance.

Graphic plotters aren't exactly new. The first plotter units erupted on the sonar market several years ago as part of the evolving Loran-C navigation system.

Noted walleye professionals Gary Parsons and Keith Kavajecz fall into a special category of GPS users. As field staff members for Lowrance Electronics, these men have logged hundreds of hours exploring the practical fishing applications of both Loran-C and GPS/plotter units.

Even before GPS technology was available to the public, Parsons and Kavajecz were provided

Gary Parsons and Keith Kavajecz were among the first walleye anglers to use GPS. Even before GPS units were available for commercial sale, these men worked with Lowrance Electronics to test prototype products.

the opportunity to use prototype units. "I guess you could say we're pioneers in the promotion and use of GPS," says Parsons. "Judged on what we've seen and learned regarding GPS/plotter systems, I'd categorize them as being a must-have item for the serious walleye angler.

"Navigation plotters are designed to show a detailed visual picture of the boat's path of movement," explains Parsons. "Like a jet stream trailing behind a supersonic jet, plotter trails make it easy to see where you've been and where you're headed."

But these units aren't just fancy maps.

"The moment an angler realizes that a GPS/plotter unit is capable of much more than the typical Loran-C/plotter, he opens the door to a whole new world of sport fishing," adds Kavajecz. "There's no comparison between GPS and Loran-C. GPS is more accurate, more dependable in all weather conditions, locks on faster and can be used not only as a navigation aid but as a road map to more successful fishing."

GPS/PLOTTERS & OPEN-WATER WALLEYES

"GPS/plotters are a must-have accessory for fishing walleyes in open-water environments," claims Parsons. "Once the first suspended fish is hooked and an icon saved a GPS/plotter allows the angler to make more precise trolling passes over the same school of fish."

In order for the angler to accurately navigate back to an icon or waypoint, the GPS plotter screen must be set on a small radius or scale. The same is true when trying to follow a previous plot trail. Adjust the scale on the plotter screen by zooming in to the 1/2- or 1/4- mile scale. The smaller the scale that is used the closer the boat can be navigated back to saved waypoints or icons.

Not all GPS plotters feature a scale that can be adjusted below one mile. These units are designed primarily for boat navigation from port to port and are less useful for fishing applications.

"One of the major problems with walleyes is they are constantly moving and following forage," comments Parsons. "Keeping tabs on a moving school of fish can be nearly impossible without the help of GPS."

GPS/plotter units help anglers keep track of moving schools and even determine the rough shape of a group of fish. Save an event marker or icon on the plotter screen for every walleye

caught. After a few trolling passes a pattern will develop that shows the rough shape of the school.

Knowing the shape of the school is important because it allows the angler to adjust trolling passes to stay in the fish for the maximum amount of time. Imagine a long and narrow shaped school of suspended walleyes positioned in a north to south orientation.

If the boat passes through the school from east to west the lures will only be in front of the fish a relatively short period of time. In comparison, when the boat passed through the school in a north to south direction, the lures are in front of the fish for a greater amount of time per trolling pass.

GPS/plot trails are also useful for anticipating the movements of suspended fish. Every fish caught and event marker saved is valuable information on the plotter screen. During the course of a day, patterns of movement develop, allowing the angler to anticipate the whereabouts of fish as they continue to move.

GPS PLOTTERS & STRUCTURE FISHING

"Once anglers get past the belief that GPS is primarily a navigation aid or open water fishing tool, they discover that GPS units are capable of aiding in structure fishing as well," says Kavajecz.

"GPS plotter units display an accurate plot trail, but for the ultimate in GPS accuracy an accessory known as a Differential or DGPS module is required," states Kavajecz. "A Differential module is a supplement to the existing GPS motor built into most units. This beacon picks up GPS signals that are amplified from ground based stations. The result is improved triangulation and signals that can provide repeatable accuracy measured down to five meters!"

The average accuracy of a normal GPS unit is approximately 100 meters. A DGPS beacon enables structure anglers to navigate along structure, then duplicate the path of the boat with follow-up passes.

"As with open-water fishing, the most accuracy is achieved when using a small plotter radius," advises Kavajecz. "To achieve the accuracy needed to use DGPS as a structure fishing aid, the plotter radius must feature a minimum radius of 1/4 mile and preferably smaller. Some of the better units feature a plotter radius measured down to a tenth of a mile or around 500 feet."

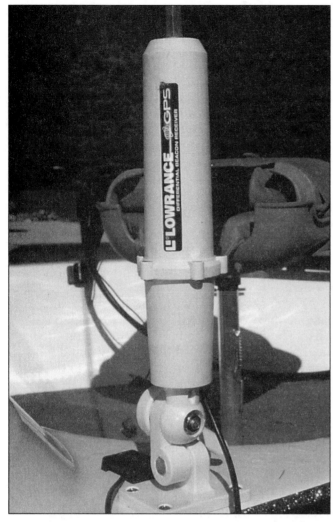

A differential beacon can transform the repeatable accuracy of a typical GPS unit from 100 meters down to five meters! Differential beacons will retro fit to most GPS units.

There are some other tricks that can help you use the GPS better.

"It's also important to set the plotter update rate at the fastest possible interval," adds Parsons. "The plot trail prints on the screen based on the rate selected within the unit's menu. For best results set the plotter to update at one-second intervals

To the structure fisherman who uses a DGPS/plotter unit, this technology is like having the ability to draw a road map on the water. Once the map is drawn, this route becomes a base line of data that can be used as reference if further exploration is required.

Structure fishermen use their sonar unit to follow bottom contours. Many DGPS/plotter units feature a split screen that allows the angler to monitor his sonar and plotter screen at the same time. In doing so, the sonar is used to follow a bottom contour while the GPS plotter screen keeps pace by recording the movement of the boat and drawing a simple base line sketch of the structure.

Thanks to the plotter screen, the structure begins to take shape, making it easy for the angler to visualize how the structure lays. Important features such as cups, bends, points and saddles become easy to spot and easy to find again when necessary.

"The quality of the signal received by a DGPS/plotter unit is what allows the plotter to record such an accurate path of boat movement," states Parsons. "Ordinary GPS units are not capable of providing this type of navigation accuracy or structure fishing ability."

DUPLICATING FISHING ROUTES

Although a DGPS/plotter unit can be used to draw the shape of bottom structure, weed edges and other cover types, its greatest value isn't in simply drawing pictures. The real value of a DGPS/plotter is that it allows an angler to analyze structure and precisely duplicate productive fishing runs.

Imagine having the ability to move the boat along the exact path where fish were previously found. With a good GPS and the knowledge of how to use it, an angler can follow every bend in a weed edge, every cup in a bottom contour and stick to the tip of a sunken point like bird dog trailing a pheasant.

"Being able to use a DGPS plot trail to accurately reproduce productive trolling passes isn't a fishing gimmick, it's the most important breakthrough in fishing technology since the invention of sonar," claims Kavajecz.

A few years ago while fishing in a tournament, Parsons and Kavajecz cemented their belief that DGPS plotter systems are the ultimate edge in fishing. The tournament was held on a natural lake featuring a meandering breakline that dropped sharply from 14 feet of water to 26 feet.

The breakline ran parallel to and approximately 1/4 mile from the shore. On top of the break a large flat gradually tapered towards shore. Many boats concentrated on the area and lots of walleyes were taken during the pre-fishing practice period.

"Before the tournament, we isolated a section of the break that held some nice walleyes on the lip and a few fish scattered along the break from 14 to

Gary Parsons took this nice walleye along a meandering break by back tracking and following his plot trail. The ability to follow a plot trail back into productive fishing spots adds a new dimension to structure fishing.

18-feet of water," explains Parsons. "We decided to fish the area during the tournament by dragging and hopping jigs along the lip using an electric trolling motor to pull the boat along the breakline."

A DGPS/plotter unit became an invaluable part of their fishing strategy. Kavajecz controlled the boat from the bow and used a Lowrance X-85 sonar unit to follow a precise depth level. When fish were marked or caught, an icon was saved on a LMS 350A GPS plotter equipped with a DGPS beacon.

"On the first pass we marked a nice group of fish and caught one walleye," recalls Kavajecz. "An icon was recorded on the GPS unit when the fish was landed. After continuing a short distance without catching another walleye we turned the boat around for a second pass. I simply followed the plot trail we established on the first pass and

lead us back over the fish. The second pass produced one additional fish and a third pass one more walleye for the livewell."

After making several more unproductive passes, the pair figured the fish moved deeper on the break. Kavajecz used the initial plot trail as a guide and positioned the boat in slightly deeper water. By paralleling the other plot trails Kavajecz was able to follow the meandering contour, only in deeper water.

"A couple passes in deeper water produced no fish," said Parsons. "It was obvious that the main body of fish had been spooked or moved and we would have to find them again."

Knowing the fish weren't deep, the next logical move was to try shallow water. The pair set their sights on the flat above the lip and eventually hit pay dirt.

"The school of fish we found on the breakline was only part of the total picture." explained Parsons. "The fish we ended up locating up on the flat may have been there all along or they could have been part of the school we found earlier in the day."

"We used the previous plot trail for reference and made a pass that paralleled the edge of the breakline approximately 30 feet into the flat," said Kavajecz. "On the first pass we caught our fourth fish and added another piece to the puzzle."

One pass on the shallow flat started what turned out to be an outstanding day on the water. The fish on the flat were easy to pattern with the help of a DGPS/plotter.

"Our plot trail became a road map that lead us back into the fish pass after pass," said Kavajecz. "The plotter allowed us to visualize the exact location of the fish and enabled us to make short and precise passes over the fish."

The pair of anglers stayed with the same school of fish the rest of the afternoon, catching walleyes almost at will.

"At the weigh-in other tournament anglers kept coming up to us and asking what lure we were using to catch all those fish," commented Parsons. "Our success wasn't because of the jigs or presentation we were using. Many other anglers in the area fished the same presentation. What we did differently was to stay on the fish better than other anglers."

An angler equipped with a DGPS/plotter can figure out where fish are located and how they are relating to available structure or cover better than ever before. Many anglers throw a marker buoy to pinpoint the location of fish. This system works in some situations, but to effectively display the layout of complicated structure would take a boat full of marker buoys.

Marker buoys also have to be picked up after each fishing trip, forcing the angler to re-learn the structure every time he fishes it. Marker buoys are also like an open fishing invitation to other anglers in the area.

"A DGPS owner can keep a permanent record of productive bottom structures by recording and naming a series of waypoints that represent key points of interest along bottom structure," says Kavajecz "Event markers or icons can also be used to map

Keith Kavajecz recommends that anglers use various icons on the plotter screen to mark important data such as the location of landed fish and major features of the structure. This information can be saved and used each time the spot is fished.

structure. Icons use up less memory than waypoints, allowing the angler to use them more freely."

"When fishing structure I plan to return to, I use waypoints to record the location of key spots such as the tips of points," says Parsons. "Event markers are used to maintain a record of spots-on-the-spot that produced fish and to mark significant changes in the structure such as cups or bends."

Saved event markers become a permanent record of structural features and indicate where specific fish were caught. When the angler leaves to fish another area these icons remain in the GPS computer memory.

The next time the angler fishes the area, waypoints and event markers saved earlier become an invaluable reference. The angler can simply jump in where he left off and fish productive parts of the structure a second time.

Electronic marker buoys are a tremendous advantage to anglers who like to fish key spots repeatedly during the course of a day, week or season on the water. Saved waypoints and icons remain permanently in the GPS computer memory until the owner chooses to erase them.

GPS MAPPING UNITS

The latest development in marine GPS technology goes well beyond graphic plotter screens. Many GPS units now feature a built-in base map of North America that's complete with major roads, land marks, permanent navigation aids, marinas and a wealth of other information.

A giant leap forward from simple plotters, a mapping unit enables anglers to see exactly where they are located in relationship to a wealth of features. Navigating to any feature on the map is easy even if a waypoint for the destination isn't readily available. With graphic plotters, a waypoint must be known to navigate to a specific destination.

The screen of a mapping unit can be altered to add important fishing information such as named waypoints or dozens of different icons that can represent where fish were caught, weed edges, hard bottom areas, navigation hazards and much more.

Mapping style GPS units are easier to use and safer for navigation purposes because potential hazards can be seen on the mapping screen. A few years ago I learned first hand how helpful GPS mapping units can be. My lesson came among the Bass Islands area of Lake Erie. This region features a number of islands, sunken reefs, ferry routes and other navigation hazards.

GPS mapping units are the latest wave in the evolution of GPS. A mapping unit features a built-in base map that enables anglers to navigate to specific spots without having a latitude and longitude coordinate.

A thick fog rolled into the area leaving visibility reduced to less than 100 feet. Boats trapped in the fog were helpless. Even those anglers with GPS plotter units couldn't navigate safely. When a waypoint is pulled up on a GPS unit a direction of travel is provided in the form of a compass bearing. The compass bearing always reads as a straight course from your current location to the waypoint. This direct route of travel could easily cause the boat to pass over shallow water, islands, and a wealth of other navigation pitfalls.

A Lowrance Global Map 2000 proved to be invaluable. To navigate, I simply zoomed out the map radius until I could see my position in relationship to other features around me. Based on my location plus the shoreline and navigation features shown on the map, it was easy to navigate through the fog with safety and confidence. When I reached fishing destinations, I simply zoomed the map scale in small enough that the unit functioned as a plotter. After using a mapping unit to

navigate safely in fog, it dawned on me how useful mapping units would be for navigating at night, during storms or other times when visibility is seriously reduced.

Most mapping units come with a base map that has enough detail to includes the outline of shorelines, major roads, shipping routes, permanent buoys and other navigation features. GPS units produced by some manufacturers accept special map cartridges that can be purchased separately. These optional after-market cartridges provide maps with much greater detail.

Lowrance Electronics amazed the industry with their latest wave of GPS mapping units. Lowrance now offers a CD-ROM disk that contains mapping data for use with their LMS 160 or LMS 1600 GPS units. An IBM compatible computer with a CD drive is required to load the data from the CD-ROM into the GPS memory. The CD-ROM mapping disk comes as standard equipment with both the Lowrance LMS 1600 and 160.

The base maps installed in many GPS mapping units may be updated to provide more detail. Special map cartridges can be purchased or CD-ROM disks that greatly enhance the data provided on the base map.

HAND-HELD GPS UNITS

Hand-held GPS units are essentially smaller versions of the permanent-mount units sold through the marine industry. Both plotter and mapping style GPS units are available in portable hand-held versions. A hand-held GPS unit makes sense when an angler often fishes from different boats, such as rental units or a friend's boat.

A hand-held GPS unit is also useful for ice fishing situations. Small enough to be mounted on the handle bars of an all-terrain vehicle or snowmobile, a hand-held GPS unit is a good investment for anglers who spend a lot of time ice fishing. Anglers who also hunt may find a hand-held unit handy for big game, turkey and waterfowl hunting situations.

The biggest disadvantage of hand-held units is the limited power source they depend upon. A GPS motor eats up batteries at an alarming rate. It's best to purchase a DC adapter that enables these units to be plugged into a cigarette lighter or other 12-volt power source.

Hand-held units also feature smaller screens that can't show as much detail as permanent mount models with full-sized screens. DGPS modules can be used with hand-held units, but a 12-volt power source from a boat, quad or snowmobile must be provided.

The cost of hand-held units range widely. Entry level products are offered for around $100, but some of the more sophisticated mapping units can run upwards of $800. Full-sized GPS units range in price from $300 to $2,000 depending on features.

GPS RIGGING OPTIONS

GPS plotter and mapping systems are effective tools for fishing walleyes on structure and in open water. To effectively use a GPS plotter or mapping unit, it must be mounted in a convenient location where the person controlling the boat can see the screen clearly and make necessary adjustments.

Structure fishermen will need their GPS unit mounted at the bow or transom depending on the method of boat control. Open-water trolling requires a GPS unit mounted on the console of the boat where it is in clear view all the time.

Anglers who fish both structure and open water can have their cake and eat it too if they're willing to purchase some extra rigging hardware. By purchasing an extra bracket, power cord and GPS antenna, a boat can be easily rigged so the GPS can be used in two different locations.

Rigged in this manner a serious angler can use his GPS/plotter effectively when fishing structure or open-water walleyes. Additional power cords, transducers and antennas are available at marine dealers or by contacting the respective manufacturer directly.

Like all elements of the computer age, GPS/plotter technology is progressing at an amazing rate. Improved computers in machines small enough to fit on the console of a fishing boat is the key to making this type of technology a reality.

In the next chapter we'll discuss the most expensive investment a walleye angler makes: the fishing boat. Like GPS technology, fishing boats have benefited from a wave of new manufacturing and design breakthroughs.

CHAPTER 8

WALLEYE DREAM MACHINES

If rods, reels and fishing line are walleye fishing tools, a boat is the ultimate tool. However you slice it, walleyes are most often caught from a boat. Some seasonal shore fishing opportunities exist and there's always ice fishing, but during most of the year fishing for this species demands a boat.

The author has watched with enthusiasm the evolution of walleye boats. A decade ago the average boat used for walleye fishing was 16 feet long and powered by a 25-horse outboard. Today a growing percentage of boats are 18 to 20 feet long and powered with V-6 outboards. His current boat, a Fisher fiberglass model, is typical of the direction many walleye anglers are going.

My first boat purchased for the purpose of walleye fishing was a 16-foot MirroCraft with a 25-horsepower tiller operated Mariner outboard. The boat had an electric motor on the transom, a flasher at the back of the boat, rod holders, pedestal seats and an aerated live well.

Modest by current standards, if memory serves me I paid around $3,000 for the whole package. At the time everyone in my fishing club was in awe of what we considered to be the ultimate boat for fishing walleyes. My current "walleye" boat is 19 feet long, made of fiberglass, powered by a 200-horsepower outboard. It has an electric motor on the bow, a four-stroke kicker motor on the transom, a Global Positioning System with a differential module on the console, three liquid crystal sonar units scattered throughout the boat, a VHF marine radio, built-in charging systems, timers on the live wells and recirculation pumps, and I'm ashamed to admit it cost 10 times more than my first boat!

The size, horsepower rating, speed and cost of fishing boats has skyrocketed in recent years. I often feel a twinge of sympathy when I see anglers shopping for a new boat at shows or marine dealers. The decision on which boat to buy can be gut-wrenching from the standpoint of picking one brand over another, wrestling with size considerations and with the realization that boats can be overwhelmingly expensive.

Before we get into a discussion about what makes a good boat for walleye fishing, lets step back to a time when boats didn't have to have three motors to be considered a craft for fishing walleyes.

I started my fishing career in a modest boat with modest equipment and I recommend that others do the same. When I first started fishing for walleyes I lived near a river that had an excellent spring and fall run of fish. A small boat was the only logical way to navigate the many shallow portions of the river and a lot of fancy accessories weren't needed to catch fish.

I depended on a flasher to find holes and depressions in the river bottom that routinely held fish and a simple transom mounted electric motor to position the boat for fishing. Most of my fish were caught on jigs or simple bottom-fishing rigs.

Gradually my desire to learn more about walleyes, where they live and how to catch them in other bodies of water forced me to consider a larger boat with more horsepower. My little Mirro-Craft served me well in the river, but in larger bodies of water it soon became obvious that bigger is better. A bigger boat is not only safer on large bodies of water, it allows anglers the speed and flexibility to explore more water while searching for fish.

My second boat was a 17-foot console design with a 90-horsepower outboard, bow-mounted electric motor and small gasoline kicker motor on the back. Compared to my MirroCraft, this 17-footer seemed like an aircraft carrier. However, it didn't take long before I was wishing for even more boat.

At about this time in my fishing career I started getting active in tournaments. Speed and performance became issues in my boat buying decisions

for the first time. I purchased a fiberglass boat and outfitted it with a 135-horsepower outboard. At the time I was one of the first anglers in the country to fish with a V-6 outboard for walleyes.

The speed this boat generated was just the ticket for making long runs and the extra power was essential for handling rough water and big waves. Eventually I moved up to a bigger boat and a 175-horsepower outboard, then a bigger boat yet with 200 ponies and eventually purchased a 20-foot class with a 225-horsepower outboard. The education I gained by running boats at both ends of the spectrum has helped me establish (at least in my mind) what makes a good boat for walleyes.

As in most pursuits, there comes a point when growth is offset with a sacrifice. In the case of walleye boats, size is a welcome luxury until the boat reaches the point that it becomes too large to launch and trailer easily, a chore to control on the water, a maintenance headache and difficult to afford. For

Most walleye anglers are well-served with a 17- to 18-foot boat. This size craft is ideal for rivers and natural lakes. A boat of this size is also capable of handling the Great Lakes and large reservoirs so long as common sense is applied.

me, a 18- to 19-foot craft is as big as I need. However, for some anglers an even bigger boat may be just the solution to their personal fishing needs.

Speaking from experience, the average recreational angler is well-equipped with a fishing boat in the 17- to 18-foot range. This size boat is easy to trailer, affordable and when equipped with an outboard motor from 75- to 125-horsepower, more than capable of handling most fishing situations.

Outboard motors are the only logical choice for a walleye fishing boat. Much of the best fishing for these species takes place early and late in the year when the threat of freezing conditions makes it risky to use inboard/outboard motors. When fishing an outboard in cold weather, make sure to tilt the motor downward to let all the water run out of the lower unit before storing the boat.

Some anglers like to start their motor out of water, throttle up the motor and let the exhaust blow any water out of the lower unit. This practice is risky business and can cause serious damage to the motor.

I recommend equipping all walleye boats with a small gasoline motor for trolling applications, a bow-mounted electric motor for other boat control chores and at least one quality sonar unit. A boat of this size with the equipment package described represents a good marriage of function and cost for most anglers.

It's hard for me to recommend smaller boats because walleyes aren't the kind of fish that are normally found on small bodies of water. There are exceptions, such as rivers, but for the most part walleyes are fish that thrive on large natural lakes, reservoirs and the Great Lakes where the potential for rough water is a constant threat.

Keeping big water in mind, anglers who spend most of their time on large bodies of water may find that a slightly larger boat, in that 19- to 20-foot range, better meets their needs. This is exactly where my personal boat needs fall. Living in the Great Lakes region, I often find myself fishing Lake Erie, Saginaw Bay and other large bodies of water. A bigger boat yields a smoother, drier and more comfortable ride in the conditions most commonly encountered on open water.

This is also why I personally have used fiberglass boats most of my fishing career. I'm often faced with boating conditions that are less than desirable. Despite some impressive advancements in aluminum hull designs, fiberglass boats offer a smoother and drier ride on the water. This fact is never more apparent than when running long distances in rough water.

In fairness to aluminum hulls, these boats can also perform well on big water, especially if larger models are selected. The Lund Barron is a classic example of an aluminum hull big water boat. This 21-footer features deep sides and a walk-through windshield that turns away spray and waves before they can soak the occupants.

One of my dearest friends, Captain Al Lesh has run this boat for more years than I can remember. The Barron is ideal for open-water trolling situations, however the high profile and windshields of this model make it tough to control in other fishing situations. No doubt this is why Captain Lesh runs two boats for his guiding and tournament fishing. The Barron is his open-water trolling boat and a 17-foot Lund is used for fishing rivers and smaller bodies of water.

Herein lies the boating compromise that all anglers are forced to make. There is no such thing as one perfect boat for fishing walleyes, because no two anglers demand the same things from their boat. Anglers who fish primarily on rivers or protected waters can get by nicely with a modest boat in the 16- to 17-foot range. The average angler who fishes a wide variety of waters, including some big water, may find that a 17- to 18-foot boat is a good choice. Those walleyes fanatics that frequent big water or who fish tournaments will no doubt be best served with a 19- to 20-foot boat.

Like Al Lesh, I've solved this dilemma by owning not one, but two boats. A 19-foot tournament boat meets my needs for fishing big water and a 16-foot aluminum boat is perfect for fishing small rivers or backwoods lakes.

Obviously, not everyone can afford or justify owning two boats. Most anglers are forced to compromise and select one fishing boat that best meets their primary needs and fishing style. This is the very reason so many anglers find themselves in boats that are on the small side.

CONSOLE VS TILLER

My first boat for fishing walleyes was a tiller design. When fishing from smaller boats, tillers offer more useable fishing space compared to console models. However, as boats increase in size the need for extra space diminishes and so does the demand for tillers.

A number of tiller boats are available in the 16-, 17-, 18- and even 19-foot class. Also, more tiller boats are offered in aluminum than fiberglass. In the case of the larger tiller models, tradi-

Tiller models were once the most common walleye boats. A tiller provides space in a rather small package.

tion has a stronger influence on design than function. Some folks simply prefer tiller boats because they are familiar with them. The truth is, a console boat can do anything a tiller can do.

The trend in the walleye fishing industry has been away from tiller boats and towards console models. Tournament influence has undoubtedly been a strong factor in the popularity of console boats that are faster, drier and more comfortable to ride in.

However, despite industry trends I don't expect to see tiller designs completely disappear. I wouldn't own a tiller boat because they are much more difficult to sell than console models, but from a fishing stand point, tiller boats are functional and affordable.

ALUMINUM VS FIBERGLASS

At some point most boat buyers are confronted with the issue of choosing an aluminum or fiberglass hull. Selecting one of these boat building materials over the other is a tricky and often painful decision. Fiberglass boats are often characterized as "higher quality" but the truth is both fiberglass and aluminum have advantages and disadvantages.

Starting with the benefits of aluminum, the market place is dominated with fishing boats made from aluminum. Not only are there more brands produced using aluminum, but there are significantly more models to choose from. From the standpoint of choice, boat buyers have a lot more to pick from if they decide to go with aluminum.

Anglers have many more brands and models of aluminum boats to choose from. Aluminum boats are also less expensive than fiberglass models in most cases.

Aluminum boats also tend to be a little less expensive when compared to fiberglass hulls. This statement is especially true when considering the small to medium-sized boats. Large aluminum boats are comparable in price to similar-sized fiberglass hulls.

Weight is another consideration worth exploring. Aluminum boats are, on the average, lighter and easier to trailer than fiberglass models. To some degree this also depends on boat size, but as a building material aluminum is somewhat lighter than fiberglass. Anglers who are limited to a modest tow vehicle such as a mini-van or sedan are going to find that a lighter aluminum boat makes the most sense.

Aluminum boats have also come a long way in recent years in the area of hull design, strength, fit and finish. New hull designs are yielding smoother riding boats, welded hulls on aluminum boats are a breakthrough that provide notable advantages in durability and performance. The better aluminum boats these days are beefed up to handle just about anything an angler might encounter. Thicker

hulls, more ribs and stronger bracing are just some of the advancements. One manufacturer, Alumacraft, even produces boats with double hulls to insure against failures.

When comparing aluminum to fiberglass the biggest difference between the two is noticed in hull design. Because fiberglass gel and mat can be molded into a wealth of shapes, 'glass hulls are the leaders in speed and performance. Most walleye boats are designed with a deep "V" hull. Fiberglass hulls incorporate a design feature known as "reverse chines" that takes water displaced by the boat and forces it to the side as the boat moves forward. Like the "V" blade on a snow plow that efficiently moves snow out of the way, the result of this hull design is a smoother and drier ride. Most fiberglass hulls also have a very sharp dead rise or angle to the "V" that helps to slice through the water smoothly, meaning the boat doesn't pound as much as more rounded aluminum hulls.

Another hull design unique to fiberglass is known as the padded hull. A padded hull is simply

It takes a full-sized vehicle to tow a full-sized walleye boat. Most anglers favor a full-sized van, pick–up truck or recreational utility vehicle.

cant damage occurs, chances are the original strength or integrity may never be restored.

Some anglers also prefer the flashy lines and endless assortment of colors offered in fiberglass boats. There's little doubt that metal-flake finishes make for eye catching and attractive boats. Fiberglass boats also tend to offer more creature comforts such as custom seats, piston operated storage lids, built-in charging systems, lighted compartments, the choice of carpeted or low maintenance fiberglass decks and many other extras.

Now that we've outlined some of the high points of fiberglass and aluminum hulls, it becomes clear there's no obvious winner in the war between boat hulls. The choice of an aluminum or fiberglass hull is largely a personal one. The decision an angler makes is no doubt going to be motivated by price, function, tradition and a dozen or more other factors.

There are so many brands, models and options available when it comes to selecting a fishing boat, the process of picking one model is difficult at best. Not unlike shopping for an automobile, a boat purchase is a big commitment for most families and one that takes a considerable amount of time and energy.

WARRANTY CONCERNS

One of the elements of boat buying that anglers should watch closely is warranty. Like boats themselves, not all warranties are created equal. Even those warranties that offer similar coverage at first glance, can look much different when the fine print is read carefully.

Boat warranties range from five years to the life of the boat. Unfortunately, lifetime or other long-term warranties are often riddled with disclaimer clauses that dilute the actual amount of coverage. Warranty agreements that span five to 10 years tend to offer more concrete coverage.

Before purchasing a boat, ask around to get a feel for which companies have good warranties and which ones are easy to work with on warranty claims. Boat dealers and boat owners are good sources for this information.

Amazingly outboard motors have rather short warranty agreements considering the cost of these products. Most outboards are only covered by a one-year warranty. Some brands offer two years of coverage.

All the major outboard manufacturers offer extended warranty programs and I highly advise

a cut-out portion of the hull located at the back of the boat and directly in front of the outboard motor. Referred to as the pad, this pocket gives the boat more lift in the water. Boats with padded hulls run on plane with only the back third of the boat touching the water.

Because more boat is lifted out of the water, friction is reduced and speed is increased. If speed is an important concern, it's worth noting that most fiberglass boats tend to offer a higher horsepower rating than similar sized aluminum hulls.

Fiberglass also has another advantage over aluminum. If a glass hull is damaged it can easily be repaired to original condition by any service center experienced in fiberglass work. Aluminum hulls are much more difficult to repair. If signifi-

Fiberglass boats have the edge on performance, especially when running in rough water. The hull designs of fiberglass boats simply enable them to slice through waves with less pounding and abuse to the occupants.

anglers to consider them. For a few hundred dollars up front, warranty agreements can be extended considerably. Not only does this coverage provide peace of mind, there's a real value if something serious such as a powerhead or lower unit fails. It seems everything that needs fixing on an outboard motor is expensive. This is especially true if V-6 style outboards are involved.

Selecting a boat and motor package is something I've done 15 times in my fishing career. Despite a considerable amount of experience in buying and running boats, each new boat purchase becomes more difficult. Frankly there are a lot more quality boats to choose from, and new models and brands are popping up every year. A few of the trusted brands that produce boats well-suited to fishing walleyes include Lund, Crestliner, Ranger, Tracker, Warrior, Alumacraft, Triton, Skeeter, Lowe, Sea Nymph, Pro Craft, Starcraft, Champion, Fisher, Smokercraft, Astro, Sylvan, Yar-Craft and Tuffy. Within these brands anglers can choose from more than 100 models that range from modest to magnificent.

In the next chapter we'll look even more closely at walleye boats. Rigging a fishing boat with electronics, rod holders, kicker motors and a wealth of other fishing accessories will be our focus.

Outboard motors are expensive items with limited warranty agreements. Anglers are well advised to consider purchasing extended warranty agreements offered by the leading manufacturers.

CHAPTER 9

RIGGING THE DREAM MACHINE

In the preceding chapter, emphasis was placed on fishing boats suitable for walleye fishing. Many hurdles must be overcome in the process of purchasing a boat. Issues dealing with size, hull type, warranties and a dozen other concerns often make boat buying a tedious and frustrating experience.

That's the bad news. The good news is once you've made your boat selection, rigging is how an ordinary boat is converted into a fishing dream machine. Accessories make the man, but accessories on a fishing boat are almost as important as the boat itself. Sonar and how it's mounted, electric motors, gasoline kickers, marine radios and rod holders are just a few of the accessories that must be purchased and later mounted in the most functional locations.

The rigging process is a service that most anglers leave in the hands of the marine dealer who sold the boat. After all, dealers are the experts at boat rigging, so why not let the experts handle these chores? If you've never rigged a boat before and you're not exactly handy with tools or the ways of electricity, leaving the rigging chores to the dealer may be the best option.

Personally, I've always considered boat rigging to be a part of my fishing education. The process of boat rigging helps me learn about new accessories and how they are used. More importantly, by doing the work myself I can be certain that things are mounted how and where I want them. This can be a major issue should the need arise to fix something while on the road or, worse yet, on the water.

Let's use electronics as an example. Your new GPS unit shuts down and you can't get it to turn back on. If you wired this piece of electronic gear you'll know exactly were the fuse cartridge is located and it's an easy job to check the fuse and replace it, if necessary. Say the fuse is okay and the unit still won't turn on. Chances are a wire connector has come loose somewhere between the unit and the battery source. Again, if you did the wiring, finding the problem isn't a big chore. However, if the wiring was done by someone else, the problem will likely have to be dealt with by a service technician.

Aside from knowing the specifics of rigging, doing the job yourself offers a great sense of satisfaction. Also, if you're anything like me, some personal preferences or biases will be involved in deciding how and where accessories are mounted. Take kicker motors for instance. I'm left-handed, so I prefer my kicker to be mounted on the starboard side of the boat so I can control the motor

Rigged and ready for action, a boat isn't a walleye boat until it's completely rigged with all the accessories that make fishing more enjoyable and successful.

with my strong arm. A kicker motor on the port side of a boat is as foreign to me as a steering wheel would be on the right side of your car.

Aside from the personal satisfaction that comes from getting involved, having input in this process makes for a boat that's user-friendly for the owner, not the marina employee who rigged it. If you decide to allow someone else to handle the rigging chores, make sure you provide a detailed list as to where and how accessories should be mounted. Better yet, make yourself available to be on hand when the rigging is taking place to make the important decisions.

Even if you don't touch a single wire, watching how the process of boat rigging is completed will help you, if problems arise down the road. Who knows, maybe you might even enjoy the process and develop enough confidence to take on the chore of rigging your next boat.

GETTING STARTED RIGGING

Before drilling the first hole or even taking accessories out of their boxes, take a few minutes and sit in the boat. Imagine how you'll be fishing and exactly where you'll get the most benefit from accessories such as sonar units, rod holders, marine radios and other items. The golden rule of boat rigging is to make absolutely sure you're mounting things in the right location before the holes are drilled.

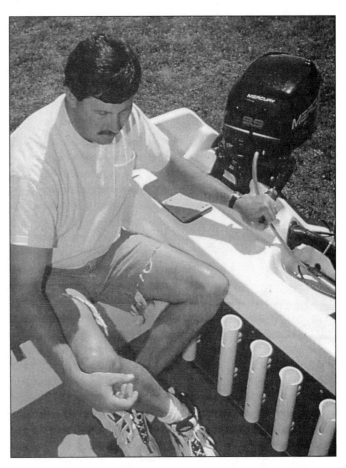

Before drilling the first hole, take some time and sit in your boat to get a feel for the location of rod holders, electronics and other accessories.

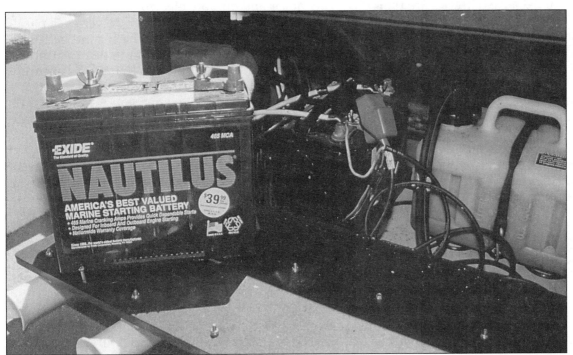

Mounting batteries is the first chore in rigging a boat. Batteries must be securely mounted to prevent them from moving while running in rough water.

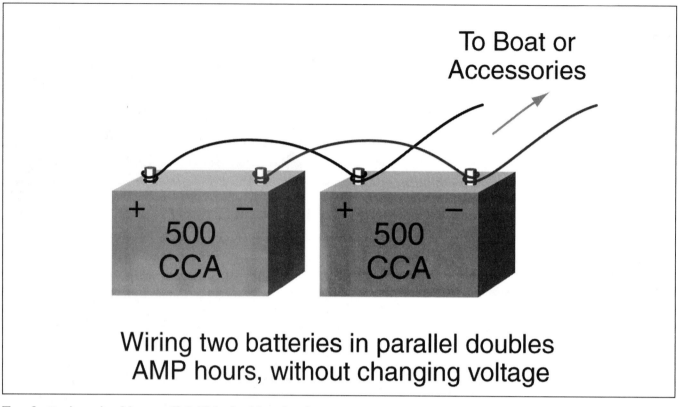

To Boat or Accessories

Wiring two batteries in parallel doubles AMP hours, without changing voltage

Two batteries wired in parallel. This doubles the time you can use your accessories.

When rigging a new boat, the less than glamorous jobs come first. Mounting battery boxes, installing batteries and securely strapping them against movement is the first step. This process is often an awkward job because batteries are typically mounted in the back of the boat near the bilge area or in dry storage boxes that are cramped and difficult to work in. What's worse, batteries are heavy and can be difficult to get into position.

Fishing boats require two different types of batteries. A cranking-style battery is used to start the outboard motor and run accessories such as sonar units. Most marine dealers use a battery with 500 cold cranking amps for this purpose. A battery this size is more than capable of starting the main outboard, but when multiple accessories are run off this battery problems quickly result. The amps it takes to run sonar units, a GPS, bilge pumps, live well pumps, recirculation pumps, auto-pilots, a VHF radio and other electronic goodies places too much strain on an ordinary 500-amp cranking battery.

This problem can be solved by installing a battery with more cold cranking amps. Models that produce up to 1,000 amps are better able to handle the chore of starting the outboard and running

accessories. Some anglers prefer to run two 500-amp batteries in parallel. Wiring the batteries in parallel doubles the amp hours (service time), but doesn't change the voltage. It takes 12 volts to start the motor and operate electronic accessories.

The problem with wiring two batteries in parallel is finding a place to mount the second battery. This can be a challenge in the cramped quarters of many boats. If there's no room to mount a second cranking battery, purchase and mount the biggest cranking style battery you can find.

Deep-cycle batteries will be needed to operate the electric motor. On boats in the 14- to 16- foot range a 12 -volt electric motor with 40 to 50 foot pounds of thrust is adequate. With larger boats a 24-volt motor that generates 50 to 65 foot pounds of thrust is required and the new 36-volt systems that generate 70 to 100 foot pounds of thrust are ideal for 19- to 20-foot tournament-style boats.

As with cranking batteries, most anglers tend to underestimate the amount of amp hours needed to operate an electric motor. I recommend that anglers invest in the biggest and best quality deep-cycle batteries they can afford. My boats are rigged with two MotorGuide Thermoil deep-cycle batteries that feature 1250 amp hours. These

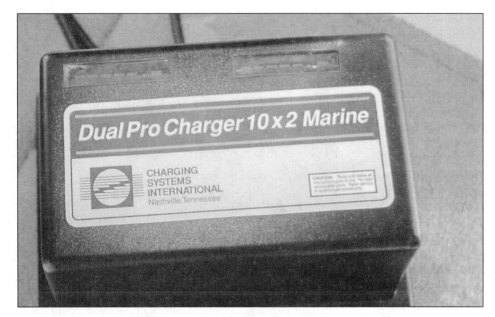

On board charging units are the most convenient and practical way to charge deep cycle batteries. Units can be purchased that charge a bank of two or three batteries at the same time.

unique batteries not only have high amp potential, they provide longer service, less maintenance and maximum efficiency in hot or cold weather.

High-amp deep-cycle batteries not only provide more power when you need it, these batteries tend to have a longer service life than smaller power sources that must be recharged more often.

Years ago I discovered that on-board chargers are the easiest and most efficient way to charge deep-cycle or cranking batteries. On-board charging systems have many benefits. Most importantly these chargers are waterproof and feature short-circuit protection. Also, most models offer some type of test feature that allows you to determine how much juice each battery contains, plus an auto-stop function that shuts off the charger when the battery reaches capacity.

These features are great, but the real value of an on-board charger is the convenience. Once wired to deep-cycle and/or cranking batteries, the angler only has to plug in a power cord to begin the charging process. Three-bank units can charge two deep-cycle and one cranking batteries at once. Two-bank chargers are designed for two deep-cycle batteries.

On-board charging units must be mounted rather close to the batteries and in a location where accessing the power cord is easy. Once batteries and charging units are installed, power leads for sonar units, marine radios, GPS units and other electronic accessories must be run.

Most electronic accessories are simple to wire. Generally a single hot wire (red) and ground wire (black) is required. Accessories such as sonar

units, GPS units and radios should be wired directly to the battery using an in-line fuse harness.

Some boat riggers wire sonar and other equipment to an accessory switch mounted on the console. Wiring to an accessory switch is asking for

VHF radios should not be wired on the same harness used to power sonar or GPS units. Electrical interference can cause these accessories to cut out when the radio is used.

trouble. Not only do these switches fail frequently, they are often connected to fuses that are too large to prevent short-circuits from damaging valuable electronics.

Two pieces of electronics such as a sonar unit and GPS can be wired to the same power lead. Avoid adding a VHF radio to the same power lead used for sonar units. This common rigging mistake can cause the graph to cut out every time the radio is keyed up. To avoid any chance of electrical interference run a separate power lead for the marine radio.

Simple power leads can be fashioned from two lengths of 12-gauge wire (one red wire and one black wire) taped together. I prefer to purchase two-strand wire designed especially for this purpose. Ring connectors that will fit over the posts of the battery are attached first using a pair of crimpers. Remember the big ring connector should be crimped onto the positive wire and the small ring connector to the negative lead.

Once these connectors are crimped in place, test them by pulling on the connector to be sure it is tight. Next thread off enough wire from the coil to be sure the power lead is long enough to easily reach the accessory it will service.

For most boats a power lead will need to be run to the console. Another power lead will need to be run if a VHF radio is to be installed. Most boat manufacturers rig a power lead to the bow of the boat suitable for wiring a sonar unit at this location. This power lead is usually hidden behind an observation plate somewhere near the bow.

To prevent screws from vibrating loose, coat the threads with a small amount of silicon before installing them.

Power leads are usually run from the back of the boat along the gunwales to the console. These wires are fished into position using a long flexible fiberglass pole with the end of the wire taped securely in place. A cheap fly rod with the guides removed has helped me rig more than a dozen boats.

MOUNTING ELECTRONIC ACCESSORIES

Once the power leads are in place, it's time to concentrate on mounting electronic accessories such as sonar and GPS units or marine radios. If your boat is a tiller model, the primary sonar unit and GPS unit will need to be mounted near the stern of the boat, and opposite the driver's seat where it can be readily seen while motoring from one location to the other. Many tiller boats feature an electronics locker that makes a convenient home for sonar and GPS units, while at the same time giving these expensive accessories some protection.

On console boats these accessories are normally mounted on the driver's console where they are easy to see and protected from the elements. Before

On console boats the primary electronics and GPS unit will be mounted on the driver's console. Not all consoles have enough room to easily mount these accessories.

The GPS antenna in this case was exactly the same size as the drink cup holder. The author mounted the antenna here to avoid drilling a large hole in the top deck.

drilling any holes, position these accessories to be sure there is enough room to mount them.

Some boats simply don't have enough console room to mount both a sonar unit and GPS. In this case mounting the GPS unit on the top of the gunwale near the driver's seat is a good second option. R-A-M brand mounts are ball-and-socket style mounts that help solve lots of sonar mounting problems. Sonar units can also be mounted flush into the dash board of some boats. This is a very clean mounting method, but only a few boat models facilitate this option.

If sonar or GPS units are mounted on top of the console, a hole must be cut that's large enough to easily thread the power cords, transducer plugs and other wires through. Normally this hole will need to be from 1 to 2 inches in diameter. A hole saw does a nice job on both fiberglass and aluminum consoles. When drilling large holes in fiberglass, place a piece of masking or duct tape over the area to be removed. The tape helps to prevent the 'glass from chipping while the hole is being cut.

The sonar or GPS unit can be mounted securely to the top of the console using the bracket that comes with the unit, but I personally prefer to use a quick-disconnect style mount such

as those produced by Johnny Ray, Ultra Mount, Tite-Lok or R-A-M. Johnny Ray has a Wire Hole Cover that not only covers the hole needed to thread power and transducer cords through, it also makes a clean connection to the Johnny Ray Swivel Mount.

A quick-disconnect style bracket makes it easy to remove electronics for storage or security purposes. The cost of these accessories ranges from $15 to $30 each.

When it's time to drill the holes and mount quick-disconnect brackets, follow the manufacturer's recommendations for screw size, type and length. Stainless steel is the only practical screw material for use on boats. To prevent the screws from chipping the fiberglass finish, use a counter sink to lightly bevel the screw holes before installing the screws and tightening them.

To insure that screws don't rattle loose, put a drop of clear silicon on the screw before threading it into position. Wipe off the excess silicon and the job is done.

GPS modules or antennas pose another mounting problem. Flush mounting them to the top of the gunwale is the most popular alternative, but this requires that a rather large hole be cut in the

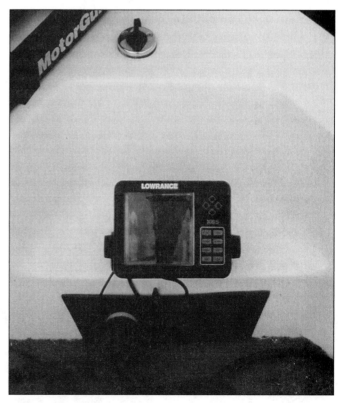

The top deck of this Fisher Boat has a spot molded in to accept a sonar unit.

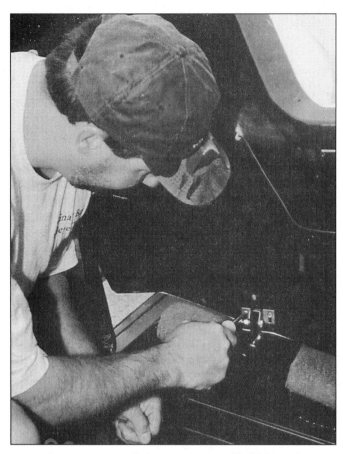

The author has no faith in through-hull style transducers. Here he has mounted an exterior transducer to the transom using two stainless steel screws.

top deck. For the last few years I've mounted GPS modules using a rail mount adapter and R-A-M ball and socket style antenna bracket. If the boat to be rigged doesn't have conveniently located rails, rails can be added if desired.

When sonar units are mounted on the bow of the boat, care must be given to insure the unit can be easily seen while fishing, but is not in the way of other accessories such as the electric motor. Most anglers choose to mount electronics on the top deck opposite the electric motor. This mounting position puts the sonar in clear view of the operator, but it also increases the chances of damaging the unit from running in rough water. Over the years, I've settled on mounting bow electronics on the casting deck near the front of the boat and close to the inside wall of the bow. Some boats also feature a spot molded into the top deck for mounting electronics. Mounted here, the sonar is visible, out of the way and protected from potential damage.

Some fiberglass boats feature through-hull style transducers for bow-mounted electronics. I feel through-hull transducers rob the equipment of valuable sensitivity or the ability to mark important details such as bait fish. An exterior-mounted transducer secured to the head of the electric motor is the best option. Special transducers or transducer brackets are available to make this mounting chore simple. The transducer cable is

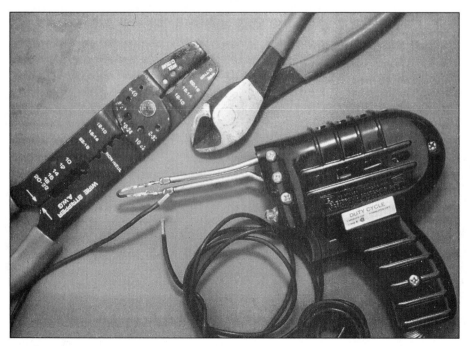

Soldering wire connections takes more time than using wire nuts or butt connectors, but the connection is much stronger. Cover the soldered wires using shrink tubing or electrical tape.

routed up the shaft of the electric motor and secured with a few wire ties. Excess transducer cable can be wrapped up and tied to the electric motor shaft where it won't get into trouble.

Marine radios pose another rigging problem. Most boats do not have a handy place to mount a radio. These accessories function best when kept dry. Mounting them under a console or in an electronics box protects the equipment from the elements. However, radios mounted in this manner can be hard to hear. An auxiliary speaker mounted in a convenient location solves this problem.

Remember when wiring a VHF radio to use a separate power lead. Radios produce electric fields that cause all kinds of problems with sonar, GPS and auto-pilots if they are wired using the same power leads. Some anglers go so far as to wire sonar and GPS units to a battery mounted solely to power these accessories.

I often wire my VHF radio to one of the deep-cycle batteries used to power the electric motor. Connecting to only one battery offers this accessory 12 volt power without fear of sending 24 volts into the marine radio.

CONNECTING POWER LEADS

Now that all the electronic accessories are mounted and power leads are run, it's time to hard wire everything together. Make sure the power leads are not connected to the battery when connecting electronics to the power source.

Butt connectors or wire nuts are commonly used to attach electronics to power leads. Both of these wire connecting methods are problems waiting to happen. Vibration is a constant problem with wire connectors. This is especially true of electronics mounted near the bow where the boat takes the most pounding.

Soldering leads together takes more time, but it also provides insurance that this vital connection won't rattle loose at the worst possible moment. Shrink tubing or electrical tape can be used to cover the bare wires once the soldering is complete.

Make sure to wire a fuse harness in-line and be sure this harness is located in an area where the fuse can be changed easily. Under the console or close to the unit it serves is the best location for a fuse harness.

Electric motors are often mounted using well nuts provided from the manufacturer. Through-bolting electric motors using 1/4-inch stainless bolts is recommended to prevent the motor from vibrating loose during heavy service.

RIGGING ELECTRIC & KICKER MOTORS

Most boat packages come with the electric motor mounted at the factory. In most cases the motor will be attached using well-nuts supplied from the electric motor manufacturer. I prefer to through-bolt my electric motors to insure they don't vibrate loose under heavy service.

If your electric motor is already mounted, it only takes a few minutes to replace the well-nuts with stainless steel bolts, washers and nuts. Use the well-nut as a spacer that keeps the bracket of the electric motor from touching the top deck of the boat. It requires four 1/4-inch bolts to securely hold the electric motor. Sometimes there's not enough room to through-bolt the electric motor. In this case a well-nut or toggle bolt must be used.

A gasoline kicker motor is one of the most important accessories on a walleye boat. If I had to choose between a gasoline motor and an electric motor, I'd have to favor the gasoline motor. Ideally a good walleye boat will be equipped with both boat-control tools.

At least four rod holders will need to be mounted near the back of the boat for trolling chores. These holders need to be mounted in convenient locations and where they won't interfere with the function of seats, rod boxes or livewell lids.

Two-cycle kickers are ready to use right out of the package. Four-stroke motors must have oil added to the crankcase before using them. This oil should be changed once a year.

Kicker motors usually bolt over the transom, but in some cases a motor mount or bracket must first be installed. If the bracket must be bolted to the transom, take great care to insure the bracket is mounted in a location where the kicker indexes freely for turning and mobility. The kicker motor and the main outboard should never touch one another.

If holes must be drilled through the transom to mount a motor bracket, it's imperative that the holes are drilled straight. Use a T-square to help guide the drill bit straight along its course. Once the holes are drilled, stainless bolts will need to be installed using plenty of silicon to insure holes in the transom are sealed.

Once the kicker bracket is secure, mounting the motor is simply a matter of lifting it onto the bracket and tightening down the threaded clamps. Once the clamps are tight, I normally put a combination lock through the holes in the clamps to prevent theft and to prevent the clamps from loosening up.

If the kicker is a two-cycle motor, mounting the prop is the only thing that needs to be done. If a four-stroke kicker motor is purchased, oil must be added to the crank case before the motor can be started. The prop will also have to be mounted on the four-stroke kicker.

Vertical rod tubes are a good way to store rods while running from one fishing spot to another. These tube type holders can also be used when fishing with planer boards.

ROD HOLDERS

Rod holders are handy and a necessary item on a walleye boat, but they also cause lots of headaches. The first problem to solve is what type of holder to choose. Rod holders are available to mount on rails, flush to the top deck or on the inside edge of the top deck.

Flush-mount holders are the cleanest design and they are frequently used on the top deck of aluminum boats. Flush-mount holders can also be used on 'glass boats, but it requires cutting some pretty big holes in the top deck. Holders that mount on the inside edge of the top deck or rails are most often used with fiberglass boats. Rail-mount rod holders are the only option that eliminates the need to drill holes.

Regardless which type of rod holders are selected, it's important to sit in the boat and explore potential mounting sites before drilling any holes. The problem with rod holders is they often are located right where a seat hits them or the lid of a live well gets in the way. Give some careful consideration to the location of rod holders before reaching for the drill.

A walleye boat will need at least four rod holders located at the back of the boat for such popular presentations as planer board trolling. Normally these holders are located in the back third of the boat with two or three mounted on each side.

A rod holder will also be handy near the bow of the boat, both on the port and starboard sides. These holders come in handy while slip sinker rigging or dragging bottom bouncers and it becomes necessary to set one rod down.

I also use tube style rod holders mounted at the back of my boat. Six tube type holders mounted across the back of the boat is a great way to insure your trolling rods stay organized and tangle free when running from spot to spot.

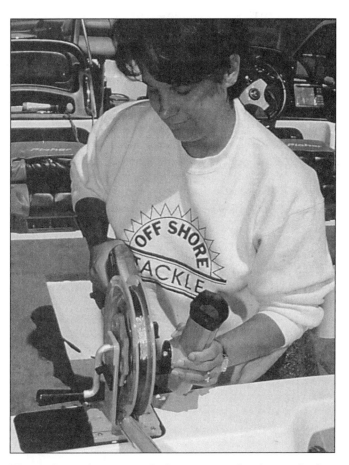

These downriggers are being mounted using swivel bases that make it easy to swivel the arms straight back when running or traveling on the road. They can be moved out to the side when fishing.

DOWNRIGGERS & PLANER BOARD MASTS

Downriggers and planer board masts are common accessories on a boat intended for walleye fishing. For most walleye fishing applications, I feel a set of manual riggers is the best choice because rarely will the angler need to reach beyond 40 or 50 feet. Riggers, like electric motors, should be through-bolted using stainless hardware and a base plate or swivel base. The most convenient location is approximately 3 feet forward of the transom on the port and starboard sides of the boat.

Mounting a base plate or swivel base allows the riggers to be removed quickly when not needed. A swivel base is handy when traveling both on and off the water.

Planer board masts see a lot of action on a walleye boat. On larger boats, the base plate for the mast is normally through-bolted near the bow. Smaller boats that have a seat base near the bow offer an even more convenient planer board mounting solution. Planer board masts can easily be adapted to fit into a standard Springfield-style seat base. This mounting method eliminates the need to bolt in a base plate and makes it very easy to install or remove the mast.

Rigging a fishing boat takes a fair amount of time and the patience to do the job right, but the satisfaction and peace of mind is worth the effort.

In the next chapter we'll take a detailed look at performance features that help make fishing boats run faster, smoother and drier.

CHAPTER 10

GETTING A PERFORMANCE BOAT TO PERFORM

When I started out fishing for walleyes, performance wasn't a term that anglers talked about at the bait shop. At the time, boats were small, outboards modest and no one had a reason to be the first boat on the spot.

The advent of tournaments changed the way anglers think about and respond to fishing. Those who don't appreciate tournaments might argue that competition and fishing aren't a good mix. I don't argue that competition often brings out the worst in folks. Money has a way of corrupting just about everything it touches. Still, tournament fishing must be credited for many improvements in our sport.

Speed is an important factor to a tournament angler. A boat that's just a few miles per hour faster translates into more fishing time. Recreational fishermen are less concerned with speed, but there are times when a little extra performance is nice when a storm suddenly approaches.

The truth is, tournaments have become the driving force that facilitates improvements in boat size, speed and performance, not to mention a wealth of advancements in terminal tackle, rods, reels and every other facet of fishing. Livewells mounted in the back of the boat, stronger hulls, better interior designs, drier riding boats and improved storage space are just some of the boating benefits made possible as a result of the influence tournament fishing imparts on the marine industry.

In the same way that professional auto racing has lead to improvements in seat belts, brakes, better tires, improved suspensions and a host of other auto performance and safety features, professional fishing has had an impact on boat design and performance. Looking at the big picture, if it weren't for tournament anglers demanding better products, the evolutionary process of sport fishing would slow down considerably.

Boat performance involves a number of issues, but speed is the driving force. Speed is an important factor in tournaments for a simple reason; it allows for more fishing time. A boat that's slightly faster than another translates into several minutes of additional fishing time. Factored over an eight-hour fishing day, speed can easily add 30 or more minutes of fishing time to the clock. The time savings provided by faster boats is very valuable to the tournament angler. However you don't have to fish tournaments to benefit from a fast boat. Recreational anglers also enjoy more time spent fishing when they purchase and use a performance style boat. In the same token, recreational anglers also benefit from better boat designs and more efficient fishing machines.

PROPS & FISHING BOATS

Props are one of those topics that generate a lot of raised eyebrows, confused looks and frustrated folks. A propeller has but one basic func-

All props including this mean-looking five-blade stainless model are a compromise. No single prop design can give maximum hole-shot and top-end speed. This Mercury High-Five offers excellent hole-shot when the boat is loaded down with passengers, gear and the livewells are full. At top end this prop offers good speed, although three- and four-blade props are faster.

One prop may be ideal for running at high speeds and with heavy loads, while a lower pitch model can help slow down trolling speeds while fishing.

UNDERSTANDING PITCH

Prop pitch is a frequently misunderstood term. Many fishermen and boaters mistakenly believe that switching to a larger pitch prop will make the boat go faster. Actually pitch refers to the distance a boat will travel forward per revolution of the propeller. In other words, a 23 pitch wheel is designed to move the boat forward 23 inches for each prop revolution.

If too large a pitch prop is used, the motor simply doesn't have enough horsepower to turn the prop adequately and the RPM level drops. Not only does the boat go slower, but the motor can load up and the plugs become fouled. If too low a pitch prop is used the prop will exceed the manufacturers recommended RPM level and engine damage can occur.

The ideal situation is to select a prop with a pitch that allows the motor to reach the maximum RPM suggested by the manufacturer without going over. If the prop selected doesn't reach the recommended RPM level, the boat will sacrifice both speed and lift.

Here's a simple rule of thumb to follow when experimenting with prop pitch. When running with the throttle wide open, increasing the prop pitch will reduce the RPM levels by roughly 200 RPM's per inch of pitch. In other words, when switching from a 23 to a 25 pitch prop, the maximum RPM level will drop approximately 400 RPM's. The reverse is true when going down in pitch size.

ALUMINUM OR STAINLESS PROPS

The first question a fisherman should ask is, "Do I need an aluminum or stainless steel prop?" In most situations aluminum props are the ideal choice for recreational fishing boats. Aluminum props cost about 1/3 the price of stainless and they can be repaired at a modest cost if damaged. The average aluminum prop costs about $150 compared to $400-$600 for stainless.

Aluminum props are the ideal choice for small to medium-size boats and motors. Available up to 23 pitch, aluminum props are also the logical choice for use in areas where prop damage comes with the territory. Those who frequently fish in riv-

tion, forward propulsion. Yet selecting the best possible prop is anything but second nature.

The problem with props is they come in a wide variety of materials, pitches and blade styles. If this situation wasn't confusing enough, virtually every prop offers a compromise of function.

In a perfect world every prop would deliver outstanding hole shot, maximum top-end speed and ideal mid-range performance. Unfortunately, a single prop can't perform flawlessly at all these levels. Fishermen are therefore forced to pick a prop that offers the best compromise of features. Not surprisingly, those who are serious about boat performance routinely carry two different props.

ers or around shallow water are wise to stick with aluminum props that can be repaired at a modest cost. If a stainless prop strikes an under water object the prop will suffer damage and there's a good chance the lower unit may also need repair.

Stainless steel props come into their own when matched with high performance boats. Designed for boats equipped with V-6 outboards, stainless steel props enable these powerhouses to achieve maximum speed and performance when hauling heavy loads.

Aluminum props are the popular choice because of their modest price, but stainless props have several advantages. Stainless props deliver more perfor-

mance and are available in larger pitch sizes suitable for higher horsepower outboard motors.

The reason stainless props provide more performance than similar pitch aluminum models is because the steel blades are rigid and they don't flex under power. The blades on an aluminum prop actually bend when the prop is in use, reducing the overall size of the prop by approximately one pitch size. Stainless props also provide increased bow lift, especially on heavy boats. The more bow lift a prop provides, the faster and smoother the boat will ride at high speed and in rough water. Stainless props can also help to reduce problems such as porpoising at all speeds.

Which is best, aluminum or stainless props? The answer depends on the type of outboard motor and how much performance the user demands.

Damaged props cost money to repair. Had this prop been a stainless model, chances are serious engine damage may have occurred.

THREE BLADES, FOUR BLADES OR FIVE BLADES

Aluminum and stainless props are available in three-blade, four-blade and five-blade models. Multiple-blade props came on the scene in response to high horsepower outboards that are typically mounted higher on the transom than smaller motors. Because the prop runs closer to the surface disturbance, the extra blades help to provide bite and stability at high speed. Most multiple-blade props are stainless, but Mercury Marine's new Typhoon is a four-blade aluminum wheel that's designed to provide extra lift for boats that have problems getting on plane.

Props with extra blades also help to reduce chime walk, provide quicker take-offs and allow the boat to be kept on plane with lower engine RPMs. It's routinely accepted that four- and five-blade props deliver better hole shot, but are slightly slower at top-end speeds. A quality three-blade prop is normally 2 or 3 MPH faster at top-

Stainless wheels are available in three-, four- and five-blade models. The best speed is offered by three-blade props and the best hole shot by five-blade versions. Four-blade props are a compromise of functions and are becoming quite popular.

end compared to the same pitch prop featuring multiple blades.

Most top walleye tournament pros favor the compromise of properties offered by the four-blade prop. Four-blade wheels offer excellent hole shot and good to excellent top-end speed. Some anglers are quick to point out that five-blade props are only 2-3 MPH slower at top-end and they provide the best low-end and mid-range performance.

A trick some anglers use to get maximum hole shot is to incorporate a small hub prop on a large size lower unit. The smaller hub size allows exhaust gases to escape both around and through the middle of the prop. The result is a little more bite and less prop slippage or blowout when powering up quickly.

All the major outboard manufacturers produce both stainless and aluminum props. In addition, independent companies such as Michigan Wheel produce outstanding props for every major I/O and outboard motor.

Unfortunately, picking props is largely a trial and error process. Since it's not practical to purchase several different sizes and try them all, it makes sense to swap with fellow fishermen and friends when selecting and testing props. Some marine dealers will allow their customers to "test" props before purchasing them, with the agreement that if the prop is damaged the customer is responsible for purchasing it. My advice is to tread lightly until you're sure you've found the right prop.

JACK PLATES

Jack plates are sandwiched between the outboard and transom of the boat. Most models span either 6 or 12 inches, increasing the overall length of the boat from the bow to prop. Originally these accessories came on the scene as a means of achieving better hole shot, more bow lift and additional speed from performance bass boats. Many walleye boats however cry out for the advantages of a jack plate.

Jack plates or set-back plates, as they are sometimes called, accomplish improved hole shot performance by slightly increasing the angle or pitch at which the outboard is mounted to the boat. This feature tends to cause most boats to plane out faster and reduce porpoising while running at mid range speeds. Jack plates also allow the engine to be mounted higher than normal for more speed or improved bite or lower than normal for running in rough water conditions.

Walleye boats are prime candidates for set-back plates because these boats are often running fully loaded and in rough water. The extra length a set-back plate adds is equivalent to running a boat that's 6 or 12 inches longer. The boat is better able to bridge the gap between waves, delivering a smoother and drier ride.

A few rules of thumb apply to the use of jack plates. Normally, jack plates are used on fiberglass performance hulls. A jack plate simply can't function to its fullest when mounted on an aluminum hull.

Also, these performance accessories are normally not required on a boat that features a built-in style set-back. Many fiberglass boats mold a 6- to 12-inch set-back right into the transom. The Fisher FX DV, Tracker Targa and Ranger Fishermen are examples of fiberglass boats that feature a molded in set-back. This set-back is part of the boat and functions like an add-on jack plate.

This fiberglass boat features a built-in set-back that improves boat performance and gives more room in the back of the boat.

Jack plates are also normally used only on boats with larger horsepower outboards. The benefit of a jack plate is hard to appreciate when incorporated with a motor less than 100 horsepower. Ideally, jack plates are used on V-6 outboards ranging from 135 to 225 horsepower.

Both manual and hydraulic style jack plates are available. Manual plates are adjusted by loosing a series of bolts and raising or lowering the engine using a threaded rod built into the jack plate. The pitch can also be adjusted on most manual plates. Generally, manual jack plates incorporate a 6- inch set back and they run around $500 installed.

A manual jack plate should be mounted at a marine dealer because it requires removing the outboard from the transom and remounting the engine. This job requires a hoist and some experience. Unless you own a hoist, impact wrench and have done this type of work before, I'd recommend leaving this chore to the experts.

Hydraulic set backs are more sophisticated and about twice as much money. Hydraulic power is used to raise, lower and tilt the engine for a wealth of performance advantages. The controls for hydraulic jack plates are normally mounted on the steering wheel where the driver can make adjustments without taking his or her hands off the wheel.

Normally used on only the largest and fastest boats, hydraulic jack plates are beyond the needs of most recreational anglers. A few tournament anglers who are serious about speed find this accessory useful.

KICKER MOTOR BRACKETS

Depending on the boat model, kicker motors are either mounted directly onto the transom or attached to a bracket that mounts to the boat. If the kicker is mounted directly to the transom, the motor will need to be supported while running to prevent the weight of the kicker motor from causing damage to the motor. Many a walleye fisherman has gotten to his favorite fishing hole only to discover the kicker motor yoke broke from running in rough water.

The gasoline motors used as kickers on walleye boats were designed for small boats, not to go speeding across rough water. The weight of the motor snapping back and forth can break the cast metal yoke used to attach the motor to the transom if the motor isn't supported securely.

Hydraulic trim units made especially for kicker motors are becoming more popular. This accessory allows the kicker motor to be trimmed up without tilting the motor at the bracket. The result is a much stronger connection to the boat and less chance of damage.

This simple kicker bracket produced by Steve Poll supports the weight of the motor and prevents kicker damage when running in rough water.

Many of the outboard manufacturers have tried to address this problem by offering special bracing units designed to protect the kicker motor while under power. The problem is, there are tons of motors in service that have no such protection built-in from the factory.

Steve Poll is a tournament angler who manufactures an excellent after-market kicker motor bracket that's simple and functional. When the kicker is in the locked up position, a welded brace mounts between the motor's lower unit and the transom. A simple strap secures the motor from bouncing and causing damage.

A growing number of anglers are using electric or hydraulic kicker motor brackets that bolt onto the transom of the boat. These brackets strengthen the kicker motor-to-boat connection and reduce damage to the motor while making it easier to raise and lower the motor.

Once installed, the kicker motor can be trimmed up without releasing the tilt feature on the motor. The result is a stronger kicker motor-to-boat connection. Minn Kota is a leader in this field of accessories. Panther also produces an excellent after-market kicker motor bracket. Trim units for kicker motors run approximately $400.

TROLLING PLATES AND HYDROFOILS

Some anglers try to avoid the cost of a kicker motor by using a trolling plate on their main outboard. Frankly, I feel add-on trolling plates are band-aids that have little value. No trolling plate can perform the function of a kicker motor. Only a kicker can allow anglers to troll slowly for such presentations as spinners, fast for trolling crankbaits or any speed in between.

Also, the gas savings a small kicker motor provides is enough to pay for the cost of this invaluable accessory. A 100-horsepower outboard can easily burn between $10 and $20 worth of fuel per day of trolling. Compared to a kicker motor that uses less than $2 per day, it's easy to see how the savings of a kicker motor add up quickly.

If you're still not convinced that you need a kicker motor, take a look at the anglers who compete in the various walleye tournaments. Not a single angler on the North American Walleye Association or Professional Walleye Trail fishes without a kicker motor.

Hydrofoils that mount on the cavitation plate of outboards are another item I feel is unnecessary. Designed to give better hole shot and reduce porpoising, these items are targeted at problems that should be corrected by other means. Most of the time when a boat is slow to rise up on plane, it's because the outboard is too small for the task. Under-powering a boat is a common problem that has lead to band-aid products, such as hydrofoils, flooding the market.

Most times hole shot can be improved by simply selecting an outboard motor that's up to the task. If problems still exist, try experimenting with different prop styles and pitches. If all else fails try mounting two 5 degree wedges between the motor and the boat transom. The added pitch will cause the motor to gave a greater bite and more power to lift the boat out of the hole.

AUTO-PILOTS

An auto-pilot is an accessory that can make fishing not only more enjoyable, but more efficient and successful. Several types of auto-pilots are available. Models that connect to the steering wheel such as the Apelco Autohelm are most often used on larger boats in the 20- to 30- foot class. Units are available for both hydraulic and cable style steering systems that retail for between $900 and $1,100.

Newcomers in the auto-pilot world are units that mount to the kicker motor. Operated using both an electronic compass and small hydraulic cylinder, this style of auto-pilot can be used for precise boat control chores such as hovering in a river, backtrolling against the wind and trolling from waypoint to waypoint.

Kicker-mounted auto-pilots can also be interfaced with four-stroke outboards to control the throttle. These units retail for around $1,600 installed. Most anglers will find that mounting an auto-pilot is a job best performed by a trained service technician.

Not every boat used for fishing walleyes is a candidate for these performance tips. Smaller boats with modest outboards benefit the least from items such as stainless props, jack plates and auto-pilots. Larger boats however can be converted in faster, smoother riding and more efficient fishing machines through the use of these performance accessories.

In the next chapter the topic switches from boat performance to boat control. Mastering boat control is more important than boat types or lure selection because without control, all fishing presentations are destined to fail.

CHAPTER 11

MASTERING BOAT CONTROL

The biggest names in walleye fishing are specialists. Mike McClelland is a master jig fisherman. Gary Parsons is an expert troller. Keith Kavajecz is a talented river fisherman. Ted Takasaki is a live bait specialist and Gary Roach is a refined slip sinker fisherman. Each of these famous anglers are considered to be tops at their niche in the walleye game, but they also have something in common.

The boat control chores required to catch walleyes are more complex than bass, pike or other species. In many cases the boat is used to drag, pull, troll or otherwise position the lure near fish.

These anglers and countless others who consistently catch walleyes share an intimate understanding of boat control.

No matter how walleyes are targeted, (jigging, rigging, trolling, casting, etc.,) boat control is the common thread that links all successful anglers together. The boat and how it's positioned in relationship to the fish is the matrix that allows lures and live baits to end up in front of fish. Without boat control, fishing for walleyes is like a bumper car without a steering wheel. Those who don't pay attention to boat control may occasionally "bump" into a walleye or two, but consistent success will be elusive.

Compared to bass, crappie and pike fishing, the boat control required to consistently catch walleyes is more complex. Most fishing presentations for these species are put into motion with the help of a bow-mounted electric motor. The boat is steered into position and the angler casts a lure to within striking distance of waiting fish.

Using an electric motor to position the boat within casting distance of walleyes is a popular form of boat control, but only one of many boat control chores a serious walleye angler must master. It's important to note that some of the most common fishing presentations for walleyes require the boat to be dragged, drifted, pulled, backed up, trolled or otherwise positioned so the lure passes by waiting fish.

With these presentations the boat becomes a vehicle that delivers the lure instead of simply a platform from which casting is conducted. If the boat is not controlled and positioned correctly, the lure has little chance of enticing walleyes.

ANCHORING

The easiest form of boat control to master is the one least practiced by anglers after walleyes. Dropping the hook is an easy and effective way to position the boat within casting distance of waiting fish. Commonly used when drifting slip bobbers across reefs, when fishing the mouth of a small stream, when casting to a cup or feature in a weed line or as a means of holding the boat while casting crankbaits or jigs to specific bottom structure or cover, every walleye boat should have two anchors aboard.

The size and type of anchor selected is the first hurdle walleyes angler must overcome. The mushroom style anchors commonly used on small boats are simply a poor design for holding a boat in any kind of wind or waves. Walleyes boats are best equipped with either a fluke or Navy style anchor. Fluke anchors are rather lightweight. Blades or flukes on the anchor dig into the bottom when the anchor line is pulled taunt. Fluke anchors provide a solid bite on the bottom and can be easily released by simply backing up and pulling on the anchor line from the opposite direction.

Navy anchors also use flukes to cut into and hold the bottom. This style of anchor is also weighted to encourage a quick bite of bottom real estate. Navy anchors suitable for walleye boats

A snap at the end of the anchor line makes it easy to remove the line from the anchor for storage.

Every walleye boat should be equipped with a fluke or Navy style anchor and plenty of anchor line.

range in size from 12 to 20 pounds. In all anchoring situations it's better to have too much weight, than not enough.

Depending on how the boat must be positioned, it's often necessary to have two anchors on board. A strong nylon line (3/8- to 1/2-inch diameter) will be required for each anchor. As a rule of thumb, figure on using at least four times as much rope as the water is deep. In other words, if the water is 25 feet deep, it will take approximately 100 feet of line to anchor securely.

Anchor line is best stored wrapped on a plastic frame intended for organizing extension cords. A strong snap at the end of the anchor line makes it easy to attach the line to the anchor when needed or to remove it for storage.

The trick to anchoring effectively is teamwork and using the wind as an aid. Set the bow anchor line first by motoring the boat slowly into position with the bow pointing into the wind. One person lowers the anchor smoothly to the bottom, while the other backs up the boat slowly or lets the wind push the boat backward.

When enough line has been played out, tie off the anchor to a cleat and, using the boat motor, drag the anchor a couple feet to securely set the flukes into the bottom. Now untie the anchor from the front cleat and back up the boat a few yards. The second anchor is slid into the water off the back of the boat. Tie off this anchor and drag it towards the first anchor to set the flukes. Finally, position the boat midway between the two anchors and tie off securely to a bow and transom cleat.

Anchored in this manner the boat can be moved back and forth between the anchors to achieve the best possible boat position.

DRIFTING

Drifting is a popular method of boat control for catching walleyes. Letting the wind silently guide the boat over sprawling flats or other large bottom structures is a good way to cover water quickly. Normally this method of boat control is used while fishing with bottom bouncers, slip sinkers or jigs that are slid along the bottom.

At first glance, drifting may appear to be a mindless form of boat control. Actually, controlled drifting is a precise form of boat control that harnesses the wind and uses it to the angler's benefit.

Obviously drift fishing requires at least some breeze to move the boat. When the wind picks up, sea anchors are often used to slow down the drifting speed.

These parachute shaped bags come in sizes ranging from 24 to 60 inches in diameter. For walleye boats ranging in size from 16 to 20 feet, a set of 48- to 60-inch bags is required. When two sea anchors are used they need to be positioned off the bow and transom of the boat, leaving the middle open to fight and net fish. If only one sea anchor is used, it must be positioned in the middle of the boat to encourage the boat to drift sideways to the wind.

Not all sea anchors are created equal, but all are rather expensive. I prefer bags that are made of lightweight nylon or polyester fabric. Synthetic fabrics are strong, mildew resistant and they dry quickly. Because the fabric is thin, the bags can be folded up and stored in a small space. The Slo-Poke produced by Quick Change Systems is among the best sea anchors I've used. With a little care this product should last for countless years.

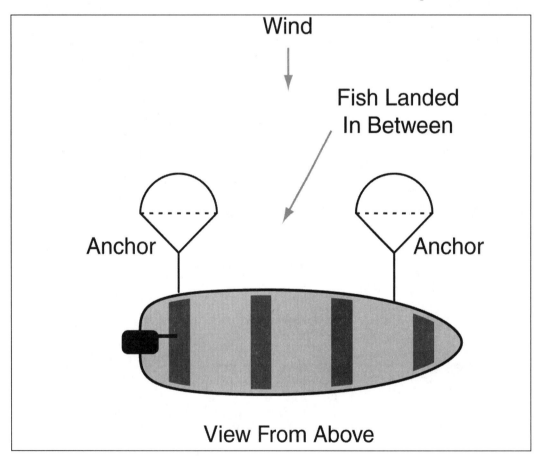

On most walleye boats it takes two sea bags to effectively control a drift in a strong wind.

When setting sea anchors it's important to let out enough line so the bag has an opportunity to open fully. The bags should be positioned from 6 to 10 feet away from the boat.

While drifting, the object is to cover water until fish are located, then make additional short and more precise drifts over the fish. Keep several marker buoys handy to mark the location where a fish is hooked. Two markers tossed 20-30 yards on opposite ends of the boat provides a target to drift towards.

Yellow is the most common color used on markers. Unfortunately, yellow is difficult to see on overcast days. Bright red or orange markers are easier to see and keep track of while fishing.

When motoring back up to make another drift, take care not to motor directly over the area to be fished. Once fish are located by drifting, a few more precise drifts can produce fast action. When the action slows chances are the fish have been

This boat is drifting between a couple of markers thrown to mark the location of fish.

spooked or caught and it's time to start drifting new water and looking for additional active fish.

FORWARD TROLLING

Forward or power trolling is without doubt the best way to cover large a mounts of water. Often practiced in cooperation with planer boards to help spread out lines, trolling has become one of the most common and productive methods of catching walleyes wherever they are found.

The first lesson in trolling is like the first lesson in setting an anchor. Never try to fight the wind while trolling. Use the wind to your advantage by trolling with the wind at your back whenever possible.

Trolling in a following sea allows the boat to be steered with less effort and allows the angler the option of slowing down to fight a hooked fish. When trolling into the wind, the boat must be steered constantly and kept moving at a steady pace to prevent the wind from pushing the boat towards a hooked fish and creating slack line.

A gasoline kicker motor (8 to 15 horsepower) is the best tool for forward trolling applications. Two-cycle motors work great, but the new four-stroke outboards that burn straight gasoline are more quiet, fuel-efficient and there's no cloud of blue smoke to breath. The extra cost of four-stroke outboards is justified considering the benefits gained.

In some respects forward trolling is like drifting. When searching for fish, long trolling passes are used to eliminate water. Once fish are located, concentrate on making short trolling passes that focus on water that's known to hold fish.

Marker buoys can be used as a guide for trolling situations, but these days a Global Positioning System (GPS unit) is the most handy means of saving locations (waypoints) and returning to spots that are holding fish. When a fish is caught a waypoint is recorded in the GPS unit or an icon or electronic marker buoy is used to identify the location of fish on the GPS screen.

The screen of a GPS unit is sort of like the screen of an Etch-A-Sketch. The boat's course of travel is shown as a plot trail. Waypoints or icons appear as symbols on the screen. The angler's chore is to steer the boat towards the icons or waypoints that represent locations of fish and come as close as possible to these electronic navigation aids.

The way to achieve the most accuracy from a GPS unit is to operate the plotter window on a

Trolling with the wind makes more sense than trying to fight the waves. This simple rule makes it easier to keep the boat under control and fight fish.

small scale. The smaller the scale or amount of water that's displayed on the screen, the more precisely the boat can be navigated to waypoints and icons. I normally troll using a 1- or 2-mile plotter scale. Once fish are located, I'll often decrease the plotter scale to 1/4 mile to provide more navigation detail.

GPS units are the only practical way to navigate in open water situations. If you don't have a GPS unit, visual floating markers will have to be used for reference. Floating markers are inconvenient because the water fished is usually deep and the span of water between markers is often expansive.

If a GPS or marker buoy isn't used as a reference, it's impossible to stay precisely on a particular location. For those anglers on a budget, a number of hand-held GPS units can be purchased for around $200. This piece of navigation equipment is more valuable than sonar once fish are located. Also, there's a safety factor in having a GPS unit aboard. Should the need arise to call the Coast Guard or sheriff marine patrol for help, you'll be able to tell them the exact coordinates of

your location, speeding up the rescue process and potentially saving lives.

BACKTROLLING

Backtrolling was all the rage when I started fishing for walleyes. Today this form of boat control has a strong following in isolated parts of the walleye heartland, especially Minnesota, northern Wisconsin, the Dakotas and Canada.

The reason backtrolling has fallen out of favor with many anglers is this form of boat control was designed around tiller-operated fishing boats. Tiller operated boats were built with backtrolling in mind. In recent years, console style boats have replaced tillers as the most common craft used for walleye fishing. While many console style boats can be backtrolled, some boats such as performance fiberglass models have padded or cupped hull designs that are not conducive to backing up. These boats are equipped with a bow mounted electric motor that in most instances can duplicate anything required of backtrolling.

Backtrolling is not as popular today as it was a decade ago. This is largely because most of the boats sold these days are console models.

Where backtrolling has the most value is when it's necessary to follow a meandering edge such as a weedline, drop off, edge of a sunken island or reef. Working from the back of the boat, an electric motor or gasoline engine is used to move the boat along a desired edge.

Unlike other forms of boat control, backtrolling is practiced into the wind. Going against the wind helps to slow down boat speed and enables the boat to be hovered in one spot as needed. The biggest problem with backtrolling is it requires a constant struggle to keep the boat precisely in position. The angler must monitor the sonar closely to insure the boat is not being pushed off the edge, cover or structure that's being targeted.

Those who are good at backtrolling can attest that this form of boat control is a deadly method for dragging jigs, rigs or bottom bouncers into the face of walleyes. Unfortunately, in most cases the boat must pass over the fish before the lures or bait can be presented. This profound limitation makes backtrolling most practical in water more than 10 feet deep.

At the risk of insulting those who favor backtrolling, this method of boat control is more difficult to learn and has less benefits than other forms of boat positioning. This technique is definitely not for beginners and even seasoned anglers struggle to backtroll effectively.

VERTICAL JIGGING RIVERS

Vertical jigging in rivers is a form of boat control and a fishing presentation rolled into one. This complex means of steering a boat into walleyes has frustrated many anglers who don't understand how to use boat control to keep jigs positioned directly below the boat.

The key to vertical jigging in current is to understand that to keep the jig vertical, the boat, jig and current must all move at the same speed. Anglers can control boat speed, but the speed of the current and the speed the jig moves in the current can't be controlled.

These facts stated, the angler's chore is to move the boat along at a speed that matches the

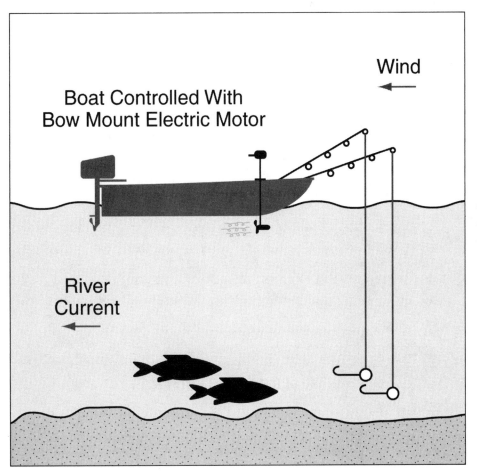

Wind

Boat Controlled With Bow Mount Electric Motor

River Current

The trick to controlling the boat while jigging is to keep the line vertical. Apply just enough power to slip through the current.

movement of the jig and current. It sounds easy, but it takes a little practice to master.

Begin by outfitting your boat with the proper equipment. A powerful bow-mounted electric motor is the ideal boat control tool for vertical jigging. Transom-mounted electric motors and small kickers can also be used for vertical jigging, but the angler will have to constantly use one hand to steer the boat, making it difficult or impossible to fish two rods at once. It's also more difficult to move the square transom of a boat against current than the pointed bow of the boat.

A bow-mounted foot controlled electric motor enables the angler to control the boat with movements from a foot petal, freeing up his hands for fishing two rods if desired.

Start by pointing the bow of the boat into the wind if a bow-mount motor is used or the transom into the wind if a tiller-operated motor is used. Let the boat drift naturally with the current for a few moments to establish the boat drifting speed.

This angler is using a bow-mounted electric motor to control his boat while vertical jigging in a river. This method of fishing is a boat control method and presentation all in one.

Now, open your reel bail and drop the jig directly to the bottom on a slack line. When the jig hits bottom, click over the reel bail and reel up the slack so the jig can be lifted up off bottom and dropped back down to touch bottom.

In a perfect world, no other means of boat control would be necessary. Unfortunately, wind catches the boat like a sail and causes the boat to move faster or slower than the current depending on which way the wind is blowing.

If the wind is blowing downstream, the boat will drift faster than the current and the electric motor will be required to slow up the boat drift. If the wind is blowing against the current, the boat won't drift as fast as the current and the electric motor will be needed to speed up the boat drifting speed.

Since the jig and current speed are constant, moving the boat as necessary is the only way to keep the line vertical. As the boat drifts either faster or slower than the current, the line to the jig will begin to angle away from the boat in one direction or another. This is the tip off that the boat needs to be moved or positioned over the top of the jig again.

Using the electric motor, move the boat towards the jig until the line is again vertical. Keeping this vertical presentation will require frequent but short bursts of power from the electric motor. If too much power is used the boat's forward momentum will carry the boat past the vertical position.

When vertical jigging it's imperative that more than one angler on board knows how to control the boat. If the angler controlling the boat catches a fish, snags bottom or otherwise temporarily stops controlling the boat, other anglers won't be able to keep their lines vertical. When the angler controlling the boat steps off the electric motor to fight a fish, clear a snag, bait a hook, etc., another angler simply steps in and takes over the boat control chores in a smooth transition.

Like drifting and trolling, the trick with drifting in rivers is to locate fish then make precise drifts back over the same water that produced walleyes. When motoring back up to make another drift, avoid driving over the water to be drifted. Make short and precise drifts using shoreline sightings and depth readings to guide your travel.

ELECTRIC MOTOR TROLLING

A wealth of walleye fishing situations call for the boat control that only a bow-mounted electric motor can perform. Positioning the boat within casting dis-

A bow-mounted electric motor is the ideal way to troll at slow speeds when pulling bottom bouncers, slip sinker rigs or jigs.

tance of cover or structure, pulling bottom bouncers along sunken islands, dragging rigs along a channel edge and silently flat-line trolling crankbaits along a shoreline are just some of the presentations that call for a bow-mounted electric motor.

A foot-control motor is the best investment because it allows both hands to be free to fish. The electric motor selected must also have enough power to fish all day. For most walleye boats in the 17- to 20-foot range a 24-volt electric motor with at least 50 pounds of thrust is required. Because walleye boats are deep-sided and ride up off the water higher than other models, a strong electric motor is required to control the boat for hour after hour.

Both cable driven and radio-controlled motors are available. Generally speaking, cable driven motors are quicker to respond to control commands and have fewer gremlins to deal with than radio-controlled units. However, radio-controlled motors offer the angler an option of fishing from any location in the boat.

Other features to look for in an electric motor is a variable speed control, constant on switch and a high bypass switch that offers up a burst of peak power when needed.

ADVANCED BOAT CONTROL METHODS

There are times when one single form of boat control isn't enough to get the job done. Some years ago while fishing the river channel in Lake Pepin, Minnesota my friend Mike Norris and I discovered an unique form of boat control that incorporates both a gasoline kicker motor and a bow-mounted electric motor.

We were dragging slip sinker rigs along the river channel and doing our best to keep the boat positioned in 12 feet of water. The wind was howling making it a constant chore to pull the boat along the break using a bow-mounted electric motor. Eventually the driving wind started winning the battle. Our battery power was fading quickly and we couldn't maintain boat control adequately.

In frustration we decided to put the gasoline kicker motor down and lock it in the forward position. The throttle was adjusted to provide just enough thrust to make slow progress against the force of the wind. Meanwhile the bow-mounted electric motor was used to steer the boat along the desired course.

The combination of the two motors worked great and allowed the boat to be positioned precisely on the depth contour that was producing fish. Since that day I've enjoyed using this means of boat control many times.

Two-motor control is also a handy way of controlling the boat while fishing wing dams. When working wing dams that project perpendicular to the river current, the boat must be held against the current then slid back and forth along the front face of the wing dam. To catch fish consistently the lures must be positioned downstream of the boat and as close to the face of the wing dam as possible.

The kicker motor provides the thrust needed to hold in the current and the electric bow-mount is an effective way of sliding the boat back and forth along the face of the wing dam. Small forward or backward movements in the current can also be accomplished using the electric motor.

Sophisticated electric motors such as the Pinpoint Positioning System are a breakthrough in

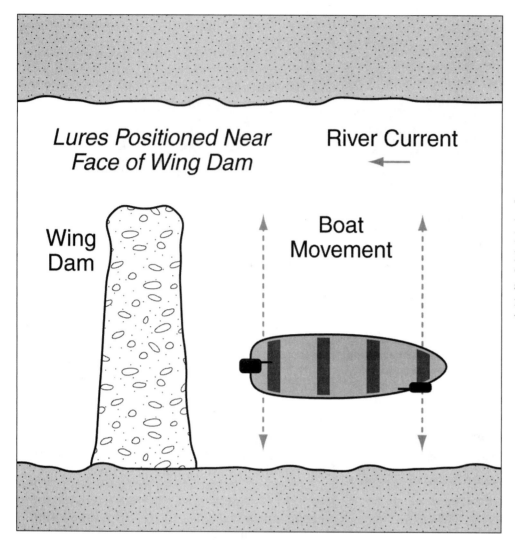

Lures Positioned Near
Face of Wing Dam

River Current

Wing
Dam

Boat
Movement

Two motors are often used to fish wing dams. The kicker motor provides the power required and the electric motor a means of sliding the boat back and forth along the face of the wing dam.

precise boat control. A series of transducers built into the powerhead are used to sense depth changes. A computer interprets the depth data and enables the motor to be programmed to follow a particular bottom contour. Imagine locating a depth contour that has fish on it and programming the electric motor to follow that contour until you program it otherwise.

This system of boat control makes for hands-free fishing that can be a real pleasure when fishing weed lines, contour breaks or other precise edges that are associated with a particular depth.

Because the Pinpoint follows depth contours like a beagle following a rabbit track, a more precise mental picture and understanding of bottom structure is provided. A Pinpoint Positioning Motor retails for around $1,600, approximately twice the cost of cable-driven manual motors. Still, this technology is an amazing thing to see in operation.

Auto-pilots are another boat-control aid that walleye anglers are starting to take advantage of. Typical auto-pilots that operate off cable or hydraulic steering systems are most likely to be used on larger boats. These systems use an electronic compass and a small pump or motor to drive the wheel as required to follow a pre-determined compass coordinate. Routes that take the boat from one coordinate to another can be programmed into these units.

The TR-1 Auto-Pilot is designed to mount to a small gasoline kicker motor. Unlike wheel-driven auto-pilots, the TR-1 is well-suited for any smaller boats. Like other auto-pilots the TR-1 uses an electronic compass to sense direction changes and a small hydraulic cylinder to turn the motor accordingly.

Used to solve a variety of boat control chores, the TR-1 is most useful as a downwind trolling aid

or as a means of holding in current. For some trolling presentations such as fishing spinners where the forward speed is slow, the thrust of the kicker motor simply isn't strong enough to keep the boat held on course against the power of the wind.

Despite this weakness, the TR-1 is a handy tool for other methods of boat control. A throttle control can also be added to four-stroke outboards that gives the operator infinite control of throttle speeds. This auto-pilot costs around $1,600 installed. A marine dealer who is familiar with the system is required to install and adjust the unit.

The methods of boat control used for catching walleyes are somewhat more extensive than other species. Perhaps that's part of what makes walleye fishing such a challenge. Meeting tough or unique boat control chores head-on and coming out successful offers a great sense of accomplishment.

In the next chapter the "how to" focus of the book begins. Chapter 12 examines casting jigs, one of the most enjoyable and effective ways to catch shallow-water walleyes.

The Pinpoint Positioning Motor is a sophisticated piece of boat control equipment that allows the boat to follow a specific depth setting with hands-free control. Useful for fishing edges and breaks, this product is gaining in popularity.

CHAPTER 12

JIG CASTING

No single lure is more associated with walleye fishing than the common lead-head jig. Nothing more than a hook with a chunk of lead molded onto the shank, jigs are as simple as walleye lures get.

As uncomplicated as jigs appear, the use of jigs is anything but simple. As one of the most versatile lures used for catching walleyes, jigs in their

Casting jigs is one of the most enjoyable ways of catching walleyes. A good method to use when walleyes invade shallow water, casting puts the angler one-on-one against the fish.

various shapes, sizes and designs are used for a wealth of presentations. Because jig designs and the applications for these designs are extensive, the only practical way to discuss jigging in the text of this book is to break down the major methods into separate chapters.

The truth is, a whole book could be written simply on the virtues of jigs and jigging. Despite the differences among jigs and presentations based around these lures, lead-heads intended for walleye fishing do have some similarities.

The size hook used on jigs is one such area. Not all jigs intended for walleye fishing use the same exact size hook, but the hooks used should be fairly large. The one lesson about walleye fishing I've learned over and over again, is that larger hooks stick and hold better than smaller hooks.

This observation is a direct contradiction to many of the early writings and theories about walleye fishing. A wealth of popular literature suggests that small hooks are easier to conceal in the live bait so often used with jigs.

This may be true, but walleyes have a large mouth that's made up primarily of bone and tough tissue. Common sense dictates that once inside the fish's mouth, a larger hook is more likely to find and hold significant real estate.

Fresh Water Fishing Hall of Fame member and popular touring walleye professional, Mike McClelland was among the first outspoken anglers to insist on jigs equipped with large hooks. "I started my fishing career as a bass angler," recalls McClelland. "Bass anglers routinely use big hooks because the hook gap or distance between the hook point and the eye tie is wider. This wider hook gap helps to insure that the hook point will contact the flesh on the inside of the mouth and penetrate deeply enough to prevent a struggling fish from tearing the jig free and escaping."

McClelland and most of the leading walleye professionals favor hooks that are at least No. 4 on their 1/16- and 1/8-ounce jigs. Larger 1/4- and 3/8-ounce models are best equipped with a No. 2 or larger hook.

A lesson the author has learned over and over again is that big hooks are an advantage in walleye fishing. Many jigs are simply equipped with hooks too small for the task.

Not only should jig hooks be fairly large, they should be made of thin wire that penetrates with only modest pressure. It's a fact of science that hooks made from thin wire are going to penetrate easier than hooks made of thicker wire. To see how this works, take an ordinary piece of paper and punch a hole using a sharp pencil. Now take a sewing needle and try the same experiment. You'll be amazed how much less pressure it takes to push the sewing needle through the paper.

The diameter of wire used on jig hooks should be thin to reduce the amount of friction and pressure required to achieve penetration. Aside from the diameter of hook wire, the hook point must also be as sharp as possible.

Hook sharpness and penetration are directly related. Fortunately for anglers this is one area where modern technology has shined brightly. Not only are fishing hooks lighter and thinner than models produced just a few years ago, the sharpness of these hooks is astonishing. Chemical sharpening processes and cutting edge-style hooks are a couple of the ways fish hooks have been made to maximize sharpness. Penetration is further enhanced by adding slick coatings such as Teflon to the hooks. Teflon helps to reduce friction and increase hooking efficiency.

Talk about hook size, wire diameter and sharpness is critical to all jigging presentations. Jig casting in particular is a presentation that requires big hooks that are made from thin and very sharp

The mouth of a walleye is full of teeth, bone and tough tissue. The only practical way to keep a fish like this from shaking free and escaping is to use a good-sized hook.

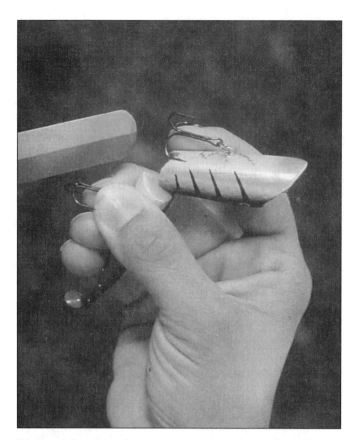

Many of the premium hooks currently produced are far sharper than ordinary hooks. Still it's necessary to keep these hooks maintained by filing an edge on them as needed.

Sometimes the hook point holds securely and the fish is landed. Sometimes the hook point literally tears through the tissue and the fish is lost.

SELECTING JIGS FOR CASTING

The weight, shape or design and location of the eye tie are also factors to be considered when selecting a jig for casting presentations. I've caught countless walleyes on ordinary round-head jigs in the 1/8- and 1/4-ounce sizes. Despite this track record of success, I prefer to cast jigs that feature a shape that allows the jig to stand-up with the hook pointing upwards when resting on the bottom. This simple feature keeps the hook positioned where it can do the most good and, to some degree, away from snags.

More jig models than could be listed accomplish this goal. I also prefer a jig equipped with a short-shank hook for casting situations that call for live bait. Jigs with a short-shank hook are compact, making the total jig and bait package small enough that interested walleyes can slurp up the entire offering. A small minnow, medium-sized leech or half a nightcrawler are the live bait choices that are most conducive to jig casting.

In addition to stand-up style jigs with short shank hooks, a jig that features an eye tie that comes out the nose of the lure is also a good feature to look for. Most jigs have an eye tie that

wire. Most of the time when a fish bites a jig that's thrown into position, the point of the hook will be a considerable distance away from the angler. At the moment the fish bites, the angler sets the hook and applies pressure to the fish.

Unlike bass anglers who often use the leverage of heavy-action rods, strong line and an aggressive hook set to drive the hook point home, walleye anglers are equipped with light action rods and thin line that has a considerable amount of stretch. Line stretch, line strength and rod flex combined make it impractical for walleye anglers to drive hooks home with authority.

This fact is why hook sharpness and design is so critical to jig casting success. Walleye anglers can't overpower the fish like a bass angler who drives the hook home in one strong jerk. Instead, the hook set is more of a rod sweep that applies pressure to the hook point and keeps the pressure on until the hook works itself into the fish.

Every head-shake and wiggle of the fish works the hook point deeper into the mouth tissue.

The author favors a select few jigs for casting applications. The Walleye Stopper Roam'r, Northland Stand-up Fire-Ball and Bait Rigs Slo-Poke are excellent products.

JIG CASTING RODS/REELS/LINES

The author recommends purchasing the best quality jig casting rod and reel combination an angler can afford. It's important to remember however that skill is just as important as equipment when it comes to jig casting.

Casting jigs appeals to so many anglers because this presentation tests the angler's skill level. The challenge is a classic one-on-one contest that pits the angler's ability to detect bites against the walleye's ability to detect danger and drop the bait.

In order to detect the bite, the angler needs a rod that's both light in weight and sensitive to every vibration telegraphed up the fishing line. High-quality graphite spinning rods are the only practical tool for serious jig casting.

The problem is that graphite rods range in price from $40 to $300. Rod advertisements lead anglers to believe that more expensive models are far better able to telegraph subtle bites than less expensive versions. Some truth exists in this advertising strategy, but the skill level and experience of the angler is just as important.

Imagine two anglers pitted in a jig casting competition. One angler has little experience in jig casting techniques, yet he is equipped with the highest quality and most expensive equipment. The second angler is an experienced jig caster, but his equipment is modest both in price and quality.

Given this situation, I'd bet on the experienced angler every time. Quality graphite spinning tackle is an aid to becoming a good jig caster, but skill and experience can't be overcome simply by purchasing an expensive rod and reel combination. I recommend that walleye anglers purchase the best quality graphite spinning rod they can afford and equip this rod with a good spinning reel. Rods for jig casting should be 5 1/2 to 6 feet long and feature a medium or medium/light action.

The spinning reel should be a fairly small model designed for fishing with 6- to 8- pound test line. Larger reels add weight to the outfit that detracts both from the sensitivity and balance of the combination. I also strongly recommend purchasing a reel that features a continuous anti-reverse feature. Reels equipped with continuous anti-reverse eliminate handle slop and slack line. This benefit makes it easier to maintain contact with the lure and control slack in the fishing line.

Slack in the fishing line is the enemy of all jig casters because it reduces an angler's ability to detect bites. Anglers can only feel bites when the line between the jig and rod tip is tight. Slack in the line enables the fish to move the jig without telegraphing this movement down the fishing line to the rod.

comes out the top of the lure. Molding the eye tie to come out the nose of the jig helps to reduce fouling problems with bottom debris and weeds.

A final feature to look for is a barbed collar on the jig to hold plastic grubs. Many jig casting situations require the use of soft plastic grubs. If the jig doesn't have a barbed collar, the plastic won't stay put on the hook shank.

Finding all these features on a single jig is challenging. Many jigs offer two or three of these features, but few deliver all four. For most casting jobs an 1/8- or 1/4-ounce jig is ideal. Jig casting is normally a shallow water presentation that's often practiced in water only a few feet deep. In water more than 20 feet deep, other jig fishing presentations are likely to be more efficient than casting.

Jig casting calls for spinning tackle and monofilament lines with low memory. The author's favorite line for casting include 6-pound test Stren Easy Cast and original Stren in the Clear/Blue High-Vis color.

Becoming a successful jig caster is about controlling slack in the line in order to better detect bites. Continuous anti-reverse reels are a useful tool in controlling line slack.

The fishing line used for casting jigs is also an important tool. Low memory monofilament in the 6- to 8-pound test range is ideal for jig casting. Low memory line comes off the reel spool smoothly and without coils. Fishing lines that coil create slack in the line that's difficult to control. The effect is like fishing with a slinky. When a fish grabs the jig, the sensation of the bite is absorbed by all the slack line created by the coils.

Usually lines with lots of coil are associated with hard-surfaced lines intended for trolling or line that's simply been on the reel for a long time. Select a line that's intended for casting and make sure the line is fresh and in good condition. For 90 percent of all jig casting applications 6-pound test is the perfect choice. When casting into heavy weeds or other snag-filled waters, slightly stronger 8-pound test makes sense.

Highly visible lines are also an advantage when jig casting, but the brightest colored lines aren't necessary in most situations. I've found that clear/blue high-visibility line offers the ideal properties of visibility above water and stealth below the water.

IDENTIFYING JIG CASTING SITUATIONS

A wealth of angling situations require a jig to be thrown into position. When fish are located in shallow water, casting is the only practical way to present lures without risk of spooking the fish. Casting is also a good way to present lures to areas not easily approached from shore or by boat. The water directly below a spillway or dam is a classic dilemma where the boat can not be positioned close to the fish. Generally the boat is anchored a short distance from the falling water and jigs are tossed up into the swirling current.

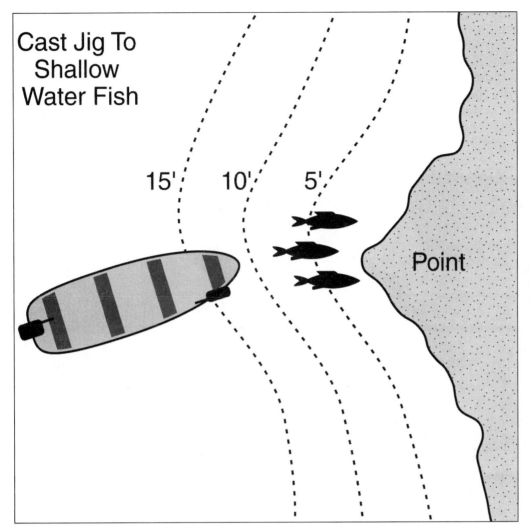

Cast Jig To Shallow Water Fish

15' 10' 5'

Point

When walleyes are in shallow water jig casting is one of the best presentations. In this situation fish are laying near the tip of a point in shallow water. The boat is positioned in deeper water to avoid spooking the fish and the jig is cast into position.

Many other applications for jig casting will be encountered. Each spring I look forward to visiting a series of Lake Erie reefs that are tailor-made for jig casting. Post spawn walleyes (mostly small males) stand guard on these reefs waiting for willing females to arrive, spawn and eventually retreat to deeper water.

No one knows for sure why males on the spawning grounds are so aggressive, but they seldom hesitate to grab a well-positioned jig and minnow combination. Perhaps the spawning ritual itself cranks these males up or maybe they are just hungry after spending a long winter in icy water. Whatever the reason, the stage is set for a jig casting experience that every angler should make a spring tradition.

On reefs that are thick with fish, hooking a walleye every cast is not uncommon. This is the ideal situation for learning the art of jig casting. It's a lot easier to learn how to cast jigs when you

can expect lots of bites to confirm the lesson. Casting a jig all day and maybe getting a couple of bites is no way to master the art of jig casting.

JIG CASTING METHODOLOGY

The techniques used for jig casting are simple, yet few anglers ever master this effective presentation. Jig casting is rather easy to learn, but it does require acute concentration. From the time the jig is cast until the retrieve is completed, the angler must pay attention to every movement the jig makes. Focusing attention on the jig helps the angler detect subtleties such as a slight sensation of weight that wasn't there before or a tick in the line that may indicate a fish has picked up the jig.

Start out by casting the jig and letting it sink on a slack line to the bottom. Don't turn the reel

The author recommends learning the art of jig casting on waters where lots of bites can be expected. If only a few bites can be expected during a day of fishing, it's tough to refine the skills needed to become an excellent jig fisherman.

handle and close the bail until the jig has touched bottom. If the bail is closed too soon, the jig will pendulum towards the angler and shave off some of the area covered by each cast.

Once the jig is on bottom the line will collapse and lay motionless on the water surface. Point yourself directly at the jig and with the rod at approximately the 10 o'clock position slowly reel up the slack line until the weight of the jig setting on bottom can be felt.

At this point, use your wrist to raise the rod tip from the 10 o'clock to 11 o'clock position. Stop the rod at 11 o'clock and watch the point where the line enters the water.

Pulling the rod tip towards you lifts the jig off the bottom slightly and causes the lure to pendulum forward a short distance before settling back on the bottom. When the jig touches down again the line will go slack on the surface, tipping off the angler to reel up the slack line and start the process over again.

This simple 10 o'clock-to-11 o'clock jigging motion is all it takes to move the jig along the bottom in a hopping motion. These short rod movements help to keep the line taunt and to prevent too much sensitivity-robbing slack line from forming. Simply repeat the process over and over again until the jig has been worked back to the boat or shore position before making the next cast.

I often vary this retrieve by using a steady pulling motion to lift the jig or a more pronounced snap of the wrist that pops the jig up off bottom. The more active the fish are, the more likely popping the jig along bottom will trigger strikes. Fish that are reluctant to bite are most likely to hit a slower moving bait that barely lifts and drops or drags along the bottom.

Mastering the mechanics of jig casting can be done in a fairly short time. The problem is, detecting bites is part physical and part intuition. If a walleye strikes the jig as it's swinging toward the angler on a taunt line the strike will be easy to detect as a crisp tick like someone used his finger to flick the tip of your rod. The feeling of a bite on taunt line is difficult to describe, but once you've felt it you'll know immediately what to look for.

Detecting bites that occur on slack line is much more difficult. If the jig is laying on the bottom and the line is slack on the surface, a walleye can suck up the jig without the angler feeling a thing. The first tip off that a fish has the bait will come when the angler reels up the slack to start the next jigging stroke.

A mushy sensation or feeling of weight is the clue that a fish has the bait. Those anglers who don't recognize this subtle feeling often mistake it for a snag. Unless the fish has swallowed the bait, chances are the fish will feel tension from the angler and drop the jig without the angler even knowing a bite occurred.

Keeping slack out of the line as much as possible helps anglers detect most of the bites that occur. Line watching can also help to detect some of the bites that occur on slack line. Sometimes the line will

When casting with nightcrawlers half a crawler is ideal. The head end of the crawler is more durable and stays on the hook better.

twitch when a fish strikes the bait. To notice this subtle line twitch, you have to be looking for it.

Most of the time when bites occur on slack line, the only way to detect these bites is through experience. The more practice an angler has at jig casting, the more detecting bites becomes second nature. Unfortunately, there are no shortcuts. Good old-fashioned experience is the best teacher.

LIVE BAIT TRICKS

As mentioned before, lead-heads tipped with live bait are one of the most popular combinations for jig casting. Early in the season, minnows are a difficult live bait to top. A 2- or 3-inch-long shiner or fathead minnow on a jig has likely accounted for more walleyes than just about all other presentations combined.

Hook the minnow lightly through both lips to insure the bait is lively. Some minnows have delicate lips that are easily ripped in the casting process. To prevent minnows from falling off the hook, take a small piece of plastic from a grub body and press it over the hook point after putting the minnow on the hook. The plastic acts like a washer, preventing the minnow from coming off.

The jig and minnow combination is tough to beat for casting situations early and late in the year. Note a piece of plastic known as a Bait Bumper has been placed over the hook to prevent the minnow from backing off the hook when casting. Bait Bumpers are available from K&E Tackle.

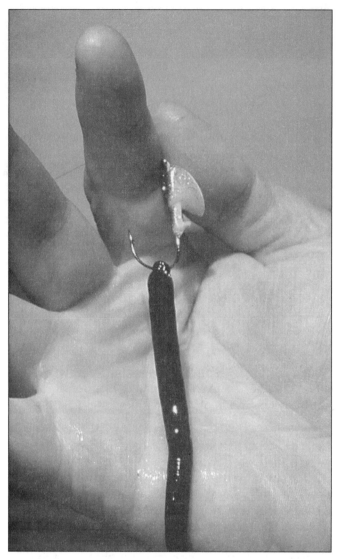

Leeches are more expensive than minnows or crawlers, but they also stay on the hook better. During the summer months leeches are an excellent bait for jig casting.

Half a nightcrawler is also an excellent bait for jig casting. Break a healthy nightcrawler in two pieces and thread the head portion onto the hook as if putting a plastic grub onto the jig. The head of the nightcrawler is tough and rubber-like, making it the better half of the nightcrawler. Push the crawler up and over the collar of the jig to insure the bait stays put.

Save the tail portion of the nightcrawler. When all the head sections have been used up, the tails are just as attractive to walleyes. Unfortunately, the tail sections are soft and more difficult to keep on the jig.

Leeches are another bait that often ends up on the business end of a jig. Medium-sized leeches are the most popular size for casting.

Leeches are attached to the jig by passing the hook point through the sucker. Hooked in this manner the leech is free to swim, wiggle and otherwise do its stuff.

The durability of leeches appeals to many anglers. This tough little creature stays on the hook well and can be cast over and over again without losing that all-important wiggle. A little more expensive than minnows or crawlers, leeches make up for the extra cost by being twice as likely to stay alive and on the hook.

At certain times in certain bodies of water, leeches will produce more walleyes than minnows or crawlers. The only logical way to approach this dilemma is to have all three bait choices handy and experiment with them until one bait emerges as the most productive at the moment.

CASTING PLASTIC BAITS

A jig tipped with live bait is hard to beat, but sometimes the fish bite so well that live bait isn't necessary. In other situations, live bait isn't allowed because of state or providence regulations. In still other cases bait simply isn't readily available.

Fly-in fishing trips are one such situation where live bait is either tough to come by or not allowed. A good assortment of plastic grub bodies is the answer when bait is out of the question or simply out of reach.

Scented grubs such as Berkley's PowerBait top the list of soft plastic lures. Not only do these baits have action, color and texture, they also smell (and apparently) taste good to fish.

Scent can also be added to ordinary grubs. A wealth of scent products are available to make plastic baits more appealing to walleyes. The early scent products were simply agents that added a powerful scent such as oil of anise. Some of the newer scent products such as those produced by Kodiac are made from actual nightcrawlers, leeches and shad minnows that are ground up, freeze-dried and mixed with a paste that helps the scent stick to lures. Fish scents are also made from oils rendered from minnows and crayfish.

A most unlikely fish scent is WD-40, a petroleum-based product designed as a household lubricant. My longtime friend and tournament partner Dr. Steven Holt swears that WD-40 helps him catch more walleyes. The spray product is easy to apply and he indeed catches lots of fish. I'm not sure if WD-40 is the answer, but I have noticed that Steve's hooks never seem to rust.

Sometimes a jig dressed with a plastic body is all that's needed to catch walleyes. Scented plastic baits can be used or scent added to a favorite grub tail.

An unlikely fishing scent product? A number of anglers feel that WD-40 helps them catch more fish. The question is does WD-40 attract fish or simply cover human scent? Either way, it seems to work.

Scented or not, plastic grubs catch walleyes. When selecting unscented plastic grubs, a few classics are must-have items. Curl tail grubs are the most popular style. A 2- or 3-inch tail is the right choice for walleyes. Grub bodies with a marabou tail like the famous Lindy Fuzz-E-Grub are often used as are 3-inch shad bodies and twin-tail grubs.

Other plastics that have a place in every walleye tackle box are the small finesse style worms often used by bass anglers. River guide Jon Bondy of Windsor, Ontario uses a 4-inch brown finesse worm when jigging for walleyes.

"Early in the season I use both the plastic worm and a live minnow," says Bondy. "Later in the season when the fish are more active, the plastic worm is all I need to catch fish."

Berkley produces a PowerBait version known as a Jig Worm that was designed to duplicate the action of using a jig with half a nightcrawler.

SUMMING IT UP

Casting jigs for walleyes rates as one of the most productive and enjoyable ways to catch fish. A great tactic for early season or any time walleyes are found in shallow water, jig casting is a simple presentation that simply takes a lot of practice to master.

In the next chapter the focus switches from jig casting to vertical jigging. A river fishing method that helps to tame current, vertical jigging is a jigging method that's based on boat control.

CHAPTER 13

VERTICAL JIGGING

Vertical jigging is a classic presentation for taking walleyes in rivers and streams. To the casual observer, this jigging technique appears to be a simple matter of drifting downstream while fishing a jig near the bottom. Actually, vertical jigging is a form of boat control that, while easy to learn, is somewhat more complicated than it looks.

Before we get into the fine points of vertical jigging, we must first examine the reasons why fishing directly below the boat is important and where this technique shines the best. We must also understand that rivers are not all created equal, but the mechanics of fishing in current are the same regardless of the size of the river, current speed or water depth.

Maintaining a vertical presentation is critical in many river fishing situations because the bottom of the river is littered with snags. Dragging a jig along the bottom is an open invitation to hang-ups that in most cases are impossible to free. Fishing vertically allows the angler to maintain contact with the bottom without dragging the jig. Each jigging stroke lowers the lure to the bottom. The moment the jig hits the bottom the line goes slack. At this moment the angler lifts the rod tip and raises the jig off the bottom.

This simple lift and drop motion allows the jig to stay in close proximity to the bottom, without actually dragging on the bottom. Anglers incorporate many variations of this lift and drop jigging action, but we're getting ahead of ourselves. The important point with vertical jigging is that snags are reduced considerably, yet the jig is always within the strike zone of waiting fish.

Most rivers are candidates for vertical jigging so long as the water is at least 6 feet deep. Since the boat is positioned directly over the top of the fish, vertical jigging isn't the ideal shallow water presentation. If the water is very shallow or exceptionally clear, the boat can spook fish.

Fortunately, most rivers aren't overly clear. The prime depths for vertical jigging range from 10 to 50 feet. At the shallow end of this spectrum 1/8- or 1/4-ounce jigs are normally used. In deeper water it may require 3/8-, 1/2- or 5/8-ounce jigs to maintain contact with the bottom. In some extreme cases where the water is deep and the current swift, jigs up to 3/4 of an ounce are required.

Vertical jigging is the easiest to master when walleyes are scattered over flats of similar depth. Once the jig is positioned near the bottom the angler can maintain contact with the bottom without having to let more line out or reel up extra

Vertical jigging is one of the most popular ways to fish for walleyes in flowing water. This nice fish was taken by keeping the jig close to the bottom and slowly lifting and dropping the bait.

Vertical jigging requires a number of different size jigs. Jigs in the 1/8- and 1/4-ounce size are used in shallow water, while 3/8-, 1/2- and 5/8-ounce jigs are used in deeper water.

line. Flats are convenient places to vertical jig or to learn the basics of this technique. However, vertical jigging can also be used to target fish on less consistent bottom structure.

Channel edges that drop sharply into deep water often hold concentrations of walleyes. This is especially true during spring spawning runs when fish seem to use the main river channel as a navigation route. Vertical jigging the edges of channel breaks is an excellent way to intercept walleyes that are constantly on the move.

Drifting along channel breaks requires more boat control than fishing the flats. A depth finder and electric motor are used to position the boat within a certain depth zone so the lures follow the contour of the break. Because the depth along the break changes rapidly, the angler must constantly let out more line to maintain contact with the bottom or reel up extra line as needed.

Anglers that take the time to learn the characteristics of breaks and stay on them will be rewarded with more bites and landed fish. Those anglers who simply let the current push the boat aimlessly along, will never rise to vertical jigging stardom.

THE MECHANICS OF VERTICAL JIGGING

Keeping a jig positioned directly below the boat doesn't happen naturally. Boat control makes vertical jigging possible. To fully appreciate vertical jigging in current, you must understand that we're dealing with three different moving objects. The boat, current and jig are all moving. The trick to vertical jigging is making sure the boat, current and jig all move at the same speed.

In a perfect world this would be easy. In the real world, one constantly changing factor messes things up. Wind is the culprit that makes staying vertical a struggle.

Think of the boat as a sail and you'll understand what happens when the wind hits the side of your boat. If the wind is blowing downstream the boat will catch the wind and drift faster than the current. If, however, the wind is blowing against the flow of water, the boat drifting speed is slowed down by the wind.

When either of these situations occur, staying vertical is impossible without the help of some boat control. If the boat moves faster than the current the line will angle upstream and the jig will be raised up off the bottom. If the boat moves slower than the current, the line will angle downstream and the force of the current on the line pulls the jig up off the bottom. When the line angles away from the boat, that's the tip-off that the boat is moving faster or slower than the current.

Simply letting more line out to maintain contact with the bottom isn't the answer. If enough line is let out to bring the jig in contact with the bottom, the jig will drag along the bottom and snags become a problem.

The only way to keep the jig directly below the boat is to position the boat over the top of the jig. This boat control chore is accomplished with an electric motor. The electric motor pushes the boat upstream or downstream as required to position the boat over the top of the jig.

Moving the boat over the top of the jig temporarily causes the boat, current and jig to move at

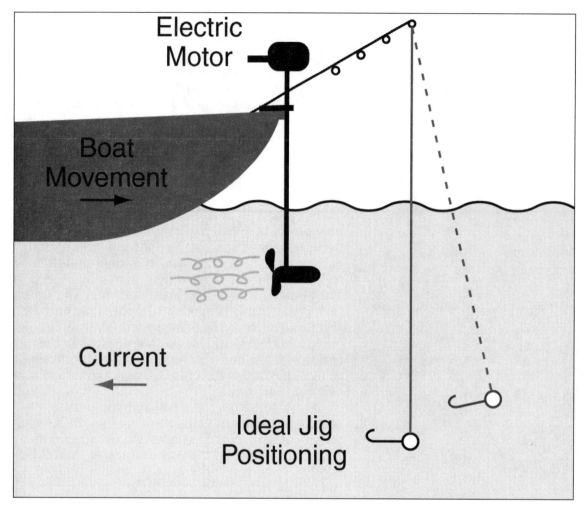

Electric Motor

Boat Movement

Current

Ideal Jig Positioning

In vertical jigging an electric motor is used to position the boat over the top of the jig as the jig and boat both drift downstream.

the same speed. The line to the jig is vertical and contact to the bottom is achieved. Unfortunately, this situation is temporary. The wind will soon cause the boat to move faster or slower than the current, forcing the angler to repeat this control measure over and over again.

FINE POINTS OF BOAT CONTROL

Understanding the mechanics of vertical jigging is the first step. The next step is to select tools that make boat control easier. We've already stated that the ideal tool for boat control while vertical jigging is an electric motor. This presentation can be mastered with both bow- and transom-mounted motors; however, the best jiggers favor bow-mounted units.

It's easier to move the pointed bow against river current, than it is to try to push the square transom of the boat. A bow mounted electric motor is vastly more efficient than a transom-mounted motor.

In addition to being more efficient, bow-mounted motors use less battery juice to accomplish the same boat control chores as a transom-mounted unit. To further increase the efficiency of the electric motor select a foot-operated model that allows the boat to be controlled using one foot. Both hands are left free to fish two rods where the law allows.

The trick to positioning the boat during vertical jigging is to point the bow (or transom if using a transom motor) into the wind and make numerous small adjustments as needed. The moment the line angles away from the boat, a small thrust of power from the electric motor will bring the boat back into position and keep the line directly vertical. If too much power or thrust is used, forward momentum will carry the boat past the vertical position.

Vertical jigging requires the angler to keep constant control of the boat. If the person controlling the boat steps away from the motor for a few moments to tie on a jig or bait up, control is lost and everyone else fishing in the boat is wasting time.

Foot-controlled bow-mounted electric motors are the logical choice for vertical jigging. A foot-controlled motor frees up both hands to fish two rods.

When fishing in tournaments, my partner Dr. Steven Holt and I take turns on boat control chores. If the person controlling the boat hooks a fish, needs to tie on a jig or bait up, he simply steps away from the motor and allows his partner to take over. This buddy system insures that boat control is always maintained.

MORE TOOLS OF THE TRADE

Vertical jigging is one of those presentations where having the right equipment makes all the difference. Rods, reels and line are all critical parts of this presentation.

As outlined in Chapter 5, Rods, Reels & Line, the rods used for vertical jigging need to be somewhat stiffer than other rods. Stiffness works to make the

rod more sensitive. If the rod bends from the weight of the jig, the rod is actually becoming a shock absorber that makes it more difficult to feel bites.

Select a graphite spinning rod that features at least a medium action. Rods from 5-1/2 feet to 6 feet are ideal. Some anglers go so far as to cut off a few inches from the tip of rods to make them a little stiffer. The tip top guide is replaced and the rod is ready for action.

Some anglers prefer to jig vertically using baitcasting tackle. Jon Bondy a guide on the Detroit River is one such angler.

"I like baitcasting tackle because the rods are a little stiffer than spinning tackle," says Bondy. "Also a baitcasting reel with a flippin' feature makes it easy to let out line and engage the reel without having to turn the handle. This feature is a

River guide Jon Bondy prefers to use baitcasting tackle for vertical jigging. The rods are a little more stiff and letting line out to maintain contact with the bottom is as simple as pushing a button.

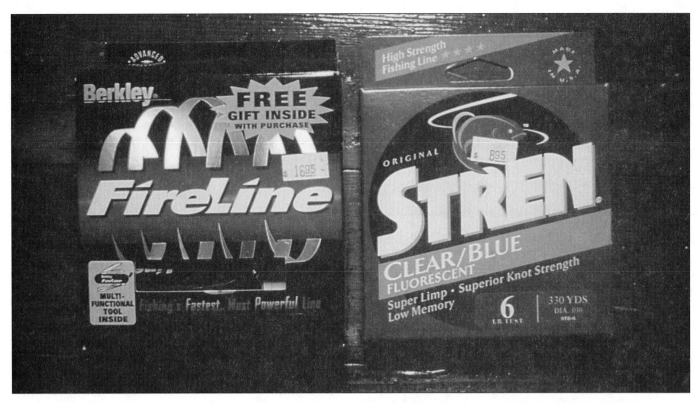

Lines used for vertical jigging need to be thin in diameter. A good 6-pound test monofilament is an excellent choice for most situations. In deep water super braids have less stretch and allow anglers to feel the bottom more easily.

great convenience when fishing bottom structure where the depth varies."

The use of spinning or baitcasting tackle is largely personal preference. The action and graphite content of the rod is the most important considerations. The higher the graphite content or quality of the graphite fibers, the lighter and more sensitive the rod becomes. Normally I have a hard time recommending expensive items, but when it comes to vertical jigging rods, I feel anglers should purchase the highest quality rod they can afford.

Good quality graphite rods range from $75 to $300 depending on the grade of graphite and brand selected. This rod should be matched with a reel that features a continuous anti-reverse feature. Continuous anti-reverse reels have none of the handle slop or play associated with other reels. With some reels the handle can turn half a rotation before the spool actually moves.

Anglers using a continuous anti-reverse reel enjoy a direct contact between reel, rod and lure that increases feel and sensitivity. If your spinning reels don't have a continuous anti-reverse feature, hold the line over your index finger while jigging to increase sensitivity.

Line is an issue that creates considerable disagreements among professional and amateur anglers alike. Despite different opinions on line type, all knowledgeable anglers agree upon one aspect of fishing line. Fishing line used for vertical jigging needs to be small in diameter to reduce resistance and drag caused by the flowing water.

Thin diameter line is exactly the reason many anglers prefer the new braided super-lines for vertical jigging. Most of these lines are a fraction of the diameter of equal break strength monofilament. Another advantage of super-lines is the lack of stretch these lines feature. Less stretch means anglers can feel the jig and anything it touches better than with monofilament lines.

Super braids suitable for vertical jigging should feature a 6- or 8-pound test break strength. Heavier line is not necessary and only creates problems in breaking the line should the jig become snagged.

Ordinary monofilament line has some properties that many anglers feel make it the logical choice for vertical jigging. The limpness of the line allows it to flow smoothly off the reel when lowering jigs to the bottom. Braided lines sometimes need a little encouragement in this department.

Monofilament is also much less expensive than super braids, and knot strength is far superior compared to braided lines. Furthermore, in normal fishing conditions most anglers can't detect a difference in sensitivity when monofilament is compared to braided super-lines.

My experience suggests that the sensitivity properties of super braids are most noticeable when fishing in deep water. The advantage of increased sensitivity is more pronounced for those who have little experience with vertical jigging. The more experience an angler has vertical jigging with monofilament, the more likely he or she will be comfortable with the feel provided by nylon lines.

In shallow water (say less than 20 feet) monofilament is easier to work with than braided lines and has adequate feel and sensitivity to detect strikes. Without sounding like I'm walking both sides of the fence, it makes sense to use braided lines in deep water situations and monofilament in shallow water. Taking this step allows anglers to enjoy the full benefits of both braided and monofilament lines.

The best monofilament line size for vertical jigging is 6-pound test. Abrasion resistant lines are the best choice and it also helps if the line is easily visible. I favor lines that are clear/blue fluorescent, but others like the bright gold or green fluorescent lines that offer maximum visibility.

A side note to monofilament lines can play a role in vertical jigging. Some of the new co-polymer lines actually have less stretch than ordinary monofilament. Stren's Sensor is an example of a co-polymer line that has approximately 50 percent less stretch than other monofilaments. In addition, Sensor features excellent knot strength, flexibility and limpness. The reduction in stretch offers greater sensitivity, especially in deep water jigging situations.

A compromise that's worth exploring, low stretch monofilament is a relatively new phenomenon on the market. No doubt additional products will be introduced that feature the handling characteristics of monofilament and the low stretch nature of braided lines.

JIGS & STINGER HOOKS

The jigs used for vertical jigging must also meet specific requirements. Since plastic grub tails are often used while vertical jigging, the lead-head selected should have a long hook shank that readily accepts twister tails, shad bodies and other plastic baits. The jig should also be equipped with a barbed collar that securely holds plastics in position.

The eye tie must come out the top of the jig head so the bait rests level when being lifted and dropped. Hooks must be thin wire and razor-sharp to maximize penetration. When jigging with light line the angler simply can't apply enough pressure at the hook set to drive hooks home. Sharp hooks

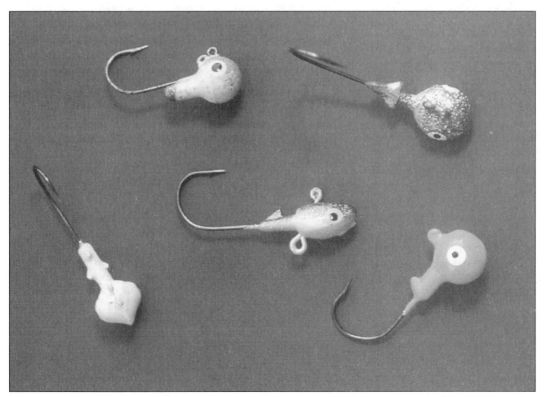

These jigs are good candidates for vertical jigging. Note each has a long shank, an eye tie that comes out the top of the jig and barbs to securely hold a plastic grub body.

Stinger hooks are not all created equal. Stingers should be long enough to easily reach the tail of the minnow and tied using light enough material that the minnow has freedom to move. The P/K Tackle stinger is one of the best available.

Stingers tied using heavy monofilament or wire are notorious for giving the minnow a lifeless profile in the water. Stinger hooks shorter than 3 inches have the same impact on action. The best stinger hooks are those that are at least 3 inches long and tied using lightweight monofilament line or braided line.

The hook used on a stinger is usually a No. 10 treble. Some specially designed trebles make for better stinger hooks. P/K Tackle uses a treble hook that features two hooks pointed forward and one hook pointed backwards. The backwards hook is imbedded into the minnow, positioning the two remaining hooks upright and ready for action.

Northland Tackle Company uses a double-barb stinger hook that helps solve the problem of the stinger pulling free from the minnow. Both of these stinger designs are excellent products.

Keeping the minnow on the jig hook is another problem associated with vertical jigging. The up and down jigging motion quickly causes the hook to tear a hole in the minnow's lips large enough that the hook and barb can easily back out.

I solve this problem by using a simple product known as Bait Bumpers produced by K&E Walleye Stopper Lures. These small round pieces of soft plastic prevent minnows from working off the hook. Run the jig hook through both the lower and upper lip of the minnow, then take a Bait Bumper and push the hook point through until the barb shows. The Bait Bumper works like a washer, preventing the minnow from working free of the jig hook. Another advantage of taking this extra step is the freedom to use more aggressive jigging strokes without fear of snapping off the all-important minnow.

INCORPORATING SOFT PLASTICS

Soft plastic grub bodies are an important part of vertical jigging. River anglers are often faced with turbid or even dirty water conditions. Not only do soft plastics increase the size of the lure, they are also available in a wealth of bright colors that are easier to see in murky water.

I use a simple guideline when selecting soft plastics for vertical jigging. The clearer the water, the smaller the plastics and the more natural shades. As the water becomes increasingly more turbid, I increase the size of plastics and switch to brightly colored or fluorescent shades.

These adjustments are based simply on the zone of awareness or ability of walleyes to see lures in the water. In clear water, walleyes can

that punch and cut their way home while the fish is struggling are often the difference between lost and landed fish.

A vertical jigging lead-head should also have an extra loop molded in that accepts a clip-on style stinger hook. Lastly, lead-heads designed for vertical jigging should come in 1/8-, 1/4-, 3/8-, 1/2- and 5/8-ounce sizes. These various features eliminate most of the popular jigs from contention. In fact, few lead-heads meet all the requirements outlined above.

Stinger hooks go together with vertical jigging like butter goes with popcorn. Some anglers claim that stinger hooks reduce the natural action of the minnow and result in fewer bites. Some truth exists in this statement. However, the type of stinger hook used is usually the reason action is reduced.

Using plastic grub bodies helps to make jigs more visible in dingy water, adds action and causes the jig to sink slightly slower.

obviously see better and farther. Smaller plastic baits and more subdued natural colors work well in this situation. If, however, the water is dirty, bigger and brighter plastics significantly increase the zone of awareness and can play a major role in angling success.

In addition to the size of plastics used, anglers have a wealth of styles to pick from. Some of the most common grub bodies include twister tails, twin-tail grubs, marabou-tailed grubs and shad bodies. Other plastics that work great in vertical jigging situations are finesse worms, tube baits and jig worms.

Scented plastics are a natural for vertical jigging and some anglers refuse to use anything less. Adding scent and taste along with action, profile and color just makes using plastics all the more effective.

Another advantage of using plastics involves the drop time as jigs are allowed to free fall to the bottom. The bulking effect of plastic makes the jig fall at a slower rate. In turn, walleyes have a longer look at the bait.

JIGGING ACTIONS

Another aspect of vertical jigging is the actual jigging motion. Again, to the casual observer the jigging action appears to be a simple lift and drop of the rod tip. Actually there's a lot of options that can change the action and how walleyes react to the bait.

In cold water conditions, walleyes are likely to be somewhat lethargic, a slow lift-and-drop jigging motion usually produces the most strikes. This jigging stoke is often called tight lining because the

jig is lifted and dropped back to the bottom on a tight line. To accomplish this jigging motion the rod must be raised in a slow steady motion and dropped in the same manner.

A slightly more aggressive jigging stroke lifts the jig off the bottom then lets the jig free fall back to the bottom. Sometimes referred to as slack lining, with this method the jig is allowed to return to bottom on a slack line created by dropping the rod tip quickly.

Even more aggressive jigging strokes pop the jig up off the bottom and allow the jig to free fall on slack line. These three basic vertical jigging strokes and dozens of variations are used to trigger walleyes into striking. Experimenting with different jigging strokes is the only way to determine if one method is going to be more productive than the other.

No matter what jigging stroke is employed, the jig should not be lifted more than about 12 inches off the bottom. Walleyes are located tight to the bottom in rivers because the current is slowest along the bottom. Friction from the water passing over the bottom reduces the rate of flow. Walleyes tuck up tight to the bottom because they can position themselves in the current while using the least amount of energy.

Keeping the jig within 12 inches of the bottom at all times greatly increases the likelihood of attracting fish. Ironically, some anglers feel the best jigging stroke is no stroke at all. Simply lifting the jig a few inches off the bottom and holding it still can be a deadly presentation. This jigging motion closely resembles the natural way a minnow would drift along in the current.

TWO-ROD JIGGING

Most states allow anglers to use up to two rods at once. Where allowed by law, using two rods for vertical jigging doubles the chances of catching fish. The second lure in the water also gives anglers an opportunity to experiment with colors, grub bodies, live baits and other options.

It takes a little effort to become comfortable jigging two rods. Once you've mastered this technique, fishing one rod will feel unnatural. Here are some tricks that help with two-rod jigging.

Lift and drop both rods at the same time. It's easier to develop a cadence when both rods are doing the same thing at the same time.

Position the rods so the jigs are fishing in two different areas. If the jigs are worked too closely together the benefit of using two jigs is lost.

If one rod becomes snagged on the bottom, reel up the other rod a few turns before setting the second rod down to deal with the snag. If you fail to take this step, chances are you'll end up with two snagged rods and a major dose of frustration. The same holds true when baiting up.

Use a jig that's heavy enough to allow you to easily feel the bottom. If too light a jig is used, maintaining contact with the bottom is a constant struggle and the likelihood of snags is greatly increased.

BAIT SELECTION

Minnows are the most common bait used for vertical jigging, but crawlers and leeches have a place as well. Some minnows are simply better candidates for jigging than others. Delicate minnows such as emerald shiners are tough to keep alive and even tougher to keep on the hook. More hardy minnow species such as fatheads or spottail shiners are a better choice.

A whole nightcrawler threaded onto the jig like a plastic grub can be a deadly bait for vertical jigging. Crawlers tend to get hot once the water temperature rises above 45 degrees. Crawlers are easy to care for and they stay on the hook amazingly well.

If short bites and missed fish become a problem, try pinching a crawler in half and threading the head section onto the jig. The rubber-like head of the crawler is tougher and it stays hooked better than the tail section.

Leeches are rarely seen used as a vertical jigging bait, but there's no reason why they can't be effective. The tradition of using minnows and crawlers is the only reason I can think of not to use leeches.

The size of bait used can also make a difference. Numerous times I've noticed that smaller minnows produced more fish than larger minnows. I've also had excellent success by hook-

Where legal, jigging with two rods doubles the chances of catching fish. To those who haven't tried fishing two rods the practice is unnatural. Once you've practiced a little, fishing just one rod feels strange.

Rigged and ready for action, this jig and minnow is armed with a stinger hook and baited with a fresh minnow. A deadly way to catch river walleyes, vertical jigging takes a little effort to master but the rewards are worth it.

ing two small minnows on the jig hook at one time. Like a twin-tail grub, this dual minnow set-up has helped me land lots of fish over the years.

There's more to vertical jigging than most anglers realize. The whole presentation is about boat control and understanding the mechanics of moving water. Beyond boat control, anglers must also be concerned with rods, reels, lines, jigs, stingers, plastics and live baits.

Vertical jigging requires some effort to master, but the rewards are worth it. In the next chapter we'll explore another method of jig fishing. Drifting, dragging and trolling jigs are other ways to take the versatile lead-head and turn it into a walleye-catching machine.

CHAPTER 14

DRIFTING, DRAGGING, TROLLING JIGS

The popularity of jig fishing can be summed up in two words: It's versatile. The lead-head jig can be fished effectively in so many ways, it's no wonder that jigging ranks as the top producer of walleyes. In addition to jig casting and vertical jigging, lead-heads are effective when drifted, dragged or trolled along the bottom. As you might expect, there's a time and place for sliding a jig along the bottom.

Before we get into the details of these different jigging presentations, it's important to note that all these techniques are about keeping jigs in contact with the bottom. All the presentations in this chapter accomplish the same function. It matters little if the boat is being pushed along by wind, current, an electric motor or a gasoline engine. If the jig is moving while in contact with the bottom, it's being dragged.

As outlined in earlier chapters, there are times when dragging jigs is nothing but a snag waiting to happen. Bottoms that are littered with broken rock, heavy weed cover or sunken wood are poor candidates for dragging presentations. However, jigs can be dragged along nicely on sand, clay, silt or gravel bottoms.

It's also nice to know that dragging jigs is the easiest of all jigging presentations to master. No special skill or technique refinement is required. Rods, reels and essential gear don't have to be excessive, expensive or elaborate.

In fact, this technique is so simple to master, I consider it my secret weapon when introducing novice anglers, newcomers, kids and other casual fishermen to the excitement of walleyes. Jig dragging should be a mandatory part of every angler's bag of tricks.

DRIFTING JIGS IN LAKES

As mentioned, dragging is dragging no matter what means is used to move the boat and jig. However, some forms of dragging are less precise than others. Drifting a wind swept lake for example is a dragging method that moves the jig along as the boat is pushed by the wind. When drifting, it's somewhat difficult to cover specific spots, follow weed edges, breaks or to return and make another drift that precisely covers the same path again.

Dragging jigs is an effective presentation that is easy to master.

When using one drift bag, the bag must be attached to the boat in the middle so the boat drifts square to the wind. When two bags are used, they are attached at the bow and transom of the boat.

This fact suggests that drifting makes the most sense when walleyes are scattered in loose groups on flats or large reefs. Drifting may be less precise than other dragging methods, but that doesn't mean that anglers can't direct or steer their drift accurately enough to stay on fish. With the help of marker buoys and GPS units, drifting can be a very effective way to both locate fish and catch them.

Some basic equipment is required for drift fishing jigs. Most importantly, the boat should be equipped with one or two drift socks or sea anchors. These parachute-like bags are used to control drifting speed.

The size drift sock required depends on the size and weight of the boat used. Small boats in the 16- to 17-foot range can get by nicely with a single 36- to 48-inch bag. Larger boats in the 18- to 20-foot class are better equipped with two sea anchors.

When a single bag is used it must be secured amidships so the boat will drift along perpendicular to the wind. When two bags are used, one must be secured to the bow and the other to the transom of the boat.

While sea anchors do a great job of slowing down drifting speed, they also pose a problem when landing fish. It seems hooked fish always find themselves between the sea bag and the boat.

When using one bag, concentrate on landing fish at the bow or transom of the boat. When two bags are deployed, work hooked fish into the middle of the boat to avoid the sea bags.

Sea bags should be equipped with a strong line that's long enough to allow the bag to open fully. The turbulence created by the boat moving over the water surface can prevent the bag from opening fully. To avoid this problem position the bag at least 6 feet from the boat. Cleats mounted in handy locations are the best way to secure sea bags to the boat.

When purchasing a sea bag, look for models made from polyester or nylon material that's lightweight, strong and resistant to rot. The bags I use are produced in South Dakota by Quick Change Systems. Called the Slow-Poke, these bags come in different sizes and are made of a fast drying nylon material. Mine have over 10 years of service on them and they will apparently last another 10 years.

A few marker buoys are also essential for drift fishing. The dumbbell-shaped floats produced by Lindy Little Joe have served me well over the years. I do, however, remove the thin line that comes on these markers and replace it with decoy anchor cord. The larger decoy cord tangles less and is easier to wind back onto the buoy.

Plan on purchasing two or three markers. Fluorescent orange is the easiest color to see on the water, followed by bright yellow. Such obvious markers can however attract visitors. Some anglers prefer to use black markers that are tough to spot unless you know where to look.

Aside from sea bags and some marker buoys, the only other essential equipment includes some favorite rods and reels, a handful of jigs and plenty of live bait.

Here's some good news: just about any rod and reel combination can be used for drifting jigs. My kids use Zebco 33 spincast combinations with great success. This moderately priced equipment often produces more fish than expensive graphite rods. The reason is simple. Less expensive rods tend to be made from fiberglass or graphite/fiberglass composites. The action on these rods is

Replace the thin line that comes on a Lindy Marker Buoy with decoy anchor cord. This larger line is easier to handle and tangles less.

A long rod, known as a dead rod, is handy for dragging jigs. The best rods are inexpensive fiberglass or fiberglass/graphite composite models.

softer than most graphite rods, making them forgiving enough to allow the jig to slide, drag and scoot perfectly along the bottom.

If you plan on using graphite rods, choose a spinning model that features a medium/light or light action. A rod from 6 to 7 feet long is ideal. The reel should be loaded with a premium monofilament in 6-or 8-pound test.

Drift fishing is one of the times I depend on a dead rod. A dead rod is simply an inexpensive 8- to 10-foot spinning rod made from fiberglass or graphite/fiberglass composite. This rod gets its name because it is normally fished by tossing a jig or split-shot rig over the side of the boat and placing the rod in a handy holder. There's nothing complicated or fancy about fishing with a dead rod. The whole idea is to get a second line, that can be fished without a lot of attention, in the water.

Steelhead rods make excellent dead rods, but there's no need to purchase the expensive graphite models. Modestly priced fiberglass versions have the ideal action for dead rod fishing.

The extra length of these rods helps to reach out away from the boat while drifting. A dead rod pointed out the bow and transom of the boat doubles the fishing coverage and helps to contact fish that may have moved away from the approaching boat.

Jigs are the next item of importance. Frankly, just about any 1/16-, 1/8- or 1/4-ounce jig can be used to drag along the bottom. Ordinary round-head jigs work well, as do the various versions of

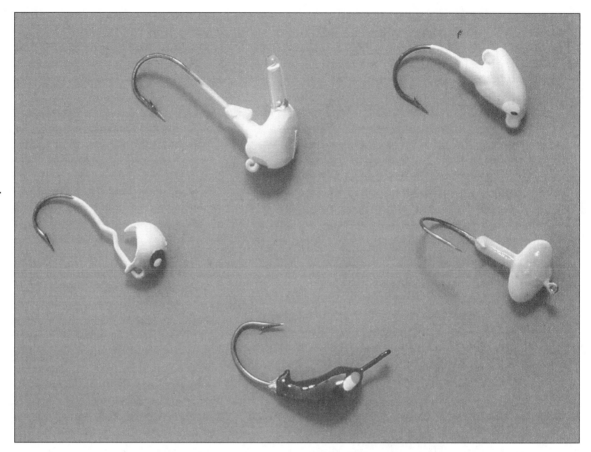

Ordinary round-head jigs can be used for dragging, but this assortment represents some jig styles that are especially productive for dragging.

Jigs can be dragged along using live bait, plastic grubs or a combination of both.

stand-up style jigs. A relatively new jighead design is among the best dragging jigs I've tested. Football-shaped jigs often used by bass anglers do an excellent job of keeping the hook pointed upwards and away from snags. The problem is, most of these jigs are built using heavy hooks suited for wrestling big bass from cover.

The Rocko Jig produced by K&E Tackle is a football-shaped head featuring a thin wire finesse-style Mustad hook. The hook is very thin wire and exceptionally sharp. I rank this jig as my favorite for dragging situations because of the upward orientation of the hook and the finesse hook that bites with the least amount of pressure.

Both live bait and plastic lures are used for dragging jigs. One of my favorite combinations is a football jig with a whole crawler hooked through the middle. This tantalizing two tailed offering is

Young Jacob Romanack is obviously proud of this walleye taken while dragging jigs.

more than most walleyes can resist. Minnows, of course, can be used and leeches are also a welcome live bait when drifting.

Some of the plastics that are good choices for dragging include twister tails, twin-tail grubs, marabou tail grubs, tube baits, finesse worms and jig worms. There's also no harm in combining plastics and live bait. The combination of action, color, scent and taste can be damaging to walleye populations.

Putting it all together, drifting jigs along the bottom is not only an effective way to trigger strikes, it's a relaxing method of fishing. Position the boat upwind of the area to be fished and let the wind push the boat along. If the wind picks up, keep a sea bag or two handy to slow down the drift.

Tie a jig on and add your favorite bait, plastic lure or bait and plastic combination. Cast the lure upwind and allow the jig to sink to the bottom. Some anglers prefer to hang onto their rods believing they can feel the bites better. I've come to the conclusion that setting the rod against the gunwale of the boat or in a rod holder is just as effective and a lot less work.

After spending a considerable amount of time holding the rod and letting the rod rest in a holder, I can see no particular advantage one way or the other. I let the rods rest in holders because it simply leaves my hands free to eat a sandwich, drink a soda or rig rods for my kids.

When the rods are resting in holders, I simply watch the rod tips as they tap out the movements of the jig dragging along the bottom. This rhythmic motion of the rod tip says the jig is moving along fine and doing its job. If the jig temporarily snags on the bottom the rod usually bends down then snaps back into position. When a fish strikes, the rod bends and starts bucking from the struggling fish.

Like I said, dragging jigs isn't complicated or a difficult presentation to master. It's simply effective and enjoyable.

When a fish is caught, toss a buoy over the side to mark the location. Drift along for a few more minutes to see if any more fish are in the area. If no bites occur, pick up lines and motor back upwind to set up for another drift. Be careful not to motor the boat directly over the area to be drifted. Set up a short distance upwind of the marker and try another drift.

Often, fish will be located in small schools or pods. The key to catching these fish is making short and rather precise drifts over the structure that seems to be holding fish.

If you own a GPS unit save an icon or waypoint for every fish caught. This information can be filed in the unit's computer and used over and over again on future fishing trips.

Even if you own a GPS, it's also a good idea to mark the location of at least some fish with a buoy. The accuracy of GPS varies depending on a service known as selective availability. Selective availability scrambles the GPS signals to various degrees of accuracy for the purpose of U.S. government security.

Generally a spot will produce a few fish before the action goes flat. Once the spot dies, continue drifting using longer passes to locate other pods of fish.

DRAGGING JIGS IN RIVERS

The chapter on vertical jigging suggested that dragging a jig on the bottom of a river is a snag waiting to happen. In many cases this is true. However, dragging jigs in rivers can be effective if the bottom composition allows for this presentation.

One of my favorite rivers is a small flow near the town of Saginaw, Michigan. The Tittabawassee River is one of the main spawning streams feeding Saginaw Bay. Each spring walleyes by the thousands run up this and other tributary streams to spawn.

After spawning, the females exit the river rather quickly, but good numbers of male fish linger in the river well into June. As these abundant males start the return journey to Saginaw Bay, they become aggressive and easy to catch.

The Tittabawassee River, like many other rivers popular with walleye anglers, features a moderate to slow current and plenty of shallow water. Flats in the 4- to 8-foot range stretch for miles. Much of the river bottom is made up of sand or gravel that makes for ideal jig-dragging conditions.

Because the river has few deep holes to concentrate fish, walleyes tend to spread out on these flats. Even slight variations in the bottom hold hungry walleyes that wait for the current to carry food within reach.

Dragging jigs along the bottom of a river is similar to drift fishing with jigs on lakes. The primary difference is the current moves the boat instead of

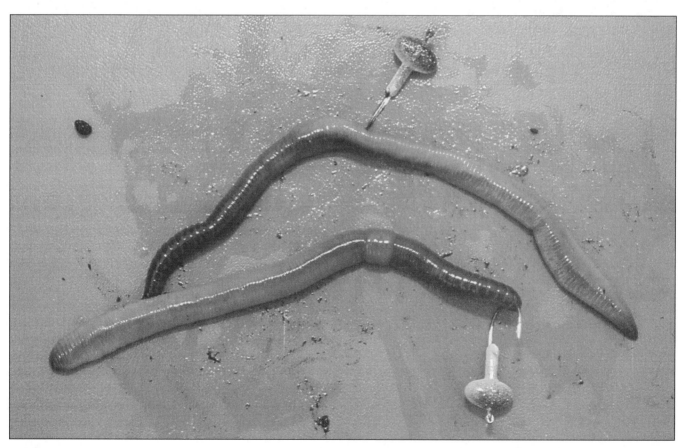

Nightcrawlers are one of the best baits when dragging jigs. A whole crawler hooked in the nose works well. Sometimes hooking the crawler in the middle and leaving two tails to wiggle produces exciting results.

the wind. The same types of rods, lines, jigs and live baits work well when dragging in rivers. There is no need for sea bags when drifting in river current.

Walleyes can turn up almost anywhere in rivers, but shallow flats in the 6- to 10-foot range are good places to start. When searching for fish I cruise slowly upstream watching the sonar unit closely. Generally I'm not looking to mark fish, but subtle changes in the bottom. Hard bottom areas such as sand or gravel attract fish and return a stronger signal. On a flasher this signal is shown as a broad red beam of light. On a Liquid Crystal Readout graph the grayline will print out a wide bottom signal.

Subtle changes in the bottom depth will also hold fish. Slight depressions are real hot spots that can produce amazing numbers of walleyes.

Once a potential fish-holding spot is located, I position the boat upstream of the area to be fished with the boat perpendicular to the current and start drifting. Jigs are baited and cast upstream and enough line is let out to allow the jig to drag along bottom. Watching the rod tips is the best way to tell if the jig is maintaining contact with the bottom.

The dead rods outlined earlier in this chapter are useful for river drifting as well. Any rod that reaches out away from the boat is going to improve lure coverage.

When a fish is caught, shoreline sightings are used to keep track of the location. When moving upstream for another drift, motor outside of the area to be drifted so as not to spook fish.

Like drifting in lakes, river drifting tends to be a spotty deal. Fish are usually located in small groups. Once a few fish have been taken from a spot, it's usually necessary to move on in search of other fish. However, remember any spot that produces walleyes. Chances are good that later the same day or another day walleyes will turn up on the spot again.

Over the years I've discovered enough spots on my favorite rivers that I simply set up a milk run and check spots that have produced fish in the past. There's no guarantee that any given spot will produce, but given enough spots you're almost certain to locate fish eventually.

One point worth noting, when water conditions rise in rivers, walleyes tend to escape the increasing current by moving closer to the bank. I've used this knowledge to take some dandy fish within feet of the bank. Areas where the water depth holds right up tight to shore tend to produce the best in high water.

For river drifting I've always felt that night-crawlers are the best bait. I like crawlers because they are inexpensive, easy to keep and effective not only on walleyes but a wealth of other species. Drifting crawlers in rivers is an open invitation to catch walleyes, plus bonus catfish, smallmouth, drum, carp and suckers will keep everyone, especially the kids, happy.

Despite the success I've enjoyed with crawlers, I must also admit that minnows, leeches and plastics produce fish as well. Drifting with the current is also a good opportunity to drag one jig along the bottom while casting a jig on another rod. Casting a diving style crankbait is yet another option that adds interest to the day and some bonus fish.

JIG TROLLING

Using the words jig and trolling in the same sentence is enough to raise the hackles of many dedicated jiggers. Those who consider jigging the ultimate means of catching walleyes are often put off by the concept of trolling.

However, combining the boat control benefits of trolling with the fish-catching virtues of jigging makes for a deadly presentation that few anglers practice. For those anglers that don't like to troll, think of this unorthodox presentation as controlled dragging.

Control is the key word. Jig trolling is about dragging jigs along clearly defined bottom structure, contour breaks or cover edges. As the most precise of all the dragging methods discussed, jig trolling combines the boat control and water covering merits of trolling with the time tested lead-head jig.

Jig trolling can be practiced in natural lakes, the Great Lakes, rivers or reservoirs. Anywhere that walleyes are found using specific pieces of bottom real estate or defined cover, jig trolling is a strong candidate for success.

Some years ago I discovered how effective jig trolling can be while fishing a favorite spawning reef in Lake Erie. Traditionally these reefs are fished by drifting and casting jig and minnow combinations and that's exactly how we started fishing. Early in the morning the air was still and conditions were ideal for casting. As the day progressed, the wind picked up. Each time we would cast our jigs, the wind blew a bow into the line, making it very difficult to feel bites. Our success dropped off to nil.

In frustration we decided to try dragging jigs along the bottom using the electric motor. It only took minutes to discover the fish were still present and willing to bite.

We simply let out enough line to maintain contact with the bottom at a trolling speed that just made headway against the wind. The electric motor worked perfectly for this presentation. We set the motor on continuous and adjusted the speed as needed.

Within minutes we were catching walleyes at will and laughing at how effective jig trolling can be. In the years that have passed since, I've refined the presentation into a system that is tough to match with any other angling method.

Unlike other jig dragging methods, jig trolling does require some special equipment and a little skill to master. For the best results, jig trolling should be practiced as a team effort with one angler in the front of the boat and one at the back of the boat.

Moving the boat quietly along is a job best suited to a powerful electric motor. Bow-mounted and foot-operated models are the logical choice because they allow the boat to be controlled with one foot, while both hands are free to fish.

A small 16-foot aluminum boat can get by nicely with a 12-volt electric motor that generates 40 to 50 foot pounds of thrust. Larger boats are best equipped with a 24-volt system that delivers 50 to 70 pounds of thrust. Many tournament anglers prefer to equip their boats with a 36-volt electric motor that generates up to 107 pounds of thrust.

Quality electronics are a must because the boat control must often be precise to enjoy the best success. Rods also need to be lightweight graphite models to help detect strikes that often occur well away from the boat. Also graphite rods are lighter and easier to hold for long hours of trolling.

Jig trolling is a team effort and the angler running the electric motor is the key. The angler running the electric motor must identify the cover, structure or contour and keep the boat moving precisely on course. It's also this angler's job to set the ideal speed that covers water, yet keeps the jigs in contact with the bottom.

To prevent anglers from tangling lines, the angler fishing from the bow uses relatively heavy

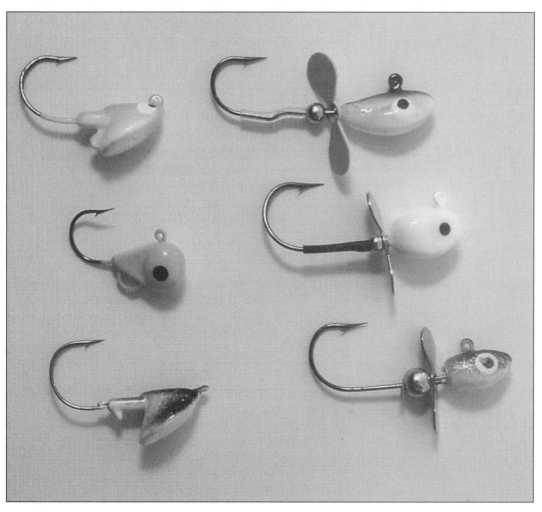

When jig trolling, short-shank jigs with a wide hook gap are among the best choices. Other jigs that can be dragged effectively include swimming jigs like the Lindy Lil Hummer, Northland Whistler and Walleye Stopper Prop jigs.

jigs fished at approximately a 45-degree angle to the bottom. Usually 3/8- or 1/2-ounce jigs are used on the bow. The angler in the back of the boat uses lighter jigs that are let out farther to maintain contact with the bottom. Jigs in the 1/8- or 1/4-ounce range work well off the back.

When fishing live bait, short-shank jigs are a good choice. The wide hook gap these jigs offer makes them bite and hold struggling fish exceptionally well. If plastic lures are used, a long shank jig with a barbed collar is needed to hold the plastic firmly in place. Stand-up, football, darter and round-head jigs can all be trolled with good results.

To further improve lure coverage, both anglers should fish two rods where allowed by law. The extra lines in the water help to cover the water more thoroughly while allowing for experimentation with color, jig style, bait and plastic body options.

Efficiency is what makes jig trolling so deadly. Four lures are presented in the strike zone 100 percent of the time. In addition, the boat is being directed along a defined path. Once fish are located along this path, it's a simple matter to make more passes over productive water.

Jig trolling works in water as shallow as 6 or 8 feet and as deep as 20 feet. As with drifting in lakes, a few marker buoys are a handy way to mark the location of fish or spots that are holding fish. When following meandering edges or contours, walleyes will often stack up in the turns or cups formed by submerged points. Dropping a few carefully placed buoys can make it much easier to visualize how the structure or cover lays out.

Drifting jigs in lakes, dragging jigs in rivers or trolling jigs on structure edges are just some of the ways lead-heads can be slid along the bottom and into more walleyes. These examples of how jigs can be versatile fishing tools are just the beginning. With a little imagination, the ways jigs can be used is without limit.

In the next chapter a classic walleye fishing method will be explored in detail. Slip sinker rigging is one of the oldest and most trusted methods for dredging up walleyes.

CHAPTER 15

REFINED SLIP SINKER RIGGING

The Lindy Rig is to walleye fishing what the plastic worm is to bass angling. Simple by design, this classic live bait rig consists of a walking-style or "L" shaped sinker threaded onto the line. A snap swivel is then tied onto the line that accepts a leader ranging from 18 to 60 inches. At the terminal end a bare hook, floating jig head or spinner is added.

Slip sinker rigging rates as one of the presentations all walleye anglers should master.

Fished with the reel bail open and the line over the index finger, live minnows, crawlers or leeches are the usual bait.

This simple rig keeps the bait near bottom and the walking sinker pulls through a variety of bottom types with amazingly few snags. When a bite occurs the angler feeds line to the fish by dropping the line from his index finger. Giving the fish line after the bite allows it to eat the bait without feeling the weight of the sinker.

After waiting a few seconds for the fish to swallow the bait, the angler slowly reels up the slack line. When the weight of the fish can be felt, the hook is set with a strong upwards sweep of the rod that lifts the sinker off bottom and drives the hook home.

Normally it's only necessary to wait a few seconds before setting the hook. This is especially true when fishing with small minnows or leeches. With crawlers or large minnows it may be necessary to wait up to half a minute to be sure the fish has the bait completely in its mouth.

While there are a lot of variations of slip sinker rigging, the basics just described have been used to take countless walleyes coast to coast. No other fishing presentation has been used by more anglers, touted as highly in the press or had more impact on walleye fishing in the past 30 years than this popular rig.

The Lindy Rig is an icon that started walleye anglers thinking about fishing in a completely different light. Some 30 years ago when the Lindy Rig was young, so was another fishing invention known as sonar. They say that timing is everything. In the case of the Lindy Rig and the first flasher units produced by Lowrance Electronics the timing couldn't have been better. Thanks to sonar, anglers could find bottom structure that held walleyes and mark the location fish.

The Lindy Rig quickly became the fishing presentation of choice among anglers who targeted this untapped resource. The Lindy Rig and flasher so complemented one another it's unlikely that any two aspects of walleye fishing will ever make a greater impact on the sport.

As you might expect it didn't take long before Lindy Little Joe Tackle Company was a booming success. Soon afterwards other companies started producing similar slip sinker rigs. Today, most of the major tackle manufacturers offer a slip sinker rig who's roots can be traced back to the original.

THE EVOLUTION OF SLIP SINKER RIGS

Over the years a number of refinements have been made to the original concept of slip sinker rigs. One of the most notable improvements was introduced with the Roach Rig from Northland Tackle. A sliding sinker stop incorporated to this product allows the leader length to be adjusted without cutting the line.

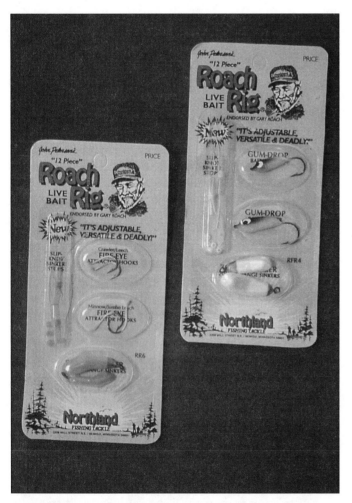

The Roach Rig introduced one of the major refinements to slip sinker rigging. A sliding sinker stop allows the leader length to be adjusted without cutting the line. Lindy Little Joe now offers a similar system.

While this improvement may sound modest, the convenience of being able to quickly add or reduce lead length should not be underestimated. In very clear waters it's often necessary to use much longer leaders. The traditional leader on a rig runs from 18 to 36 inches, but leads as long as 6, 7 or 8 feet are sometimes required. The Roach Rig helped to popularize the use of long snells on slip sinker rigs.

Also unique to the Roach Rig, the sinkers used feature a soft wire loop that can be easily bent open and closed so weights may be changed without cutting the leader. These weights are available in natural lead color or in painted versions designed to act as attractants.

Lindy Little Joe also offers a sliding weight stop that makes rigging more convenient. Soft Stops are soft plastic beads that act like a sinker stop. The beads are held in place with a removable peg that allows anglers to adjust leads to any length desired without cutting the line and retying. Easy to use and durable enough to be used over and over again, Soft Stops are small enough that they don't catch on weeds or otherwise interfere with the normal function of the rig.

Quick Change Systems of Pierre, South Dakota lays claim to another major advancement in slip sinker rigging. Known best for the Quick Change spinner clevis, this company also produces a weight clip that, when threaded onto the line ahead of a snap swivel, allows rigging weights to be changed by simply snapping them on or off this convenient clip.

This sinker clip can be used with the two designs of walking-style sinkers produced by Quick Change. The first design is similar to the traditional walking sinker except it has a wire eye molded into the sinker instead of a hole for the line to pass through. This wire snaps cleanly onto the weight clip.

A second style of rigging weight features a painted sinker on the bottom with a short wire arm molded into the top. Again this wire arm is designed to accept the weight clip. Available in both orange and chartreuse, these weights act not only as a sinker but also an attractant.

Anglers have a third weight option when using these Quick Change clips. A single-arm bottom bouncer can also be used, lifting the bait farther off the bottom and making it more practical to use in areas where the bottom is littered with snags or moss that can quickly foul hooks. The single-arm bottom bouncer is also ideal for fishing crawler harnesses. This rig also converts an ordinary bot-

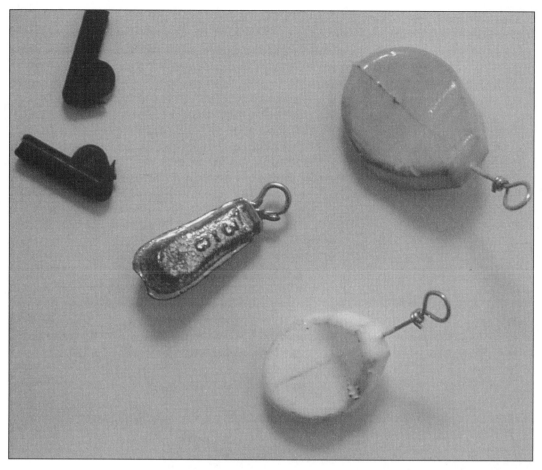

The Quick Change Systems weight clip made it possible to change weight sizes and styles without cutting and retying. This weight clip can be used with walking-style sinkers or single-arm bottom bouncers.

Lindy's new No-Snagg sinker is among the hottest concepts to hit the rigging scene. This unique slip weight fishes through cover and structure that would eat up ordinary sinkers.

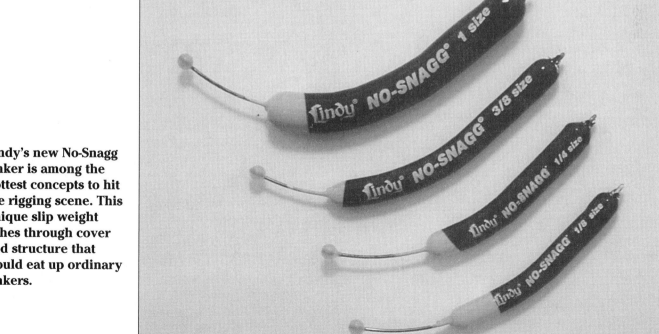

tom bouncer into a slip sinker rig that's often productive when fishing conditions are especially tough.

Like the Quick Change clevis, this weight clip is as handy as handy gets. Only pennies each, every tackle box should be equipped with a few of these rigging accessories.

If most slip sinker rigs have a failing, it's that they are prone to snag. The best solution I've seen to this problem comes in the form of a product recently introduced by Lindy Little Joe. Called the No-Snagg sinker it looks like a pencil weight, slightly bent with a short piece of wire coming out the bottom. The bottom part of the weight is lead, but the top half is a buoyant material.

The result is a sinker that rides upright in the water giving it a remarkable ability to pull through rocks and other snags without hanging on the bottom. Touted as the most snag-resistant bottom sinker ever developed, this unique product is used exactly the same way as a traditional walking sinker. Available in a wide variety of sizes, this new product has already become popular.

The Snake Weight is another rigging sinker that is designed to be snag-resistant. The weight is made from a short length of hollow parachute cord filled with lead balls. The nylon cord is heated at one end to melt the cord and trap the lead balls inside. At the other end a snap swivel is clipped through the nylon material to close it and provide an eyelet suitable for threading the line through.

The Snake Weight slithers through rocks, brush and other snags amazingly well and is fished like a normal slip sinker rig. Various weights are produced to handle all common rigging situations.

When rigging in weed cover, the walking-style sinker used on most rigs is often removed and a bullet-style weight substituted. The pointed bullet weight pulls through weed cover with less hang-ups. Ordinary lead bullet weights work fine, but anglers also have the option of using brass or steel weights that add sound to the presentation.

Ultra Steel 2000 produces a three-piece weight including a nose cone, small clacker weight and rear weight that completes the sound chamber. The line is threaded first through the nose cone, then the clacker and finally through the rear weight. When pulled along the bottom the clacker makes a clicking sound as it contacts the front and back pieces of the bullet-shaped weight.

This system is easy to use, it pulls through weeds well and is a great way to add sound to a slip sinker presentation.

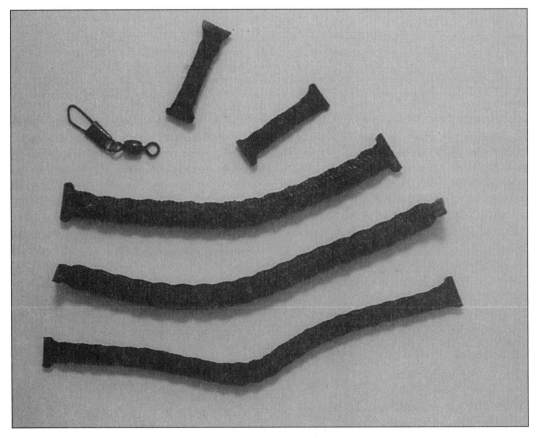

Snake Weights are snag-resistant slip weights that are designed for fishing in tough cover. The weights are fashioned from lead balls placed inside a length of parachute cord.

Rigging in weed cover calls for a bullet-style weight. The pointed shape of these weights allows them to pull through weed cover with few hang-ups.

It's important to note that the normal hook size for a slip sinker rig is a No. 4 for small minnows, crawlers or leeches and a No. 2 for bigger minnows. When rigging in weeds, big hooks tend to readily catch on weed cover. To reduce problems with the hooks catching on weeds, consider using a smaller No. 6 hook on rigs fished in weed cover.

Weedless-style single hooks can also be used. The Eagle Claw 449WA hook in No. 6 or 4 is a good option for those who like to tie up their own rigs. Lindy Little Joe produces a weedless slip sinker rig that comes complete with bullet weight, leader and weed-guard hooks for fishing in the salad.

EQUIPMENT NEEDS

The rods and reels required for slip sinker rigging are similar to that recommended for casting slip bobbers. The primary difference is a slip sinker rod needs to be highly sensitive because bites must be detected by feel.

A high-quality graphite spinning combination in the 6-1/2-to 7-foot range is ideal for slip sinker rigging. A rod that ranges from medium to medium/light action is recommended. The reel should be spooled with 6- or 8-pound test monofilament for best results.

Slip sinker rigging is one presentation that clearly calls for the forgiving properties of

Mark Moore of Cadillac, Michigan used a soft, floating jig head tipped with a leech to catch this northern Michigan walleye.

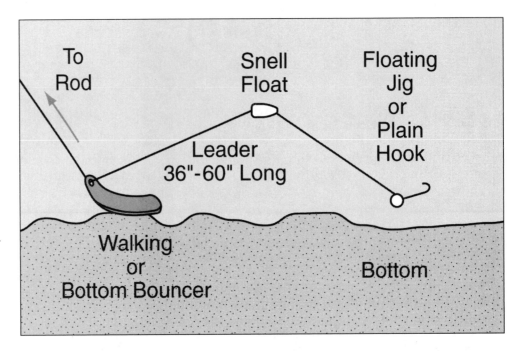

To Rod

Snell Float

Floating Jig or Plain Hook

Leader 36"-60" Long

Walking or Bottom Bouncer

Bottom

Rigging a snell float in the middle of a snell helps to build slack into the leader that makes it easier for walleyes to inhale the bait.

monofilament. Monofilament is preferred for rigging because the line has a small amount of natural stretch. When a walleye picks up a bait fished on monofilament, the elastic properties of the line prevents the fish from detecting the angler at the other end.

The low-stretch properties of braided super lines create a situation where the fish feels resistance immediately and, in many cases, the fish rejects the bait before the angler has time to set the hook. Braided lines have lots of niches in the world of walleye fishing, but slip sinker rigging isn't one of them.

Outside of the spinning combination outlined and an assortment of various types of slip sinker rigs, no other special equipment is required. It is however necessary to stock up on the various components used in slip sinker rigging.

Every angler will need an assortment of weights including 1/4-, 3/8-, 1/2- and 3/4-ounce variants. A number of small snap swivels will also be needed to attach rig snells. Some anglers prefer to place a small plastic bead between the sliding weight and the swivel to insure the line isn't damaged by the sinker.

As far as terminal tackle goes, a number of commercially prepared snells are offered by companies such as Northland, Lindy, Quick Change Systems, Owner and Mustad. Those anglers who enjoy tying their own snells will need an assortment of beak-style hooks in sizes No. 6, 4 and 2.

My favorite rigging hooks are thin wire styles that are lightweight and extra sharp. A few of the outstanding products available include the Eagle Claw Featherlight, Mustad Finesse and Gamakatsu Octopus. Soft floating jig heads such as the Northland Gun-Drop Floater are also must-have items.

The unique sinker clips produced by Quick Change systems also rank as mandatory items for rigging. Other useful items are snell floats. These small foam floats are designed to add buoyancy to the rig and prevent the hook from dragging on bottom. Lindy, Northland and Quick Change Systems all produce snell floats that are sold as components.

A snell float trick taught to me by Fishing Hall of Fame member Bob Propst has produced countless fish over the years. Instead of attaching the snell float near the hook, slide it up the harness about halfway between the hook and snap swivel. Use a piece of tooth pick pushed into the end of the snell float to peg it in place.

Rigged in this manner the snell float will rise up off bottom when the boat's forward momentum stalls for a moment. This creates a tiny bit of slack line in the snell that makes it easier for walleyes to suck the bait completely into their mouth.

It's little tips like this that can make a big difference in the success anglers enjoy while slip sinker rigging.

USING SLIP SINKER RIGS

Drifting, using an electric motor and back-trolling with a gasoline engine are the traditional ways of presenting slip sinker rigs. Unlike other fishing presentations where the angler casts the bait into position and imparts action to the lure, the boat is used to pull or drag slip sinker rigs into position.

The key to fishing these rigs is to move slowly, stay in contact with bottom and watch the sonar closely for fish. In many instances fish that are marked on the sonar can be caught by using the boat to pull the bait past waiting fish.

Enough weight should be used so the bottom can be easily felt. To maximize the effectiveness of slip sinker rigs they must be fished relatively close to the boat. I like to fish rigs at roughly a 45- to 60-degree angle behind the boat. If too light a sinker is used, lots of line must be let out to feel the bottom. This situation presents the bait so far behind the boat, it's tough to steer the bait into good-looking bottom structure or fish marks.

This is especially true when working sharp dropping breaks, the tips of points, cups in a contour edge and other spots-on-the-spot. Rigging is an excellent way to fish these types of bottom structure, but the boat must be under control and positioned in exactly the right spot.

The fact that precise boat control is required for rigging is one of the major reasons backtrolling has become a standard method of presenting rigs. A boat moving backwards can be steered to follow meandering contours closely. This is especially true when using a transom-mounted electric motor. Electric motors enable the boat to be turned at much sharper angles than gasoline motors which suffer from the limitations of a narrow steering radius.

It's important to note, however, that backtrolling can only be accomplished with boats that feature a square transom. Many of the performance fiberglass boats on the market feature built-in set-back plates or padded hulls that make it nearly impossible to drive the boat backwards. Fortunately, an electric motor mounted on the bow can be used to steer these boats accurately.

Speed control is the other reason backtrolling became so popular in the early days of slip sinker rigging. Most boats back then were not equipped with electric motors. Instead the boat was controlled using a tiller-handle outboard. To reduce speed so the rigs could be positioned on the bottom, the boat is worked into the wind and the motor kicked in and out of gear as needed.

In some instances a small sea bag can be used to slow boat speed. The father of walleye fishing, Bob Propst Sr., often uses a small sea anchor tied to the rear cleat of his boat. When Bob needs to backtroll at a super-slow speed he tosses the bag over the side. The bag is attached to a short cord that keeps it positioned under the boat and out of the way.

As you might guess splash guards were invented soon after backtrolling became popular. Splash guards prevent water from sloshing into the back of the boat and soaking the occupants. Backtrolling is one of the few instances when walleye anglers are advised to work against the forces of the wind.

OTHER RIGGING OPTIONS

To be effective a rig doesn't have to be of the slip sinker variety. A split-shot pinched on the line 18 to 36 inches ahead of a single hook is a simple, yet effective, example of a rig. This type of fishing is rarely practiced, but this no-nonsense rig makes a lot of sense in some walleye fishing situations.

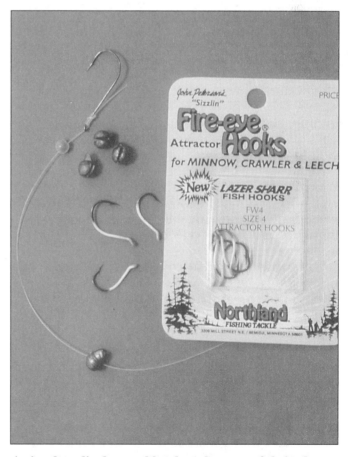

A simple split-shot and hook makes a useful rig that can be cast into position. Because split-shot rigs are inexpensive to make, many anglers use them when fishing snag-filled waters.

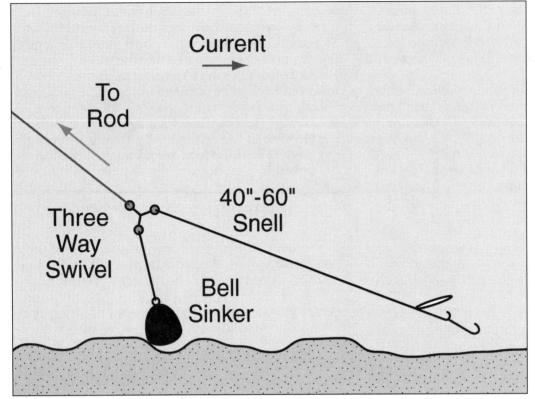

Current

To Rod

Three Way Swivel

40"-60" Snell

Bell Sinker

Three-way rigs are good options for fishing the bottom in swift current. Three-way rigs are also a good way to position the bait a little farther off bottom than is possible with a bottom bouncer.

I depend on split-shot rigs when fishing in snag filled waters where I would be likely to lose more expensive slip sinker rigs. Losing slip sinker rigs is not only more expensive than a split-shot rig, it takes away more valuable fishing time to rig up each time a snag is encountered.

It's amazing how a split-shot rig can be fished through obvious snags with few hang-ups. The trick is to let out just enough line to touch bottom when dragging these rigs. If casting, use just enough weight so the rig will sink to the bottom and no more.

Often used on a dead rod, a split-shot rig needs little tending. If a soft wire hook, such as an Aberdeen, is used most snags can be recovered simply by using a steady pull that bends open the hook. Once the rig is recovered, bend the hook back into shape with a pair of pliers, sharpen the hook, bait up and you're back in business.

A dead rod can be any rod, but a long steelhead-style rod with a very soft action is the best option. The long rod helps to present the bait out away from the boat and the soft action reduces the chances that a walleye will detect something unnatural and drop the bait before the angler can set the hook.

Three-way rigs are another useful tool for fishing walleyes. A three-way rig performs a function

similar to the bottom bouncer. The main line is attached to one end of a three-way swivel. On the second swivel a snell ranging from 36 to 60 inches is added. On the last swivel a dropper lead with a lead sinker is added. The rig is then drifted or trolled with the weight ticking along the bottom.

Unlike a bottom bouncer, a three-way rig can be adjusted so the trailing harness fishes the desired distance from bottom. By simply adding a longer length of dropper leader, a three-way rig can be used to fish well above the bottom. This technique is especially useful when fishing in clear water or places where zebra mussels are plentiful. Anywhere these bottom-dwellers live they play havoc with anglers who try to fish the bottom for walleyes.

If the hooks touch the bottom they are quickly fouled with zebra mussels. Fishing a three-way rig with a 24- to 36-inch dropper is a good way to position spinners and other terminal rigs well off the bottom and solve this common problem.

The weight used on a three-way rig can be a bell sinker or split-shot pinched onto the dropper line. It's also a good idea to use a dropper line that's lighter than the main line. Should the sinker become snagged on bottom, the dropper line can be broken off without losing the entire rig.

The popularity of the bottom bouncer has led many anglers to abandon three-way rigs. I believe, in certain situations, three-way rigs can be more effective than bottom bouncers. In deep water it's easier to maintain contact with the bottom by using a three-way rig because they have less drag in the water. Also, if fish are especially spooky, a three-way is less likely to alarm fish.

Two anglers can use three-way rigs in combination with slip sinker rigs. Set a couple slip sinker rigs as normal, then incorporate two three-way rigs using much heavier weights. The heavier three-way rigs fish down below the boat, while the lighter slip sinker rigs are positioned out a short distance behind the boat.

Put the three-way rigs in rod holders and hold the slip sinker rigs in your hands. Combining three-ways and slip sinker rigs covers the water with a couple different presentations. This effective four-rod rigging option also allows anglers to experiment with a number of different live baits and terminal tackle options.

Three-way rigs can be fished using spinning tackle until heavy weights are incorporated. When weights above 1 ounce are used, anglers are better equipped using baitcasting rods and reels armed with 10-pound test monofilament.

I often use downrigger rods when fishing three-ways with 2-, 3- or 4-ounce weights. These versatile rods are equipped with line-counter reels and also used for fishing bottom bouncers and crankbaits behind in-line planer boards.

Slip sinker rigging is one of the oldest and most respected ways to catch walleyes. Simple by design and functional on all bodies of water, this classic presentation takes fish on natural lakes, rivers, reservoirs and the Great Lakes.

In the next chapter we'll discuss another bottom-fishing method. Bottom bouncers got their start in the Dakotas, but anglers coast-to-coast currently enjoy the fish-catching powers of these bottom weights.

CHAPTER 16

BOTTOM BOUNCERS: THE BASICS AND BEYOND

The art of locating and catching walleyes starts at the bottom. This species isn't always located where the mud meets the water, but you can bet that any lake with significant numbers of

On any given body of water at least some walleyes are going to be found living on the bottom. Bottom bouncers are one of the best ways to stay in contact with bottom while quickly covering water.

fish will always have at least some specimens hugging the bottom.

Even in bodies of water where walleyes widely suspend in the water column, a significant number relate to the bottom on any given day. Lake Erie is the best example of a fishery that supports a substantial number of suspended walleyes. Despite the fact that walleyes can be located suspended in the water column 12 months of the year, there are always some fish that for reasons only the fish fully understand, choose to live on the bottom.

The most logical solution to this mystery suggests that walleyes turn up where food is available. Walleyes suspend in the water column to take advantage of pelagic (free-swimming) forages such as emerald shiners, alewives, smelt, ciscoes or shad, but it's just as obvious that suspended fish are not always in a feeding mood. To some degree the location of the most abundant food sources will dictate the location of some walleyes and perhaps even the majority of walleyes in a given body of water.

Still, there are situations were walleyes take to the bottom, despite abundant suspended forage species. Perhaps the bottom is a convenient place to rest or hide from predators? Maybe walleyes use the bottom as a place to lay in ambush for passing prey? Perhaps the bottom is a travel route complete with landmarks? Could it be that the bottom gives walleyes a sense of security? Some anglers even believe that bottom-dwelling walleyes and suspended walleyes are two different strains of the same species.

The last theory is a little far-fetched, but who knows for sure? Why some walleyes favor the bottom while others don't is a mystery that's not likely to be answered any time soon. What we do know is that walleyes frequently turn up on bottom. In my humble opinion, the bottom is the focal point that allows walleyes to function both as a benthic (bottom-dwelling) and pelagic (free-swimming) species.

Because walleyes have evolved into an adaptable species, they are opportunistic. Not unlike northern pike, muskie, smallmouth bass, stripers and other predators, walleyes feed where and when they can.

This survival equation means that sometimes walleyes will be suspended and sometimes they will be found on the bottom. Our immediate focus is to determine the most efficient means of locating and catching walleyes on bottom. Why these fish so often are found on the bottom we'll leave to the philosophers.

INTRODUCING THE BOTTOM BOUNCER

When it comes to fishing the bottom, there are lots of options to pick from. Jigs, slip sinker rigs, three-way rigs, spoons and even crankbaits can be used to fish the bottom. However, all of these lure or rig options are weak when compared to the strengths of the bottom bouncer.

Simple by design and function, a bottom bouncer is nothing more than a length of wire bent to form a long leg (approximately 12 inches) and short arm (approximately 3 inches). A lead weight

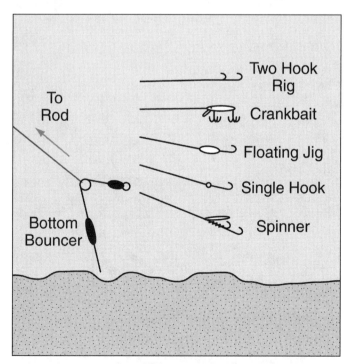

A wealth of snell options can be used with a bottom bouncer weight. Spinners are the most common snell option, but floating jigheads, single hooks, two-hook rigs and even crankbaits can be used.

is molded midway onto the long leg and a snap swivel is attached to the end of the short arm. The line tie or attachment point becomes the apex where the leg and arm come together.

Normally a snell with a single hook or crawler harness is attached to the snap swivel and allowed to trail behind the bottom bouncer as the rig is drifted or slow trolled. However, other options such as flutter spoons, stickbaits and floating jig heads can also be used.

When deployed, the weight sinks rapidly to bottom. The wire leg ticks along bottom, tripping over rocks, logs and other debris with amazing efficiency. Meanwhile, the trailing lure, bait or harness is positioned a few inches off the bottom, right where waiting fish can see it.

Not only are bottom bouncers an effective way to present a wide variety of lures and live baits near the bottom, they are without a doubt the most efficient means of fishing the bottom. Bottom bouncers are efficient because they present baits near, but not on, the bottom. They move along bottom with few snags. They enable anglers to fish a wide variety of depth ranges and most importantly, bottom bouncers impart action to rigs and lures that trigger strike responses.

Let's take a close look at how bottom bouncers present lures or baits close to, but not directly on the bottom. Unlike walking sinkers, keel sinkers, split shots, worm weights, egg sinkers and other fishing weights, the bottom bouncer incorporates a 12-inch length of wire that helps to present the bait a little bit up off the bottom.

The weight is normally balanced about midway on the wire arm, leaving several inches of wire sticking out below the weight. This wire rides along the bottom and is less likely to wedge between rocks and other snags than a weight that contacts the bottom.

The Dan Gapen Bottom Walker uses a similar design except the weight rests on the bottom and the wire used only lifts the lure a couple inches off bottom. A useful sinker design on snag free bottoms, the Bottom Walker has not become popular among hard-core walleye anglers largely because it is less snag resistant than other sinker types.

Needle weight style sinkers function similar to bottom bouncers. The weight is positioned midway on the wire and a three way swivel used to add leaders and the main line. Like bottom bouncers, needle weights are available in a wealth of sizes suitable for different depths.

Single-arm bottom bouncers are yet another product that function much the same as tradi-

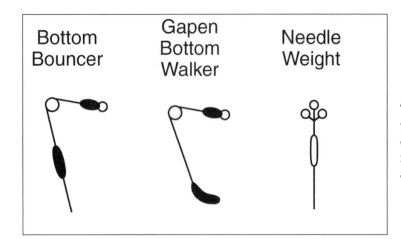

Bottom Bouncer

Gapen Bottom Walker

Needle Weight

The Gapen Bottom Walker and needle weights function similarly to bottom bouncers, but these trolling/drifting weights have not become as popular with walleye anglers.

tional bottom bouncers. A number of manufacturers now offer single-arm bottom bouncers, but Quick Change Systems of Pierre, South Dakota originally introduced the design in cooperation with their molded Quick Change Sinker Snap.

The Sinker Snap is threaded onto the line and a snap swivel tied to the end of the line. A spinner rig or other snelled rig is attached to the snap swivel and the single arm bottom bouncer is snapped into the plastic Sinker Snap.

The chief difference between this and other bottom bouncers is that the weight slides freely on the line like a slip sinker rig. When a fish bites, the angler can drop the rod tip and feed line to the fish. A cross

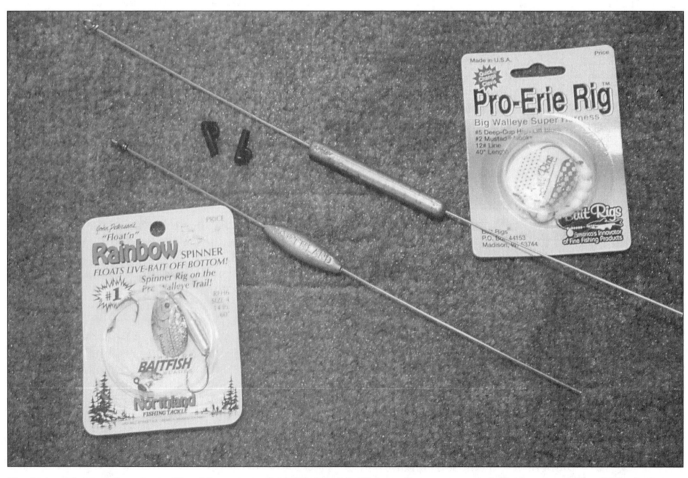

Single-arm bottom bouncers like this one produced by Quick Change Systems are gaining in popularity. This rig functions like a slip sinker rig, yet the weight is tall enough to position spinners and other hardware up off the bottom.

between a slip sinker rig and traditional bottom bouncer, single-arm bottom bouncers have become very popular. These weights are more convenient to store and they can be easily removed from the line when motoring from one location to another.

In addition to positioning baits up off the bottom and reducing the chances of snags, bottom bouncers are also produced in a wide variety of weights suitable for any walleye fishing situation. The size of bottom bouncer selected is relative to both water depth and drifting or trolling speed.

When using a bottom bouncer to fish a snell with a single hook and leech combination, speeds similar to slip sinker rigging are employed. A small 1/2- to 5/8-ounce bouncer could be used easily in water up to 20 feet deep. However, the same size bottom bouncer wouldn't be adequate for trolling spinner harnesses. The extra speed required to turn the spinner blade forces the use of a somewhat heavier bottom bouncer to maintain contact with bottom.

Because bottom bouncers are used with a variety of rigs, harnesses and lures at a wealth of speeds, there's no set size that's ideal for a spe-cific water depth. The most common sizes offered include 1/2-, 5/8-, 3/4-, 1-, 1-1/2-, 2- and 3-ounce models. Of these sizes, the most-used models are the 1/2-, 1- and 2-ounce versions. Armed with a good selection of bottom bouncers in these sizes, anglers can be confident while fishing waters from 10 to 40 feet deep.

When selecting bottom bouncer sizes, the rule of thumb is to select a weight that's heavy enough to maintain contact with the bottom when the weight is positioned at approximately a 45-degree angle behind the boat. This helps to insure the bouncer is staying in close contact with the bottom and functioning properly.

Note that I said, "...in close contact with the bottom." I did not say, "...dragging on the bottom." To fish effectively, a bottom bouncer should be set so it trips along the bottom with the wire touching down every few feet. Accomplishing this goal can be a little tricky.

Bottom bouncers do have a failing. If these sinkers are fished too far behind the boat, the bottom bouncer will not skip along the bottom in an upright position, but will lay over on its side and simply slide along the bottom. The bait is not positioned above

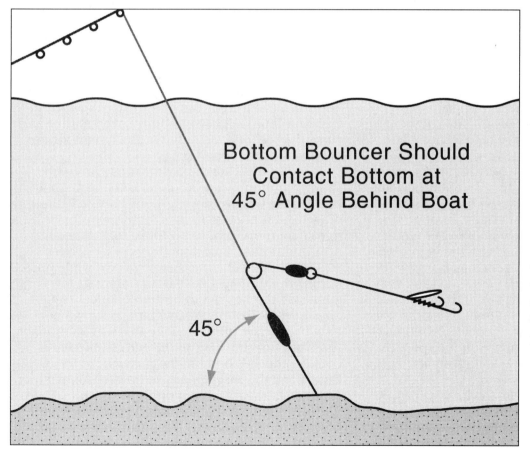

Bottom Bouncer Should Contact Bottom at 45° Angle Behind Boat

45°

The rule of 45 suggests that a bottom bouncer should be fished behind the boat at approximately a 45-degree angle to the bottom.

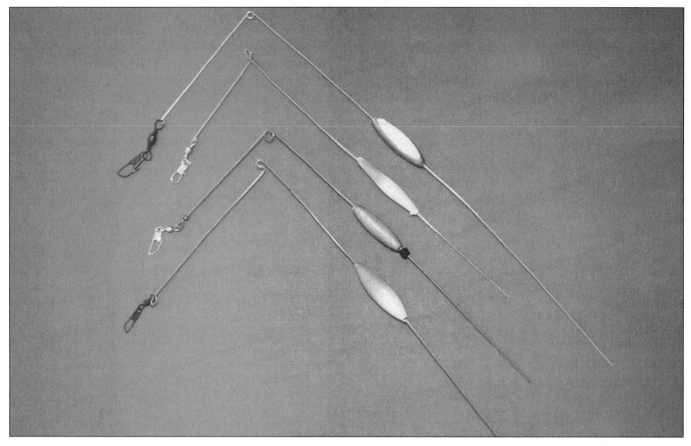

All the major tackle manufacturers produce bottom bouncers. These examples are produced by Northland, Walleye Stopper, Lindy, Quick Change Systems and Bait Rigs.

the bottom, snags are increased and the whole purpose of using the bottom bouncer is lost.

Here's the tricky part. How do you know exactly how much line to let out to insure a bottom bouncer is fishing effectively? To insure that bottom bouncers are working correctly it's important to establish a boat speed before setting a line.

If you plan on drifting, let the boat drift for a moment or two before setting lines. If you're trolling with an electric motor or small kicker motor, establish the trolling speed to be used before setting the lines. Once a boat speed has been established, stick with this speed.

Set lines by free spooling the bottom bouncer and trailing harness to the bottom. When the bottom bouncer hits bottom the spool will stop turning momentarily. Put your finger on the spool to prevent additional line from playing out and hold the rod still for a moment.

The forward movement of the boat will apply considerable water resistance to the line and bottom bouncer, forcing the bouncer to swing backwards and lift up off the bottom. Try dropping the

rod tip back to see if the weight can be felt hitting bottom. If the weight can't be felt hitting bottom, free spool the weight to bottom a second time and close the reel bail the moment the weight strikes bottom for the second time.

Usually, allowing the bottom bouncer to free spool to bottom twice is a good working method of keeping the weight tripping along bottom without dragging. In very deep water it may be necessary to free spool the weight to bottom a third time.

Carefully set, a bottom bouncer ticks over rock, sand, gravel and other structure while positioning the trailing lure, bait or harness a few inches off the bottom. A bottom bouncer weight does a fine job of presenting lures near the bottom, but there's more value to this versatile sinker.

Every time the wire on the end of a bottom bouncer touches bottom, the sinker stops for an instant and the weight starts to tip over. Momentum causes the trailing spinner or other lure to hesitate. The forward motion of the boat jerks the bottom bouncer to attention and the trailing harness darts forward again. This stop-and-go motion is absolutely lethal on walleyes that may have noticed the spinning blade or bait and cruised up for a closer look.

The beauty of a bottom bouncer is this important strike-triggering element is built into the natural function of these drifting/trolling weights. The rod can be held in the angler's hand or placed in a rod holder with equal success.

SUGGESTIONS FOR RODS/REELS/LINES

Now that the basic function and benefit of the bottom bouncer has been explored, it's time to examine some specific equipment that make fishing with a bottom bouncer more enjoyable and practical.

Just about any rod and reel combination can be used to fish bottom bouncers. However for the most part these weights are heavy enough to eliminate spinning and spincasting tackle. Baitcasting tackle not unlike that used by avid bass anglers is ideally suited to fishing bottom bouncers.

Rods often range in length from 6-1/2- to 8-1/2-feet. Shorter rods are more comfortable and practical if the angler elects to hold the rod. Longer rods reach out away from the boat to cover more water and are best used in a convenient rod holder.

Graphite rods are often used for bottom bouncer fishing because they are light to hold and sensitive to subtle strikes. If the rod will be used primarily in a rod holder, I'd suggest a fiberglass model or graphite/fiberglass composite. Glass or composite rods are a little less expensive and they function well in situations where the rod is not depended upon to telegraph strikes.

A good quality baitcasting reel capable of handling 200 yards of 10- to 12-pound test monofilament should be matched to this rod. The best monofilament for bottom bouncer fishing is premium quality line that features excellent abrasion resistance and toughness. Line watching is not important with bottom bouncer fishing, so clear or low-visibility green lines are the best choice.

If a bottom bouncer rod will be held in the angler's hand, I'd recommend using a lightweight graphite triggerstick with a baitcasting style reel. A 7-foot model with a medium or medium/light action is a good choice.

When fished in deep water, thin diameter braided super lines make it easier to maintain a light contact with the bottom.

Anglers who fish in deep water will find that braided super lines make it easier to set bottom bouncers properly. The thin diameter of these lines combined with low stretch makes it easier to set bottom bouncers at that perfect 45-degree angle. Super lines with a 10- to 15-pound break strength are ideal for deep-water fishing with bottom bouncers.

A WORD ON HARNESSES

Bottom bouncers are most often used in cooperation with spinner rigs or crawler harnesses. The 12-inch harnesses sold in tackle shops aren't the answer for fishing bottom bouncers. A bottom bouncer requires a longer harness, usually from 36 to 60 inches long. Harnesses shorter than 36 inches place the bait too close to the weight and reduce somewhat the natural stop-and-go action of the moving bottom bouncer.

Harnesses longer than 60 inches tend to stretch back so far they drag on the bottom. Many anglers believe that when they are fishing a blade, the resistance on the blade causes the bait to raise in the water column. Actually, the reverse occurs. Water flowing over the blade forces the blade towards the bottom. The weight of the blade,

hooks and bait further force the business end of a harness to sink.

In my experience, the most useful harness length for fishing with bottom bouncer varies from 40 to 60 inches, depending on water clarity. In clear water, snells on the longer side of these recommendations tend to work better than those on the shorter side. In darker water, shorter harnesses are a little easier to work with and very effective.

A single hook snelled with between 40 and 60 inches of monofilament is a common way to fish leeches, crawlers or minnows on a bottom bouncer. For leeches I favor a very light wire hook in the No. 4 size. Light wire hooks allow the leech freedom to swim about. Thin wire hooks can also be bent out and recovered if the bait snags.

For crawler fishing, two compact beak-style hooks in size No. 4 or 2 work great. I often thread a single colorful bead onto the snell just to add a touch of color. The same beak hook is ideal for minnows. A snell with a single No. 2 hook works best.

Commercially produced snells with hooks suitable for leeches, crawlers and minnows are offered by a wealth of trusted companies. Most of these snells are long enough to allow them to be cut for specific purposes. If you enjoy tying your own snells, the best material to use is fluorocar-

There is a staggering number of options of spinner harnesses available. All the major tackle manufactures produce good products or anglers can tie their own using a several different components.

bon. This special monofilament is tough yet flexible and it virtually disappears in the water.

Stren is the leading manufacturer of fluorocarbon lines. It is currently available in small leader spools, the best sizes for bottom bouncer fishing range from 10- to 12-pound test.

STORING BOTTOM BOUNCERS AND SNELLS

A bottom bouncer is a wonderful fishing tool, but they are a nightmare in a tackle box. The long wires don't fit neatly into tackle box compartments and when on the rod, bottom bouncers are a pain to keep from tangling while motoring from one spot to another.

The best storage system I've seen for bottom bouncers is produced by K&E Walleye Stopper Lures. The system resembles a cloth tool roll but

it's made from heavy Cordura nylon and vinyl material. When rolled out on the deck of the boat, several pockets made from clear vinyl accept bottom bouncers in different sizes. When rolled up, the whole package takes up very little room and can be stored in traditional tackle boxes, dry storage compartments or just about anywhere.

Storing harnesses is also a trouble spot in a tackle box. Most harnesses come in blister packages that are of no use once the product has been unwrapped. If the harness isn't stored neatly in some fashion, a tangle among tangles is eminent.

Some anglers simply roll up the harness and slip it into a ziplock style plastic bag. This system works pretty good, but the little bags blow out of the boat the moment the tackle is removed.

Other anglers favor wrapping the harness around a foam, rubber or plastic storage device that holds the snells neatly. This system works too, but most are limited to half a dozen snells.

Lindy Little Joe has a round plastic snell holder that accepts one snell. Because one snell is placed on one holder, there's never a tangle problem. The snell holders are small enough that they easily drop into the compartment of a Plano or Woodstream utility box. I usually store a dozen or more pre-tied snells ready for action.

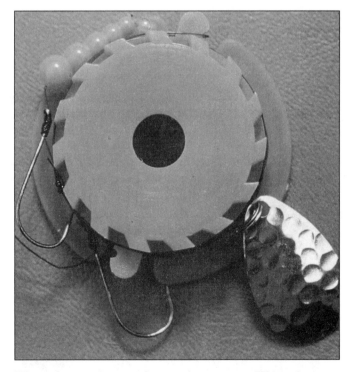

Worm harnesses can be a pain to store. Wrapping them up is about the best way to avoid tangles.

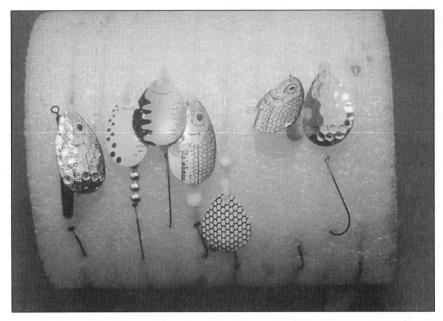

Foam wheels and plastic leader wheels are some of the more popular and practical ways to store harnesses.

When a bottom bouncer is attached to a rod and the harness is in place, these fishing tools are a handful to keep organized. Padded foam devices that wrap around the bottom bouncer and rod blank are a good tool for keeping snarls to a minimum. A strip of Velcro holds the foam wrap in place, protecting the rod from the bottom bouncer and helping to insure the leader stays in place.

UNORTHODOX BOTTOM BOUNCER METHODS

Longtime friend Mike McClelland once won a walleye tournament using bottom bouncers in an unorthodox means. The tournament was on Lake Erie and the walleyes were both suspended in the water and cruising near bottom on mud flats ranging from 30 to 40 feet of water.

It was early in April and fishing was sporadic. The spawn had just finished up and the big females were just beginning to bite. Fish were widely scattered, making the job of consistently catching good numbers and good size fish tough.

Frustrated by the hit and miss fishing, Mike theorized that the key to success would be moving quickly until a pod of fish could be located, then slowing down to fish the area. Mike and his amateur partner set two 3-ounce bottom bouncers armed with spinner rigs out the back of the boat and put the rods in holders at each corner. Next, a pair of 2-ounce bottom bouncers were set farther back and attached to Off Shore Tackle Side-Planer

boards. The boards helped to position the lighter bouncers out to the side to increase lure coverage.

These four rods were dragged along at 6 or 8 miles an hour while Mike watched his sonar unit closely. When Mike started marking fish he slowed down and let the bottom bouncer and spinner rigs sink towards bottom. The heavy bouncers set on the corners fished the bottom, while the lighter bouncers rigged to the side with boards fished up off the bottom a few feet.

"Some pods of fish were biters and others weren't," recalls McClelland. "If a pod of fish didn't seem interested in biting, I sped up and went looking for another group of fish. When I found more fish on the graph, I simply slowed down and let the fish tell me if they were interested. When I caught small fish I moved on and when I caught larger fish I worked the area thoroughly."

This unusual bottom bouncer fishing technique proved to be effective enough to easily win the event. While McClelland's bottom bouncer brain child might not apply to every situation, it clearly was a good idea at that location and time.

The point is that bottom bouncers are versatile fishing tools that have produced countless fish for as many anglers. Next to the lead-head jig no other single walleye fishing method can lay claim to as many fish. What's even more exciting is that bottom bouncers make for an easy and relaxing method of fishing.

In the next chapter we'll take a detailed look at the worm harnesses so often used in combination with bottom bouncers.

CHAPTER 17
WORM HARNESS KNOW-HOW

Walleye anglers can't take credit for inventing crawler harnesses or spinners, as they are often called, but we can claim to have refined them and found more ways to use them. For me, the 12-inch long three-hook harnesses sold in sport shops caught more than fish. These jewelry-like fishing tools also caught my imagination and started me on a lifetime of tackle crafting.

Some of my earliest fishing memories centered on building my own fishing harnesses, using a hodge-podge of beads from my mother's sewing basket, hooks I scrounged from rusty metal tackle boxes and fishing line salvaged from a dusty reel that hung in the garage.

Not satisfied with these mix-and-match spinners, I wanted my harnesses to look like the ones in the sport shops. My youthful motivation to build spinner rigs came to life when I discovered an outdoor supply catalog called Herter's. Inside the pages of this catalog were more fishing tackle

Recently the author was asked to design a signature series of fishing tackle for Walleye Stopper Lures. The line includes several jig styles, finesse spinner rigs, open-water spinners and bottom bouncers.

components than I dreamed possible. Everything including beads, clevises, hooks, blades and knot tying tools were laid out on the pages.

I begged enough cash from my parents to purchase a kit that contained all the supplies needed to make professional-looking crawler harnesses. Fortunately, my parents had a soft spot for a youngest son that lived to fish. I waited every afternoon for the UPS man to finally deliver my package.

Over the years, the tackle building bug I caught as a child has grown into a full fledged passion. In addition to my crawler harness beginning, I've made from scratch just about everything in a tackle box, including molding my own sinkers and jig heads, carving crankbait bodies, painting lures and building fishing rods. I even went through a period when I made my own soft plastic lures. What a mess! Some jobs are best left to the professionals!

My passion for building fishing tackle recently hit a peak when K&E Tackle of Hastings, Michigan approached me and asked if I could help them design a line of walleye fishing tackle. I jumped at the opportunity to share my tackle creations with other anglers, but for the most part, building fishing tackle connects me to the sport I love.

There's no better way to become a successful angler than to study fishing tackle, watch how it functions and imagine how it can be improved. I spend countless hours studying and thinking about fishing tackle refinements because I'm never satisfied that the lures we use are as good as they can be.

The crawler harnesses used for walleyes are an example of how refinements in tackle design help everyone hook and land more fish. When I first started fishing for walleyes seriously, spinners used for this species were equipped primarily with No. 8 and 6 hooks. It was a formula for failure. In previous chapters I've expressed my feelings about fishing with small hooks. Walleyes are tough fish to hook and hold. Hooks smaller than No. 4 are an evil thing on a crawler harness intended for fishing walleyes.

In addition to being built with small hooks, most spinner harnesses were rather short, usually less than 36 inches long. The popular harnesses used for walleyes today range in length from 36 to 72 inches long.

Many anglers also recognized a problem with the placement of hooks on spinner rigs. Most harnesses are tied using two or three hooks spaced about 2 inches apart. This hook spacing leaves more than half of the nightcrawler unprotected by a hook. Spacing the hooks 6 inches apart helps to

The author learned about bottom bouncers from Bob Propst, Sr., who many consider to be the father of modern walleye fishing. Bob, who fished tournaments most of his life, now runs a guiding business out of Pierre, South Dakota.

insure that when a walleye smacks a crawler harness, it will end up with a hook in its mouth.

Spinner harnesses have been producing walleyes for as long as anyone can remember, but the popularity of these lures can be linked to the rise in popularity of bottom bouncers. No two fishing tackle products are more compatible than bottom bouncers and nightcrawler harnesses. The bottom bouncer keeps the bait near the bottom and moving along snag-free. Meanwhile, the spinner blade attracts fish setting up the nightcrawler as the deal closer.

Bottom bouncers can be traced to roots in the Dakotas, where anglers used them to drift spinners over large flats or to fish the deep water tips of points. Gradually, the use of bottom bouncers spread across all North American walleye waters. Tournaments were a major influence in spreading

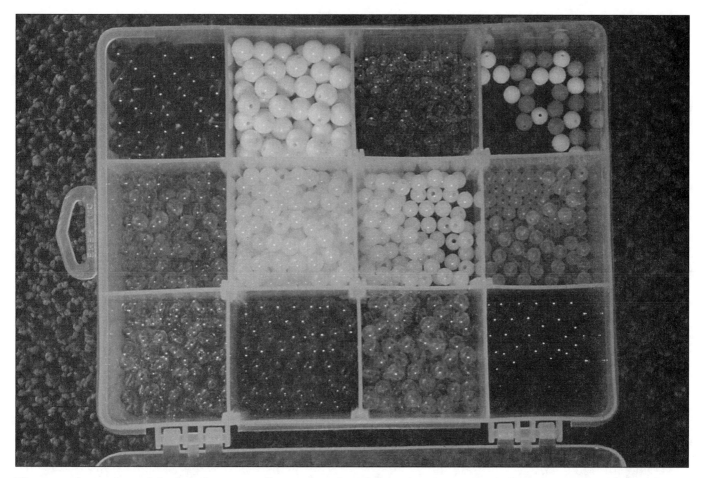

These are just a few of the beads commonly used to tie spinner rigs. An angler is limited only by imagination.

bottom bouncers. Anglers from the Dakotas, Nebraska and Kansas who were familiar with these fishing weights brought them along on trips north, south, east and west.

The first time I saw a bottom bouncer was during the early 1980s while fishing with a walleye legend and Fresh Water Fishing Hall of Fame member Bob Propst, Sr. On the floor of Bob's boat was a five gallon bucket filled with various sizes of bottom bouncers.

Bob graciously showed me how to rig up the bottom bouncer with a spinner harness, then he explained how these sinkers could be used for drifting or slow trolling. He went on to explain why the stop-and-go motion of the bottom bouncer helped to trigger strikes.

Thanks to Bob's coaching, it took less than five minutes to catch my first fish. I've been hooked on these unique bottom weights ever since and I shudder to think of all the walleyes this angling method has brought to net. I'm not alone in my praise of the bottom bouncer and spinner combination. This dynamic duo has become one of the most faithful

walleye fishing presentations in the nation. Effective anywhere that walleyes are found on or near bottom, combining bottom bouncers, spinner harnesses and crawlers is a formula for success.

WHAT MAKES A GOOD WALLEYE HARNESS?

Over the years I've developed some strong ideas on what makes a walleye spinner effective. Quality components are a big part of the equation. Everything from the beads, clevis, blade, floats, hooks and line must be the right size and of top quality.

Let's take a look at each of these components. Beads come in a wide variety of sizes, shapes, colors and materials. Both glass and plastic beads are good choices for harnesses. However, plastic beads are more readily available and offered in a wider range of sizes, colors and shapes.

The most common beads used on walleye harnesses are round 4 mm or 5 mm models. The most

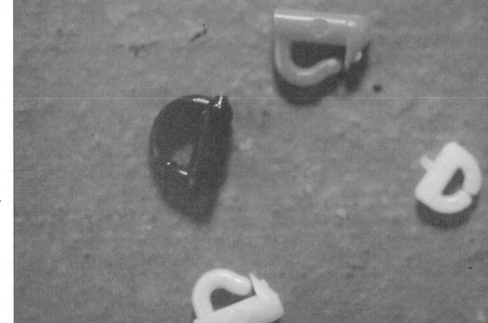

Plastic spinner clevises revolutionized the use of spinner rigs. Both Quick Change Systems and Lindy Little Joe produce plastic clevises that allow blades to be changed easily.

popular colors are green, chartreuse, orange, red and white. Thankfully anglers are not required to stick with these basics. Faceted beads, elongated beads and stacked beads add interest and a different look to harnesses. The elongated and stacked beads also have the advantage of being easier to thread onto the line. Because each bead takes up the space of several round beads, the time required to build harnesses is reduced.

Color choices are almost without end. Some of my favorite bead colors to build with include glow, pearl, purple, blue and pink. Essentially the sky is the limit when it comes to bead shape, color and style.

Clevises are an important part of any spinner rig. The device that connects the blade to the monofilament snell, clevises are produced from both metal and plastic. Most metal clevises are either folded styles or those punched out of a single piece of metal. Both styles work well, but the problem with these traditional clevises is they force the angler to cut the harness if the blade size, shape or color is to be changed.

Plastic clevises, like the famous Quick Change clevis, enable the angler to snap blades on and off the clevis as needed. It only takes a matter of seconds to change blade size, shape or color when using one of these unique clevises.

A revolution in spinner fishing, it was no surprise when other companies developed similar products. Lindy Little Joe offers the X-Change clevis that functions much like the Quick Change clevis. Both clevises are offered in small and large sizes to suit a wide range of blade sizes. These products are also very inexpensive, making them the obvious choice for spinner building.

The blade types used on spinner rigs are almost as abundant as beads. The three standard blade types used on spinner rigs include Colorado, Indiana and willow shaped blades. Of these standards, Colorado blades are nearly round in shape and spin at the slowest speeds, followed closely by oblong Indiana blades and willow leaf shaped blades becoming a distant third.

The most common blade sizes are 1, 2 or 3. Larger blades are often used when fish are very active or if larger fish are the target. When fish seem to be active and biting well, bumping up in blade size will produce larger fish. If the bite is tough, smaller blades are more likely to produce action.

In addition to these classic blade shapes, a wealth of other designs are waiting for anglers to try. A few worth experimenting with include deep cup Colorado blades, tomahawk style blades, thumper or pear-shaped blades and French-style blades. There are dozens of others that can add a little different thump, vibration and flash to a spinner rig.

The big news with blades isn't so much shape as color. The variety of colors and color finishes

Blades suitable for spinner rigs come in a wealth of sizes, shapes and colors.

available on spinner blades is staggering. The leaders in unique blade color patterns have come from the big three in walleye tackle manufacturing: Northland Tackle, Lindy Little Joe and Bait Rigs. Each of these trusted companies offers blades that are light years ahead of standard green, chartreuse or orange painted blades.

Some of these finishes incorporate glitter, scale patterns, air brushed multi-color designs, flash tape, holograms, die coats and even metallic finishes including genuine silver and gold plate. Another metallic finish, Palladium is catching on because it's actually brighter than genuine silver plating. Currently the only source for Palladium plated blades is PK Tackle. The best way to get information about these blades is by checking out their web site at http://www.ool.com/walleye.

There seems to be no limit to the unique colors, finishes and patterns that can be applied to blades. What's better is the cost of these blades isn't out of reach. Even genuine silver and gold plated blades can be purchased for pocket change.

Floats are a frequent addition on spinner harnesses. The idea of adding a small foam float to a rig to give it buoyancy or lift in the water has lured countless anglers to purchase spinner rigs with floats. Unfortunately, these floats don't function as you might expect. The buoyancy provided by the float is negated when the spinner rig is pulled through the water. Water rushing over the blade and harness actually forces the rig downward even if a number of floats are threaded onto the harness. The only time the floats can lift the harness is when it stops moving.

Despite these comments, in-line floats aren't useless. Floats have a functional niche on spinner harnesses. These colorful additions are a convenient means of adding color and bulk to a harness without having to thread on so many beads. Added color and bulk makes harnesses easier to see in dirty water. Floats can make spinner rigs neutrally buoyant. This helps to keep the bait and hooks from quickly settling to bottom when the boat is slowed to fight a fish or during turns.

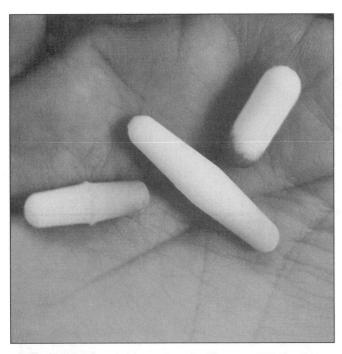

Snell floats are often used on harnesses. While these floats can't give the bait significant lift, they can make the bait more buoyant in the water. Plus, they add fish-attracting color.

Hooks are the one element of spinner harnesses that have seen the greatest improvement. Not only are commercially prepared harnesses built using larger hooks, the hooks used are sharper and lighter than ever before.

The standard No. 6 bait-holder hooks that were so common on spinner harnesses have been replaced by No. 4 or 2 beak-style hooks with razor sharp points. All the leading tackle manufacturers are using quality hooks as part of their spinner rigs. Anglers who enjoy tying their own harnesses can purchase several brands that are ideal for spinner building.

A few of the hooks recommended for tying spinners include Mustad's 92569 Neon Beak Hook, Cabela's AC9523 Accupoint, VMC V7199BN Octopus, Eagle Claw L226BKG, Gamakatsu Octopus and Owner 5111. There are many other good choices. Many of these hooks are offered in nickel, bronze, red or neon painted finishes. All the major tackle manufacturers also sell hooks as components.

The line used to tie spinners is the final component to consider. Both monofilament and the new braided super lines are being used to build walleyes spinners. Monofilament is still the most

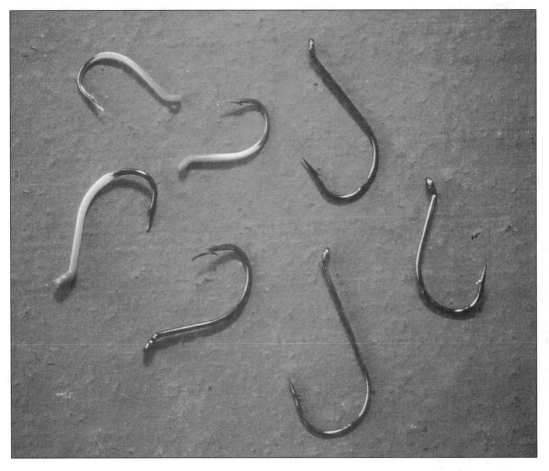

The best hooks for building harnesses are No. 4 or No. 2 beak or octopus-style hooks. Most of the manufactures produce premium hooks that are as sharp as physically possible.

popular option, but a number of anglers favor harnesses built from braided materials. More on braided lines in a minute.

The size of monofilament used on harnesses varies greatly. Some manufacturers feel that limp 8- or 10-pound test is the answer, while others figure that more durable 14- to 17-pound test line is best. I've become convinced that line diameter has little or no influence on how walleyes react to spinner rigs. This observation stated, harnesses tied using somewhat heavier line are just as effective, more durable, easier to keep untangled and they have a longer life.

I recommend that anglers purchase rigs tied using at least 12-pound test line. Anglers who want to tie their own rigs using 12- to 17-pound test can do so with the confidence of knowing they will function well and walleyes won't know the difference.

However, the types of monofilament used can make a difference. Soft and limp line designed for use on spinning reels doesn't have the abrasion resistance required for a spinner harness. Lines that feature an abrasion resistant outer coating for spinner tying include Stren Super Tough, Berkley XT, Maxima, Ande Premium and Silver Thread Excalibur.

A newcomer on the line market, fluorocarbon is becoming popular for tying spinner rigs. Fluorocarbon is tough, yet virtually invisible in water. Stren is the leading manufacturer of fluorocarbon leader material. Stren also produces a saltwater leader that's excellent for tying spinners. Known as High Impact Hard Mono Leader, this stuff is so tuff saltwater anglers use it straight to the hook when fishing baracuda! Unfortunately, salt water products are not widely available where walleye anglers do most of their shopping. You'll have to special order this product or purchase it from a saltwater tackle supply catalog.

I've been using hard mono leader material for my harnesses for some years and have found this material to be superior. Most of the anglers who have fished spinners in my boat would agree.

Braided super lines such as Fireline, Spiderwire Fusion and Bass Pro Shops Excell Nitro are finding themselves used on spinner harnesses as well. The toughness of these lines combined with the lack of stretch makes them good choices for harness rigging. These lines do however have a tendency to tangle and must be kept stored on a leader wheel to avoid problems.

Commercially available harnesses tied using super braids are currently offered by Bait Rigs, PK Tackle and Cabela's. Commercially available harnesses produced using fluorocarbon line are offered through Cabela's. Harnesses tied using hard mono leader are currently offered by K&E Walleye Stopper Lures.

OPEN-WATER SPINNERS

The weight-forward spinner has been used to catch walleyes on Lake Erie for generations. Designed to be cast, counted down to the desired depth and retrieved just fast enough to make the blade turn, weight-forward spinners are a good way to fish open water, but these lures are not the most efficient way to get fish.

Trolling is the answer to fishing suspended walleyes with spinner rigs. The only practical way to cover large amounts of open water, trolling is

A wealth of lines including monofilament, hard monofilament, fluorocarbon and super braids can be used for tying spinner rigs.

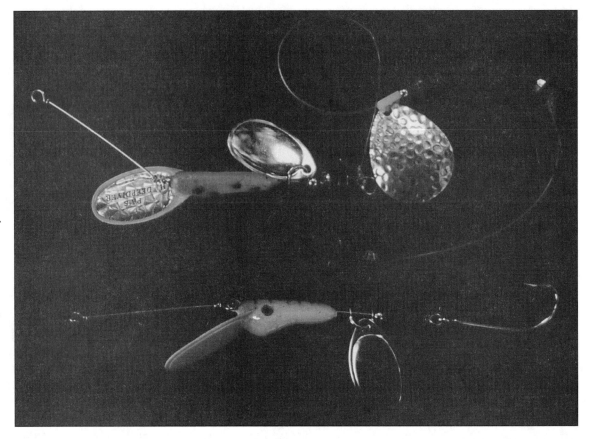

The Pa's Double Trouble and Crawler Connection are open water spinners that can be trolled effectively at speeds up to 2 miles per hour.

especially effective when fish are scattered at a variety of depths.

In defense of weight-forward spinners, these lures can be trolled. An exceptional product known as the Pa's Double Trouble features a diving lip that causes this lure to dig like a crankbait. The Pa's Double Trouble is a useful trolling product and one of the most popular lures on big waters such as Lake Erie and Saginaw Bay.

Available in both a single-hook version and the Crawler Connection which incorporates a short harness attached to the Pa's diving head, the lip design of these lures allows them to be trolled at speeds up to 2 miles per hour.

Two-hook snelled spinners similar to those used on bottom bouncers are the workhorses of open-water trolling. Instead of using a bottom bouncer as a sinker, a relatively new in-line trolling sinker known as a Snap Weight is used to position the harness at the desired depth range.

A Snap Weight is a pinch pad style line clip similar to those used as downrigger or planer board releases. A weight is attached to the clip via a split ring. Various size weights can be attached to the split ring to achieve depths ranging from a few feet to 40 feet or more.

The spring tension of a Snap Weight is designed to be strong enough to hold the weight securely on the line when trolling and fighting fish. Because Snap Weights can be conveniently put on and taken off the line, they are often placed well ahead of the lure giving this trolling weight far more flexibility than keel sinkers, rubber core weight, split-shots or other weights that must be fixed to the line.

When trolling in open water it's common for anglers to let out a 50-foot lead and attach a Snap Weight to the line. Additional line is let out and the whole rig is slowly trolled. Depth can be influenced by varying lead lengths, using different size weights or by manipulating trolling speed.

When a fish is hooked, the angler reels in the fish until the Snap Weight can be reached and removed from the line. The process of removing a Snap Weight from the line takes less than a second, further making these products user-friendly.

Snap Weights are one of those ideas that anglers wonder: why didn't I think of that? A simple and easy way to add weight to trolling lines, Snap Weights and open water spinner fishing go together like ham and eggs. Not only has Snap Weight trolling become popular on Lake Erie, but

Snap Weights are a common trolling weight used to fish spinners in open water. These trolling weights are easy to put on and take off the line and they come in sizes ranging from 1/2 to 3 ounces.

anglers are using this method coast-to-coast to troll up suspended walleyes.

A book could be written on the variations of Snap Weight trolling and why this angling method is so effective. The most common question asked about Snap Weight trolling is how deep will they fish? The depth that Snap Weights achieve depends on the weight used, lead length and trolling speed. The book *Precision Trolling* provides a useful guide to trolling Snap Weights that can help anglers answer some of the "how deep" questions. Testing was conducted using Snap Weights from 1/2 ounce to 3 ounces. A trolling method that has become known as the 50/50 system was used as a data base line.

With the 50/50 system, a spinner harness is let out behind the boat 50 feet and a Snap Weight is attached to the line. Another 50 feet of lead is let out and the entire 100 feet is trolled at speeds ranging

from .5 to 1.5 miles per hour. A simple chart shows the depth ranges Snap Weights can be expected to run based on the amount of weight used and the trolling speed. Copies of *Precision Trolling* are available for $24.95 by calling 1-800-353-6958.

Despite the popularity of the 50/50 system, don't hesitate to experiment with a variety of lead lengths when trolling with Snap Weights. It's important however to keep track of lead lengths, so they can be duplicated when fish are hooked. Line counter reels are the most convenient method for monitoring trolling leads.

THE FINE POINTS OF OPEN WATER SPINNERS

The same spinners used on bottom bouncers can be used for open-water trolling with good success. Problems can develop however. Trolling puts a lot of pressure on hooked fish. Shake-offs are common and fish lost at the net are a fact of life. The single hooks used on most harnesses are not up to the task of serious open-water trolling.

Tying spinner harnesses with treble hooks instead of single hooks makes these rigs more functional. If using treble hooks on a spinner rig seems unorthodox, think of open-water spinners as crankbaits. These lures are moving quickly through the water. Fish slash at the baits as they go by and in order to get hooked consistently, treble hooks are required.

A No. 4 or No. 6 round-bend treble hook is a far better choice than single hooks. Still, many anglers prefer the premium grade of treble hooks available such as the Mustad Triple Grip, Heddon Excalibur, Gamakatsu Extra Wide Gap or Eagle Claw Kahle. These offset style hooks are not only exceptionally sharp, the hook design helps hold onto the fish that strike.

Open-water rigs can be tied using a single hook at the front and a treble hook at the back or with two treble hooks. Commercially tied open-water spinners are currently offered by K&E Walleye Stopper, P/K Tackle, Bait Rigs and Cabelas.

The blades used while fishing open water are larger than normal. Open-water fish tend to be bigger fish and they are often aggressive. Instead of the size 1, 2 and 3 blades used in combination with bottom bouncers, open-water trollers favor 4, 5, 6 and even size 7 blades.

Larger blades give off more vibration and flash to call fish from greater distances. Also, it's impor-

Open-water spinners are best equipped with treble hooks. A No. 6 or No. 4 round bend or wide bend style treble hook works great.

tant to note that open-water trolling often takes place in clear water where fish will travel a considerable distance to check out a passing spinner. Large blades with lots of flash are usually the ticket for open-water trolling success. Some of the best choices include genuine silver or gold plate and Palladium.

The blade types used for open-water trolling also vary. Anglers fishing bottom bouncers and spinners often stick with Colorado blades because this design spins at the slowest speeds. Open-water anglers generally troll a little faster, opening the door to Indiana and willow leaf blades.

Gang or multiple spinners are also a common sight in on open water. Many anglers will rig two or three blades on a harness using a few beads or a snell float as spacers between the blades. Some open-water anglers even go so far as to tie their rigs using steel leader material to produce the most durable harnesses possible. Others rig two or three blades on a short length of stainless steel

wire, then attach the hooks using a heavy monofilament harness.

All of these options are more effective when trolled in combination with planer boards. Both portable in-line boards and full sized dual board skis are useful tools in helping to cover more water with spinners.

In addition to using Snap Weights to present open-water spinners, two other trolling techniques are effective in open water. Both downriggers and diving planers are useful tools for fishing spinners in open water.

Downriggers are the leaders in depth control. Spinners fished in cooperation with downriggers can be positioned at precise depth levels or in close proximity to bottom without fear of snagging. When fishing spinners with downriggers, leads from 50 to 75 feet seem to produce the most fish.

Both the small diving disks such as the Big Jon Diver Disk, Luhr Jensen Mini Dipsy or Jet Diver and larger divers can be used for trolling up walleyes. Smaller diver disks are often used in combination with planer boards to present spinners below the surface and out to the side of the boat.

A spinner harness from 40 to 72 inches long is attached to the back of the diver. Various trolling leads are used to cover depth ranges from near the surface to approximately 30 feet.

Larger divers such as the Luhr Jensen Dipsy, Slide Diver and Kastaway Magnetic Diver can be used to reach fish in deeper water. These are popular trolling tools on the Eastern Basin of Lake Erie where anglers must fish 40 to 70 feet below the surface to catch walleyes during the summer months when these fish often suspend at or slightly above the thermocline.

The diving planers outlined are also directional. By adjusting a weight on the diver these devices can be adjusted to plane out to the side of the boat. Divers can't cover the kind of water possible with planer boards, but they do fill a unique niche between planer boards and downrigger lines.

TIPS ON BAIT

The common nightcrawler is what walleye harnesses are all about. Certainly spinner rigs can be used with minnows, leeches and even soft plastic lures, but these baits only represent a small part of the spinner fishing world. When using minnows or leeches, a single hook harness is the best option. A No. 4 hook works best for leeches and a No. 2 is ideal for minnows.

Day-in and day-out, the best live bait for a spinner harness is going to be a fat nightcrawler. Mother Nature's most perfect fishing bait, it's hard to do better than healthy nightcrawlers. Those of us who use spinner rigs frequently are convinced that bigger crawlers produce better than smaller ones. Bait should also be replaced regularly to maximize the smell and wiggle only a nightcrawler can offer.

Worm harnesses and the way they are fished have come a long way in the last few years. Not only have spinner rigs changed to meet the needs of more demanding anglers, these effective lures are being used in a wealth of places and ways to take walleyes. The garden-variety harnesses we grew up with don't cut it any more. A new breed of spinners has arrived.

In the next chapter, learning to troll crankbaits in and around structure is the goal. This seldom-practiced trolling method is a good way to catch more walleyes.

Diving planers, especially the new mini-disks are great tools for trolling spinners in open water. The small mini-disks can be fished in cooperation with planer boards.

CHAPTER 18

STRUCTURE TROLLING

Fishing bottom structure is a job that most often goes to jigs, slip sinker rigs or bottom bouncers. These time-tested fishing methods do an excellent job of presenting bait near the bottom. Despite the effectiveness and popularity of these fishing presentations, one problem plagues their use: Traditional bottom-fishing methods are slow presentations that can be a time-consuming and tedious ways to hunt for walleyes.

Much of the time spent on walleye water is dedicated to finding fish. Ideally this process involves quickly moving from one likely spot to another until fish are located. It would be nice if walleyes were homebodies like largemouth bass that often live near the same log, stump or weed patch all season. Unfortunately, walleyes are a free-roaming species that seldom takes up residence anywhere for long.

The hot spot one day is often a waste of time the next. This is one of the reasons so many anglers get frustrated with the walleye game. It's also the reason many of us keep coming back for more. Walleye fishing is a never-ending challenge that has something to offer every angler, expert or novice.

Traditional bottom-fishing methods work well once fish are located, but finding fish fast calls for an approach that covers lots of water quickly. Structure trolling crankbaits is one of the best ways to cover water both rapidly and efficiently.

Amazingly, few anglers have discovered the fine art of structure trolling. Effective in natural lakes, rivers, reservoirs and the Great Lakes, there's hardly a place where walleyes live that crankbaits can't be used to locate their whereabouts.

Think about the virtues of structure trolling for a moment. This method eats up water at a rate of 1 to 3 miles per hour, presents a lure that looks like the walleyes' favorite forage near the bottom and follows bottom contours, turns and breaks like a beagle follows a rabbit track.

Both fast-paced and precise, structure trolling is an ideal method for checking "spots" that may or may not hold fish. Often, fish holding on structure rest so tightly to the bottom that fishing for them is the only way to determine their presence. Sonar units have a difficult time separating walleyes from bottom, when this species plants its fins in the sand. Also, rock-covered bottoms or sloping contours work to hide walleyes from sonar detection.

In a nutshell, structure or contour trolling boils down to presenting crankbaits close enough to the bottom that fish will strike at them as they go by. The fact is, most anglers have no idea how deep various crankbaits dive. Without this valuable data, it's easy to see why anglers are reluctant to "experiment" with their expensive crankbaits.

Structure trolling is one of the least-practiced methods of catching walleyes. This fast-paced presentation is an excellent way to cover water quickly.

Wouldn't it be nice if anglers could determine exactly how deep the various models and brands of crankbaits dive? This information would be invaluable.

The truth is, testing crankbaits to determine their diving depth isn't a new concept. According to Joe Hughes, press relations manager for PRADCO the manufacturers of Rebel, Heddon, Cotton Cordell, Bomber, Excalibur, Smithwick, Fred Arbogast and other popular crankbait brands, his firm has been involved in research to determine crankbait depth since the early 1970s.

"Sonar detection is a method we use to determine the maximum diving depth of crankbaits, says Hughes. "The data collected is then published on the package as a guideline for consumers."

Unfortunately, the data collected by PRADCO only involved lures produced by this company. Also the data collected was never published in book or chart form that consumers could purchase.

Some years later, noted walleye angler Mike McClelland used sonar detection methods similar to those used by PRADCO to test the maximum depth of some 200 crankbaits. His findings were published in the book *Crankbaits: A Guide to the Trolling and Casting Depths of Popular Crankbaits.*

The data produced by McClelland was based on one lead length of 120 feet which Mike felt produced maximum or near maximum diving depth. The four-color book was well-received in the trolling community, but there was criticism that the data produced was limited to one lead length. The 98-cent question became, how deep do crankbaits dive on various lead lengths? Eventually McClelland's book went out of print.

The desire to know how deep crankbaits dive and the desire to reduce annoying and costly snags is exactly the reason three Michigan anglers set forth to test the diving depths of popular crankbaits. Avid crankbait trollers, Tom Irwin, Dr. Steven Holt and yours truly, theorized that sonar detection wasn't the answer to determining crankbait depth. Instead, this threesome went to work using scuba techniques to test crankbaits on leads ranging from 15 to 250 feet.

To test the baits, a floating buoy was placed on the surface of the water with a descent line attached to the buoy and to a weight positioned 50 feet below the surface. A tape measure was then attached to the descent line. As baits were trolled past the buoy, the diver submerged and noted the point where the lure passed by the tape measure.

Using scuba gear to test lure depth is a very accurate method of collecting data. Each lure was hand tuned to insure maximum diving depth. In addition, baits were trolled on leads ranging from 15 to 250 feet to determine the total spectrum of diving depths of which each lure was capable.

The base line data was performed using 10-pound test monofilament, but testing was also conducted with heavier lines and braided super lines to help develop a line conversion chart that allows anglers to accurately factor the depth of their cranks no matter what line size is used.

Using scuba equipment to actually see how crankbaits dive and react in the water has proved invaluable.

"We were amazed to discover that monofilament attached to a crankbait doesn't dive down into the water in a smooth curve as you might expect," says Dr. Holt. "Actually most of the line floats on the surface and only the last few yards angles down into the water."

Other interesting observations were also noted.

"We soon learned that baits have to be properly tuned to achieve consistent results," added Irwin. "A crankbait must dive straight down into the water to achieve maximum depth and to deliver the action it was designed to offer."

Holt also noted that even a small piece of weed caught on the hooks of the lure, reduced the diving depth considerably.

"Many anglers like to place half a nightcrawler on the hooks of their cranks," notes Holt. "Even a small piece of a nightcrawler cuts the diving depth of a crankbait in half."

The first book, *Crankbaits In-Depth*, contained 50 lures and was released in 1992. Each year more lures have been tested and revised editions published. Eventually, other trolling devices such as Snap Weights, diving planers, and lead core line were added along with informative text on trolling methods. The book title was changed to *Precision Trolling*. Now in its 5th edition, *Precision Trolling* includes diving data for 140 popular crankbaits and trolling devices.

Easy to read "dive curve" charts are used to show how deep various lures dive on all popular lead lengths. A life-size picture of the lure appears next to the dive curve for easy reference.

In order to achieve a specific target depth, anglers only need to find the target depth on the chart then run across the scale to find the suitable lead length required to achieve the target depth.

Used and endorsed by thousands of anglers, *Precision Trolling* has a dedicated following that anxiously awaits each new edition. As new lures and

The book *Precision Trolling* is a popular guide to the trolling depths of over 140 crankbaits.

IMPORTANT EQUIPMENT

Before we get into the many lures that are suitable for structure trolling and the mechanics of this presentation, a few words on required equipment is in order.

Quality sonar is absolutely a must for structure trolling. Picking a depth range and following it, sticking tight to sharply sloping edges or walking a meandering edge can not be accomplished without dependable sonar. Liquid crystal units are the most common type of sonar available. The technology that made liquid crystal sonar possible has come a long way in recent years. Models currently being produced have resolution matching that of paper graphs, plus a lot of more useful features.

Despite the dominance of liquid crystal sonar units, flashers and video sonar are also readily available. Flashers these days are used mostly on the dash of a boat as a guide to high speed running, however some die-hards still prefer to locate fish and structure with a flasher. Those anglers who understand how to use a flasher can get all the information they need including instantaneous read outs. Unfortunately, most anglers don't know how to interpret the bleeps of light that show up on the dial of a flasher.

The two-dimensional picture drawn by liquid crystal and video units is easier for most anglers to interpret and benefit from. Video units offer an excellent color picture, good resolution and dependability. Somewhat higher in cost than liquid crystal units, the chief drawback to video sonar is the size. Two or three times as large as other sonar units, there is simply no room to mount these products in many open-bow boats.

Like other products, sonar units are not all created equal. Some brands and models offer clearer screens, more resolution, easier to use menu systems and higher dependability. The more features a unit offers, the higher the price is likely to be.

It's wise to spend the extra funds required for quality sonar. Saving a few bucks is tempting, but the savings often are at the expense of functional equipment.

Think of sonar as a long-term investment in your fishing boat. It's best to buy quality up-front than to be forced to upgrade down the road. A number of good products suitable for walleyes and structure fishing are available. Some anglers prefer stand-alone sonar, while others choose to combine sonar and Global Positioning Systems (GPS) technology in the same unit.

trolling devices are introduced, they are tested and the information included in subsequent editions.

The value of knowing how deep various crankbaits dive when trolled can not be overemphasized when structure trolling. If too long a trolling lead is used and the bait snags bottom, not only is the risk of losing expensive tackle increased, but time is lost as well.

If the baits aren't fished close enough to the bottom, they can pass right over fish without producing the desired strike response. It's important to keep the crankbaits within 2 feet of bottom in clear water and within 12 inches of the bottom when the water is off color.

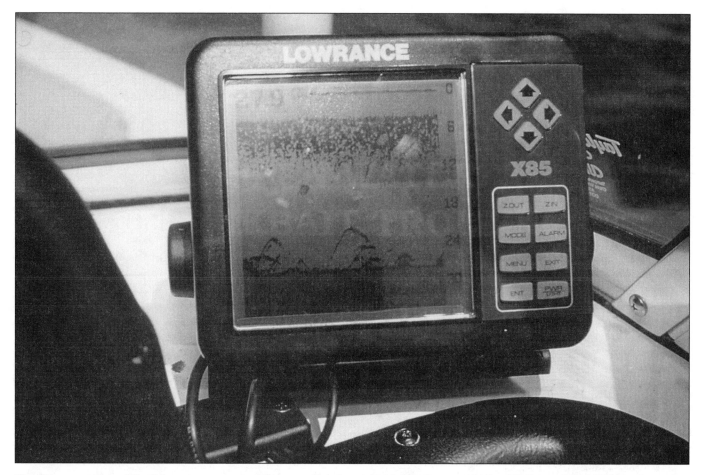

Quality sonar is critical for structure trolling applications. Both Flashers and Liquid Crystal Readout style units can be used to follow bottom contours.

The Lowrance LMS 350A is one of the most popular products that combines both a quality sonar and GPS plotter in the same unit. Lowrance also offers a sonar module for their Global Map 2000 and LMS 160 that offer GPS mapping units.

On my boats I've elected to purchase stand-alone sonar and GPS units for the past several years. The products are mounted next to one another on the boat console in clear view. Combined units such as the 350A saves space on the console of the boat, but in order to use both sonar and GPS functions at the same time the screen must be split in half. Splitting the screen reduces the viewing image for both sonar and GPS. Mounting a sonar and GPS unit side-by-side allows both products to function at full capacity.

The advantage of using two stand-alone units is never more appreciated than when structure trolling. The full screen sonar unit provides a detailed picture of the underwater environment, showing bottom contours, bottom hardness, weeds or other submerged items and, of course, fish and bait fish.

I'm currently using a Lowrance X-85 because this product offers some of the highest resolution available. The full 240-vertical-pixel screen gives this product impeccable resolution, excellent gray line helps separate targets from bottom and a digital depth readout is instantaneous. An instantaneous digital depth readout allows me to determine subtle changes in depth that wouldn't be easy to identify on the liquid crystal screen.

A primary liquid crystal sonar unit should offer from 200 to 300 vertical pixels. Lesser products simply don't have the ability to mark fish as readily, especially fish that may be holding tight to the bottom or cover.

Rigged with the right sonar, anglers are equipped to follow depth contours accurately. Without these aids, structure trolling is a shot in the dark.

Next to sonar equipment, the most important item for structure trolling is an electric or gasoline motor.

Quiet electric motors are often used by anglers fishing at night along rocky shorelines, break

Using a stand-alone sonar and a GPS unit enables both products to be operated using their full screen capabilities. Units that combine sonar and GPS require the screen to be split into two smaller pieces.

walls, weed edges and other spots that attract walleyes. The stealth these motors offer allows the boat to be positioned without spooking fish.

Gasoline motors are the workhorses of structure trolling. Best able to pull baits at a wide range of speeds for hours on end, a small gasoline kicker motor is the ideal tool for structure trolling.

In some cases, larger primary outboards can also be used as a trolling aid. Mercury's popular 100- and 115-horsepower outboards are four-cylinder designs that run on two cylinders at low RPM levels. This feature allows the engine to run at slow trolling speeds without fouling. When it's time to head for home, the other two cylinders kick in when the engine is throttled above 2,000 RPM.

Other larger outboards can also be used for structure trolling, but the fuel burned can be considerable. The fuel burned trolling with larger motors is enough to justify the expense of purchasing a kicker motor.

In addition to an electric or gasoline trolling motor, boats used for structure trolling will need several conveniently located rod holders. Many anglers enjoy holding the rod while fishing, but it's not practical to hold the rods all the time. Also, in states where more than one line can be used per angler, rod holders are the best way to keep lines organized and tangle-free.

Rod holders need to be located at the back of the boat and within easy reach of anglers. Models are available that can be mounted on the inside of the gunwale, on top of the gunwale or on rails mounted to the gunwale. Be sure these holders are mounted in locations where they won't interfere with other accessories such as livewell lids, boat seats, etc.

The rods and reels used for structure trolling should be light enough to hold in your hand. Graphite bass-style triggersticks in the 6- to 8-foot range are ideal for structure trolling. Shorter rods are handy for hand-holding rods, while longer rods help reach out away from the boat to increase trolling coverage.

These rods should be equipped with line-counter reels. It's critical to monitor lead length

Kicker motors are the workhorses of structure trolling. Here a kicker motor is being used to follow a contour line adjacent to a major point.

triangular shaped clip. Ball bearing swivels are also problems. The extra weight of the swivel can make tuning lures more difficult. A simple cross-lock snap is the best option.

SORTING CRANKBAITS

The list of crankbaits that are suitable for structure trolling is longer than this chapter. What makes a crankbait suitable for structure trolling isn't so much the brand, color, action or shape. What matters is if the bait floats at rest and dives when trolled. Sinking style crankbaits are poor choices for structure trolling because these baits are dependent on speed. The slower they are trolled the deeper these lures run. When the trolling speed is increased, diving ability is sacrificed.

Since it's difficult to accurately control trolling speed, sinking baits are tough to present near the bottom without fear of snagging. Floating/diving

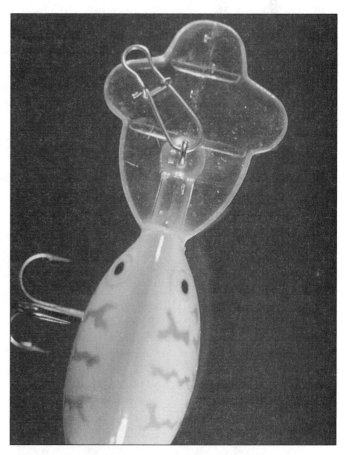

Cross-lock style snaps are the best way to attach crankbaits to fishing line. A round snap such as this allows the bait freedom to wiggle, while making it easy to change lures as needed.

when structure trolling. Lead length is one of the most important variables that determines lure diving depth.

Many of the line-counter reels on the market are rather large, bulky and heavy. In recent years some newer editions that are more streamlined have appeared. Good examples of smaller line counter reels are produced by Cabela's, Shimano, Penn, Marado and South Bend.

One more item will be needed for structure trolling cranks. A good assortment of cross-lock style snaps are the best way to attach crankbaits to your fishing line. Snaps allow baits to have freedom of movement so important to their action and baits can be changed quickly as needed.

Note that I recommend a cross-lock snap not a snap swivel. Snap swivels are notorious for causing crankbaits to run out of tune. The worst models are the inexpensive ones that feature the

crankbaits can be set to run at whatever depth is desired by manipulating lead length and line diameter. If the boat speed is slowed or increased the lure's running depth will not be changed.

Of the hundreds of lures that potentially could be used for structure trolling walleyes, a few rise as trusted companions. One of the easiest ways to categorize these lures is by body shape.

Baits with long minnow-like profiles are some of the most productive crankbaits for walleyes. A few models that feature small lips with modest diving depths and models with larger lips that dive to considerable depths will be needed. In the shallow diving category some of the classics include the Storm ThunderStick and ThunderStick Jr., Bomber Long A, Smithwick Super Rogue, Bagley Bang-O-Lure, Rapala Husky Jerk, Reef Runner Ripper and Little Ripper, Mann's Stretch 1 and Rebel Minnow are good choices.

Deeper diving minnow profile baits include the Storm Deep Diving ThunderStick Jr. and Deep ThunderStick, Bomber 24 and 25 A, Smithwick Diving Rogue, Rebel Spoonbill, Reef Runner Deep Diver, Bagley's Deep Diving Top Gun and Luhr Jensen Power Dive Minnow.

All of these baits can be trolled at a wide range of speeds. Minnow profile baits can also be used effectively at any time of year. Especially effective early and late in the season, this body shape lends itself to a subtle top to bottom roll that walleyes simply can't resist.

Shad-shaped crankbaits are the next category of floating/diving lures to consider. Must-have brands and models include the Rapala Risto Rap and Shad Rap series, Bomber Long A series, Cotton Cordell Wally Diver series, Luhr Jensen Fingerling, Mann's Wally-Trac, Excalibur Fat Free Shad, Storm Rattlin' Thin Fin and Lightnin' Shad.

All of these lures do a good job on bodies of water where gizzard and thread fin shad or alewives are abundant. Shad-body lures are versatile baits, can be trolled at a wide range of speeds and are useful throughout the year.

The final category of crankbaits can be called fat-bodies or high-action lures. These lures tend to perform best when trolled at high speeds. The clear choice for fishing in warm weather when walleyes are most active, good fat-bodies include Storm's Hot n' Tot series and Wiggle Wart series, Bagley Diving

Sinking or countdown style crankbaits such as these are not a good choice for structure trolling. Lures that sink are dependent on speed. In other words the depth level depends on trolling speed.

Floating/diving style lures are the best crankbaits for structure trolling. A selection of stickbaits, diving minnows, shad-bodies and fat-body lures is required.

Killer B-II, Luhr Jensen Hot Lips series, Mann's Plus series and Rapala Rattlin' Fat Rap.

PUTTING IT ALL TOGETHER

Not every fishing situation is suited for structure trolling. It's difficult to accurately present crankbaits near the bottom when breaks twist and turn unexpectedly or the depth level changes rapidly.

The ideal situations for structure trolling include large areas that feature a defined break or drop off, sprawling lake or river flats, the edges of well-defined reefs, long tapering points, river channel edges, gentle meandering weed lines and saddles between islands or points.

To begin contour trolling, select a depth range where walleyes are suspected to be present. After sticking with a particular depth contour and thoroughly covering this depth range, other depth contours can be explored as required until fish are located.

Swinging in and out of different depth ranges isn't practical because the trailing lures will either be positioned too deep or too shallow. This practice is considered sloppy boat control and will almost certainly lead to snags, lost lures and lost fishing time.

The depth range selected often depends on the time of day. When fishing early in the morning, in the evenings or after dark walleyes often move into shallow water. The tops of reefs, points and other areas can be productive areas to search. Later in the day, walleyes often drop into deeper water where they hang out until the urge to feed encourages them to make another shallow move.

During the summer and fall walleyes often favor deep water. Good places to hunt for fish on the bottom are where points taper out into deep water, the deep edges of reefs or mud basins.

Once a depth range has been selected, lures that run deep enough to reach the desired depth must be selected. In clear waters set the baits to run within 2 feet of the bottom. In murky waters the lures must run within 12 inches of the bottom for consistent success.

Selecting baits can be as simple as paging through the book *Precision Trolling* to see which models are capable of reaching the required depth. Note the lead length required to achieve the desired depth and set the bait the appropriate distance behind the boat.

If the law allows that more than one line may be used, select a second bait and set it back the required lead length. Running multiple lines increases the likelihood of contacting fish and allows for experimentation with lure shapes, sizes and colors.

It's not difficult to present cranks near the bottom on flats or edges that are relatively straight. However, some of the most productive structure isn't so easy to fish. Here's where the men and boys part company.

More difficult structure trolling chores often require the angler to sweep cranks into the back of a cup formed where a point juts out from the shoreline. The tips of points are another situation where fish are often stacked up in a very small target area. Simply following the desired depth contour will actually cause the trailing baits to miss these targets entirely!

Worse yet, if the bait misses the target on the shallow side, the lure will almost certainly hang on the bottom or foul in weeds and other debris. If the lure misses the mark on the deep side of the target area, the bait will pass through open water too far away to interest fish.

To hit these targets the angler must know the key moment to move the boat outside the desired depth level, in order to swing the trailing baits into the target area. Working cold turkey, it's all but impossible to anticipate these turns, bends or cups in a piece of structure. To effectively fish these areas the angler must spend some time becoming familiar with specific spots.

Once the angler has a general feel for the structure, a game plan can be formed to structure troll key areas. Using the cup formed on the inside edge of a submerged point as an example, imagine the boat approaching the cup and the crankbait trailing behind the boat at the desired depth level. Think of the cup as a triangle with one leg leading into the cup and another coming out. To insure the crank hits the mark, the boat must be turned to pass inside the desired depth contour just before the boat reaches the cup, then swung back outside joining the desired depth contour well beyond the cup.

The dog leg formed will force the trailing crankbait to swing into the bottom of the cup where walleyes are most likely to be waiting. This maneuver is easier to perform when trailing deep-diving cranks fished on relatively short leads. If the bait is positioned a considerable distance behind the boat to achieve the desired depth, it's more difficult to steer the lure into position.

Pulling baits straight across the tip of a point is another challenge. Most anglers simply follow the depth contour straight off the end of a point that extends into open water. When the boat hits deep water the angler turns around and runs up the opposite edge of the point.

Working down the both edges of the point works some key water, but the tip of the point is missed completely. To hit the tip of the point, the boat must be turned out as it approaches the end of the point, then turned at a 90-degree angle and run perpendicular to the direction of the point.

This maneuver swings the trailing crankbait out into open water then, pulls the bait straight across the tip of the point. If the tip of the point suddenly drops off into deep water or there are

Structure trolling is a lot of work, but it can also be an effective way to find and catch walleyes. Fish like this are a common result of structure trolling crankbaits.

rocks or other cover on the tip of the point, most of the fish will stack up in this small area.

The better an angler learns a particular piece of structure, the more accurately the target areas can be fished. Despite the fact that obvious cups and points are often well-known spots, few anglers fish them accurately enough to catch anything but the stragglers. Fishing the spot-on-the-spot is the key to making the best catches.

As you no doubt can appreciate, structure trolling is a complex angling method that requires both boat control and lure depth control. Despite the fact that structure trolling isn't an easy way to fish, this technique is one of the fastest ways to cover water while searching for walleyes. Think of structure trolling as a spot checker. Don't stay in one spot too long and keep moving until fish are located.

In the next chapter we expand on crankbait fishing tactics by examining open-water trolling methods.

Chapter 19

OPEN-WATER CRANKBAIT TROLLING

Big walleyes and lots of them. That's what we want. The rules of walleye fishing have changed in recent years. A game that once was played on classic structure and cover such as points, reefs, sunken islands and weed edges, is now conducted on a new court.

Open-water trolling is perhaps the most exciting development in walleye fishing history. This style of searching for big fish got a foothold on the Great Lakes at such popular sites as Saginaw Bay, Little Bay de Noc and Lake Erie. In recent years this fishing technique has expanded to countless

Big walleyes, and lots of them, are the reward for fishing crankbaits in open water. This fine fish taken by Gary Parsons is typical of those taken from open

larger natural lakes and reservoirs from New York to Montana.

Anywhere walleyes feed on forage species that roam the open water, trolling crankbaits is likely to produce fast action and big fish. Fueled by enormous populations of pelagic forage species such as gizzard shad, alewives, smelt, emerald shiners and ciscoes, the unlimited dinner buffet walleyes benefit from pays off both in big fish and rapid growth rates.

Saginaw Bay located in southeastern Michigan boasts one of the fastest growth rates for walleyes on record. Walleyes reach 20-22 inches in only three years, thanks to an almost unlimited diet of shad and shiners! Trophy fish are so common that local taxidermists rarely receive fish less than the 11-pound minimum for Michigan's Master Angler program. Apparently, local anglers feel there is no need to mount 9-10 pound fish when 11-pound giants are taken so often.

You could say the anglers of Saginaw Bay are spoiled, but they aren't alone. Lake Erie produces so many walleyes in the 10-pound range that they are just considered good fish, not exceptional trophy class specimens! The same could be said for dozens of other fisheries.

What all these bodies of water have in common is a pelagic forage base that keeps growth rates high and the open-water trolling bite exciting.

SAFETY & BIG WATER

Open-water walleye fishing offers anglers some amazing opportunities. The lure of catching lots of fish and big fish is enough to make anglers travel hundreds of miles. It's also enough to encourage them to fish in poor weather conditions, use boats that are too small for the task and to take risks that can lead to disaster.

Any time big water and small boats are combined, the potential for disaster exists. Bad weather turns these waters into more than a mean chop. Many anglers have lost their lives because the wind and waves were more than a match for their boat.

Two days prior to my writing this chapter, a pair of anglers died on Lake Erie when a northeast wind capsized their boat. No one knows for sure exactly how this disaster happened, but similar mishaps are all too frequent. Headlines in local papers report drownings and missing anglers, but these warnings don't seem to prevent others from making similar mistakes.

Fishing fatalities associated with big water are real, but most of the accidents that occur take place because anglers take unnecessary risks or they are unprepared for fishing in open water. Getting caught in open water when bad weather approaches is a fact of fishing. Leaving the dock to fish in bad weather is fool hardy.

Following some basic safety rules is the best way to insure that open-water fishing is a fun and rewarding experience. A small craft advisory is a clear warning not to fish. If you're caught on the

Safety should be a primary concern when fishing big water. Threatening weather can turn an otherwise calm body of water into a dangerous mix of wind and waves.

water when a small craft advisory is posted, leave the water immediately.

Every time you leave the dock make sure your boat is equipped with a basic list of safety equipment including life vests, a throw cushion, flare kit, compass, anchor and anchor rope. In addition to these safety essentials, I'd recommend adding a VHF radio to your boat. Should the need arise to call for help, a VHF radio can be a life saver. I also recommend using a GPS unit as a safety device. Knowing your exact location can be a big time-saver in getting help on the scene fast. Hand-held GPS units are available for less than $200.

Adding a second or auxiliary bilge pump can help keep the water at bay long enough for help to arrive should your boat begin taking on water.

Being safe on the water is serious business no matter where you fish, but when fishing big water safety is a matter of life and death.

ELECTRONICS

Open-water walleye fishing takes place on some of the largest bodies of water North America has to offer. Finding fish among the endless miles of white caps can be an overwhelming task to those who are not familiar with this fishing style. Like any other search, the process begins by spreading out, moving quickly and not duplicating coverage.

It helps to break down huge expanses of water into smaller and more manageable pieces, then think of the selected area as a grid with parallel lines. By following these imaginary lines, water can be thoroughly searched using electronics until fish are located.

Quality electronics are vital to finding fish in open water, but the process isn't as simple as putting the boat on plane and cruising until fish are spotted on the sonar. Unfortunately, to effectively mark fish most sonar units must be moving less than 10 miles per hour. At high speed too much turbulence from the prop and boat occurs to achieve dependable results.

To speed up the search process, try putting the boat on plane and running at high speed for 1/4 mile, then slowing down and cruising at less than 10 miles per hour for 1/4 mile. This run-and-gun method covers water quickly, yet provides an opportunity to thoroughly check for suspended fish. If two, three or more boats spread out and work together, a lot of water can be searched for suspended fish in short order.

Compared are a typical 50 kHz (wide-angle) and 192 kHz (narrow angle) transducer. Wide angle transducers are sometimes used to search for suspended fish; however, 50 kHz transducers are actually designed for deep water use.

Despite the need to cover lots of water, suspended walleyes can't hide. The fact that they are suspended in the water column makes them easy to mark on most sonar equipment. It's important to note that fish suspended near the surface aren't likely to appear on the sonar screen.

Imagine how a walleye suspended within a few feet of the surface reacts when a boat suddenly approaches. The fish uses its lateral line to sense the boat and while the fish probably doesn't have the ability to decipher what the object is, it certainly knows the object is big. In the eat-or-be-eaten world fish live in, a big object moving through the water sends a clear message.

That's exactly what happens when a boat passes through a school of suspended walleyes. Fish located near the surface sense the approaching boat and simply move out of harm's way. Fish well below the surface aren't disturbed by the passing boat. As a result, the boat marks few fish suspended near the surface and lots of fish hanging deeper.

Just because the graph doesn't mark fish in the upper water column, doesn't mean they aren't

there. Any time fish are marked in the top 15 feet, assume that walleyes are also suspended closer to the surface. The only way to confirm the presence of these high fish is to set lines and catch some.

Some open-water anglers often use wide-angle transducers to achieve more sonar coverage. A typical 50 kHz transducer offers approximately twice the water coverage as a 192 kHz transducer. However, because the pulse widths used in 50 kHz transducers are farther apart, the resolution or ability to mark fish close to the bottom is somewhat sacrificed. The best all around transducer is a 192 kHz or similar model that produces approximately a 20-degree cone angle.

In addition to quality sonar, a GPS unit is invaluable for open-water fishing. Frankly, without this navigation aid or a Loran-C system, open-water fishing is a waste of time. Loran-C is a ground-based navigation system that uses signals broadcast from towers. A GPS system uses signals transmitted from satellites orbiting the Earth.

Both navigation systems function in a similar manner, but because Loran-C signals are ground-based they are susceptible to weather fronts. The signals for Loran-C navigation can fail during foul weather, leaving boaters helpless at the moment they need the navigation system most. Satellite based GPS systems are the most dependable marine navigation systems available.

As you might expect, GPS systems can be rather expensive. Thanks to competition within the industry and less expensive components, the price of GPS units has dropped sharply in recent years. Lowrance Electronics is a leading manufacturer of recreational GPS units, producing some of the products most popular with walleye anglers.

"The technology available for GPS is rising at an astonishing level, yet the prices on many units are dropping," comments Mike Carney, Marketing Manager for Lowrance Electronics. "Our model LMS 1600 is a classic example. This state-of-the-art GPS unit features a 12-channel receiver, CD-ROM mapping unit, storage of 750 waypoints and 1,000 icons,

plus a price tag that's hundreds of dollars less than our comparable units produced just one year ago."

Good news for walleye anglers, quality and high-tech GPS units are now more affordable than ever before. A few years ago mapping-type GPS units were luxury items used by tournament pros and a handful of serious anglers. Today mapping-style GPS units are within the price range of most recreational anglers.

The need for a navigation system such as GPS exists because in open water there are no land marks to use as reference. It's all but impossible to stay on a school of open-water walleyes without the help of a Loran-C or a GPS unit. Marker buoys are not practical when fishing large basins of water because the fish are constantly on the move. A school of fish found one day is likely to be miles away the next.

PLANER BOARDS

Next to sonar and GPS, planer boards are the next most essential piece of equipment for open-water crankbait trolling. Boards allow anglers to spread lines out to the side where huge amounts of water can be covered in a minimum amount of time.

Two basic types of planer boards are available including catamaran-style boards and in-line skis. Catamaran or dual boards are normally fished in cooperation with a planer board mast mounted in the front of the boat. A tow line is run from the mast to the planer board and individual lines are set using pinch-pad line releases.

This planer board system has been around for decades and has proven itself as a fish-harvesting system. Many charters on the Great Lakes will run as many as 10-12 lines at a time using catamaran-style boards.

Those who are intrigued with the use of catamaran-style planer boards should note that a couple of developments have made this style of fishing more user-friendly. Boards that collapse for storage are the hot ticket. Nothing is more difficult to store on a boat than a bulky set of dual-ski planer boards. Collapsible boards can be tucked into storage compartments when not in use, making them the obvious choice.

Reeling in planer boards at the end of the day is another area where significant advancements have been made. Most planer masts feature a set of reels that are used to store the tow line. When it's time to pick up for the day, the boards must be reeled in by hand. This chore is no big deal on

This boat is equipped with a GPS unit. Frankly, without GPS or another navigation aid, fishing in open water is a waste of time.

This collapsible Riviera planer board can be stored easily even in small boats.

calm days, but bouncing around in the bow of a boat on rough water is no picnic.

An automatic tow line retrieval system produced by Riviera Downriggers is the most unique system I've seen for deploying and picking up planer boards. A set of spring-loaded reels are mounted to a planer mast. Tow line is loaded onto the reels and threaded through a pulley system on the mast and attached to the board using a heavy snap swivel. The distance boards are run out to the side is controlled by letting the boards out a desired length, then wrapping the tow line around a stop feature molded into the reel housing.

Once the stop feature has been set, deploying boards is as simple as dropping them over the side and trolling away. The spring tension reels feed line out until the pre-set stop is reached. When turning, the spring loaded reels pick up slack in the tow cable, then as the boat straightens out line is fed back out to the pre-set stop.

At the end of the day, picking up the boards is simply a process of driving the boat directly at one board. The slack line is automatically reeled up. When the first board has been retrieved, sim-

ply turn the boat and drive towards the second board. Again the spring loaded reels pick up the line automatically. There's never any need to work off the bow when setting or picking up boards.

Marketed as the Riviera/Kachman Automatic Planer Mast, this advancement in planer fishing is more handy than a pair of first mates.

Despite the advancements in planer boarding equipment, catamaran-style planer fishing systems are only as good as the weakest link in the system. The line releases used can make or break success on the water.

Over the years I've used just about every kind of line release produced. For my money nothing beats a quality pinch-pad release that uses spring tension to hold the line firmly between two rubber pads.

Bruce DeShano is the owner of Off Shore Tackle Company, the nation's leading manufacturer of pinch-pad style line releases.

The Riviera/Kachman Automatic Planer Mast is a useful and convenient tool for deploying and picking up dual style planer boards.

"Line releases have a simple job that's tough to perform," says DeShano. "The pinch pads must hold the line securely enough that wave action and deep diving cranks don't cause false releases, yet cradle the line gently enough so as not to damage the line. When a fish strikes, the release must provide enough tension to insure a solid hookset before releasing the line."

All this sounds elementary, but achieving the ideal amount of spring tension in a planer board line release isn't simple. "Variables such as line diameter, line stretch, wave conditions and trolling speed influence the function of planer board releases," explains DeShano. "There's no such thing as one release that functions in all conditions. That's why Off Shore Tackle produces a whole family of line releases designed to meet the needs of walleye anglers."

The OR-10 (yellow) is the most popular walleye trolling release in the Off Shore Tackle line. This release has both a light and moderate tension setting. The OR-14 (black) has a little stronger tension than the OR-10 and is popular with anglers who troll large baits at fast speeds. Finally, the OR-3 (white) features a larger pad surface that functions well with a wide variety of line sizes.

The OR-3 has enough tension that walleyes will rarely trigger the release at the strike. Instead the boat drags the fish for a moment until the angler pops the line free from the release by snapping the rod tip. Charter captains who troll several lines per side favor this release because if more than one walleye is hooked at the same time, fish can be dragged until the captain trips the releases one at a time. This way all the fish don't end up at the back of the boat at the same time, tangles are reduced, netting is more relaxed and charter life less stressful.

As you might have guessed, catamaran-style boards are most popular with anglers who own larger boats. Catamaran boards are the only practical way to run four, five or six lines per side.

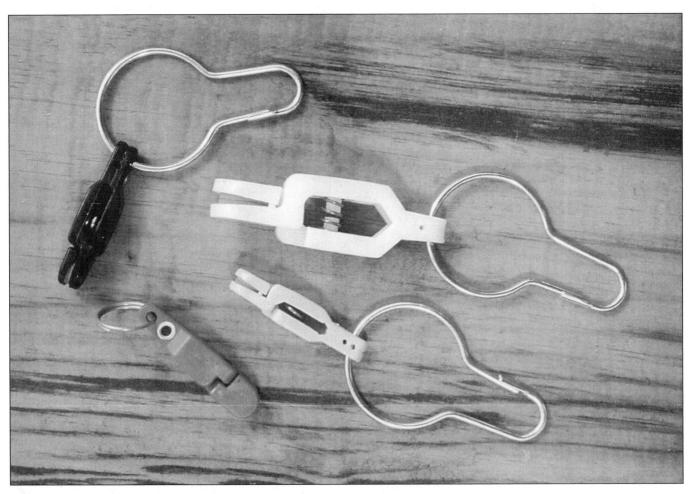

Planer board releases come in all sizes, shapes and tension adjustments. The author feels that pinch-pad style releases such as these are among the most functional and dependable.

The Tattle Flag is an after-market kit that converts the flag on an Off Shore Side-Planer into a spring-loaded flag that pulls down when a fish is hooked. This little item makes it much easier to detect small fish that have been hooked when using in-line boards.

Anglers who fish from smaller boats that typically fish a total of four to six lines may want to consider in-line style planer boards. Not only are these boards less expensive than catamaran planer systems, they can be trolled at a wider range of trolling speeds.

In-line boards attach directly onto the line. The crankbait is set the desired distance behind the boat, then the board is attached to the line. Again, the pinch-pad style line release is the most popular method of attaching the board onto the line. Once the board is attached to the line and dropped into the water, line is played off the reel until the board works itself out the desired distance to the side.

How far out to the side an in-line board is fished depends on wave conditions. On calm days boards can be set up to 100 or 150 feet to the side.

In rough seas mini boards function best when fished within 50 or 75 feet of the boat.

When a walleye is hooked on an in-line board, the weight of the struggling fish causes the board to pull backwards in the water. The board and fish are then reeled in together until the board is close enough to the boat to remove it. It only takes a second to remove the board from the line and free the angler to complete the fight.

The primary criticism of in-line boards comes from anglers who have a hard time telling when they have hooked a fish. When a big walleye is hooked, the board reacts noticeably. However, when small fish bite, it's surprisingly easy to drag a hooked fish and not know it.

As an answer to this problem, Off Shore Tackle recently introduced a spring loaded flag that pulls down when a fish bites. Marketed as the Tattle Flag, this after-market kit includes a flag, linkage bar, springs and necessary hardware to fit the Off Shore Tackle Side-Planer. Unfortunately, the Tattle Flag kits don't fit other brands of planer boards.

The Tattle Flag kits are so sensitive that small fish such as yellow perch, white bass or sheephead pull the flag down. Even a piece of weed caught on the crankbait causes the flag to register at half mast.

A wide variety of in-line boards are on the market, but not all are suitable for open-water walleye trolling. Features to look for on in-line boards include a ballast or weight system that causes the board to rest upright in the water at rest or slow trolling speeds. If the board doesn't rest upright in the water the tracking or planning ability of the board is sacrificed. Also, boards without proper ballast tend to dive when fishing in rough seas.

Size is another consideration when shopping for in-line boards. Boards on the small side are light and easy to reel in, but their lack of size prevents them from pulling deep diving crankbaits, lead-core line, snap weights and other trolling gear so common to walleye fishing. A good in-line board should also be equipped with a flag. A flag makes it easier to see the boards so strikes can be detected and also so other anglers won't run over your lines.

RODS/REELS/LINE

The rods and reels used for crankbait trolling must also meet certain standards. The rods themselves must be sturdy enough to handle the drag of planer boards and big fish. The good news is that expensive graphite rods are not required for trolling situations. More affordable fiberglass or

emphasized how important lead length is to open-water trolling. Lead lengths are one of the most important variables that influence crankbait running depth. Also, when a successful lead length is discovered, line-counter reels make it easy to duplicate that lead again and again, or to run the same lead length on other rods.

When selecting rods and reels, buy all the same brand and model rod and match them up with reels that are the same brand and model. The reason it's important to match these tackle items involves the reels more than the rods.

Unfortunately, the gear ratios and spool diameters of different line-counter reels are not the same. Some reels record in feet and others in meters. This creates a situation where various brands of line-counters don't provide identical readings.

In-line planer boards are an effective and affordable way to troll for walleyes.

fiberglass/graphite composite rods make the best tools for planer board fishing. I use 8-foot downrigger-style rods and have found them to be durable with the ideal action for fighting big walleyes.

The bad news is, walleye anglers need more trolling rods than other rod types. A set of at least four trolling rods is required to get started open-water fishing. Many anglers carry six or eight rods on board.

The reels used on these trolling rods should be one of the various brands of line-counter reels. Companies that produce line counter reels include Daiwa, Penn, Shimano, Marado, Okuma, South Bend and Cabela's. The prices on most of these reels range from $60 to $120.

Despite the substantial investment required for these reels, line counters are the only practical way to monitor lead lengths. It can't be over

Downrigger-style rods equipped with line-counter reels are the obvious choice for open-water trolling chores.

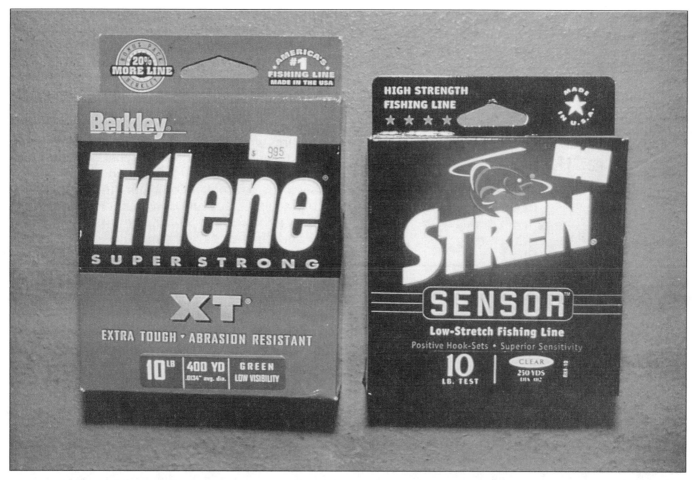

The best lines for trolling are hard-surfaced lines designed to be abrasion-resistant. Two of the most popular lines include Stren's Sensor and Berkley XT.

In other words when a Daiwa SG27LC and Marado Compass C 631 play out 50 feet of lead, both reels don't necessarily let out the same amount of line. The variances experienced on lead length between major brands can be minor or significant enough to influence lure diving depth. Fortunately, within a brand or model of reel, consistently is not a problem.

Serious trollers tend to match their rods and reels so nothing is left to chance. The next step is to calibrate the reels by making sure each is loaded with exactly the same amount and diameter of line. The best way to do this is to fill each reel to capacity. Because the counters on most reels are based on spool diameter, filling the spool to capacity provides the most accurate lead length data.

Lines used for trolling are also an important consideration. The thin, limp lines favored for casting are poor choices for trolling. More durable, hard-surfaced monofilament lines are best for

trolling situations. A few of the excellent trolling lines to pick from include Stren's Super Tough and Sensor, Berkley XT, Maxima, Ande Premium, Mason T-Line and Abu Garcia Royal Bonnyl II.

Most open-water trollers favor 10- to 12-pound test line. These line sizes provide the ideal combination of modest diameter and strength.

It's best to purchase these lines in money-saving 2,000-yard filler spools. It takes a considerable amount of line to fill trolling reels. Once a reel has been filled to capacity, there's no need to strip off all the line when it's time to install fresh line. Simply peel off 200 yards of the old line and discard it. Tie a spool of fresh line onto the old line using a double overhand knot and spool up enough line to fill the spool.

CRANKBAITS

The choices of crankbaits available is one of the most overwhelming aspects of crankbait troll-

A large assortment of crankbaits are useful for open-water trolling. The Storm Hot n' Tot family used to catch this fish is one of the author's all time favorites.

ing. What's even more confusing is that many of these lures are marketed as species-specific baits. Ironically, some of the most popular lures designed to be bass jerkbaits also happen to be prime walleye producers.

Specific crankbaits tend to become popular on certain bodies of water. For instance, on Saginaw Bay the most popular walleye crankbait is the Storm Hot 'n Tot. This family of lures has produced countless walleyes on Saginaw Bay, but you'll rarely find anglers fishing Lake Winnebago in central Wisconsin using Hot 'n Tots. On this popular fishery the bait of choice is a Cotton Cordell Wally Diver.

In Port Clinton, Ohio, Lake Erie trollers won't leave the dock without a good selection of Reef

Runner Deep Divers, at Lake Pepin on the Wisconsin and Minnesota border, you can bet locals will have a box full of Rapala No. 7 Shad Raps. The examples of local anglers sticking with one bait go on and on.

Certain lures become popular on certain bodies of water because they consistently produce and are readily available. However, that's not to say that other lures can't be just as productive. Fishermen aren't known for greasing wheels that don't squeak.

When traveling to new fishing destinations it's always wise to stock up on baits the local anglers recommend. Crankbaits don't get locally popular without good reason. Still, it's not wise to put all your faith in one or two crankbaits. Experiment with various baits. Sometimes baits that are locally popular pay off and sometimes they don't. The key is to let the fish decide which baits they want instead of trying to force feed them something they are supposed to like!

Open-water walleye trolling doesn't require a huge selection of crankbaits. To be honest, my most productive lures can be counted on the fingers of both hands. So why do I have boxes and boxes of crankbaits to choose from?

It happens like this; you're on the water and fish start smacking a 1/4-ounce Hot n' Tot in the blue and silver with the red lip. You look in your box to see if you have another one. As luck would have it you have every other color but. Despite trying similar baits of different colors, that one bait continues to be the hot producer.

In frustration you stop on the way home and buy three more 1/4-ounce Hot n' Tots in the same color for the next fishing trip. The next time you go fishing, the walleyes won't touch the Hot n' Tot. This time the bait they want is a shad-colored Reef Runner and you only have one. On the way home you stop at the bait shop. Repeat this process over the course of several seasons of fishing and you can see why the tackle companies love fishermen.

No matter how many crankbaits an angler owns, there will always be a reason to buy more. Over time, serious crankbait trollers collect more baits than they are likely to use, but they won't admit it. I think of my crankbait collection as a necessity. My wife has a pair of shoes for every outfit and I have crankbaits for every fishing situation!

On a more practical note, anglers just starting to fish open water can get by nicely with a modest selection of lures. I recommend that anglers purchase a few baits from each of four categories I'll dub as stickbaits, minnow divers, shad bodies and fat bodies.

STICKBAITS

Stickbaits are slender baits with a small diving lip. Most of these baits are made from plastic, but a few wooden models are available. Many of the most popular models are marketed as bass fishing jerkbaits.

All stickbaits are run fairly shallow, with most reaching only 6 to 8 feet below the surface. To achieve extra diving depth these baits are frequently used in combination with trolling weights such as Snap Weights, keel sinkers or lead-core line. Stickbaits are also fished frequently with downriggers and diving planers.

Must-have stickbaits include Storm's ThunderStick and ThunderStick Jr., Rapala's Husky Jerk series, Reef Runners Rip Stick and Baby Rip Stick, Bomber's Long A, Bagley's Bang-O-Lure and Mann's Minus One.

Stickbaits produce walleyes in a wide variety of trolling situations, but they are absolutely deadly in cool to cold water. The subtle top-to-bottom roll these baits produce is especially effective early and late in the season when trolling speeds are often slowed to 1.5 miles per hour or slower.

DIVING MINNOWS

Take a stickbait and put a larger diving lip on it and you've got a diving minnow bait. Among the most versatile of all walleye trolling cranks, diving minnows have the same top-to-bottom roll of a stickbait with a greater diving range.

Diving minnows can be trolled effectively at slow, moderate and fast speeds. Not surprisingly, diving minnows are productive all year long and, because they have a greater depth range than stickbaits, they are most often used without excess weights on the line.

Most of the major lure manufacturers have good baits to choose from. Some of the most popular models include the Storm Deep ThunderStick and Deep ThunderStick Jr., Bomber 24 A and 25 A, Rebel Spoonbill, Reef Runner Deep Diver, Mann's Stretch Series and Luhr Jensen Power Dive Minnow.

Diving minnows produce good results in a wide variety of waters. The profile of these lures does an excellent job of imitating common forage species such as emerald shiners, smelt, alewives, ciscoes and spottail shiners.

SHAD BODIES

Crankbaits designed to look like shad are an essential part of any walleye tackle box. Gizzard and thread fin shad are widespread and in many waters they are the primary forage of walleyes. Not only are these soft-rayed fish abundant, they are relatively easy for walleyes to catch, high in protein and easy to digest. When shad are abundant, walleyes will often ignore all other forages in favor of a steady diet of shad.

As you might expect such a popular forage species is bound to have a lot of crankbaits built to imitate it. Over the years a few models of shad-shaped cranks have become standard trolling baits. Classic choices include the Storm Lightnin' Shad and ThinFin, Rapala Shad Rap and Risto Rap series, Excalibur Fat Free Shad, Cotton Cordell Wally Diver and CC Shad.

Shad bodies are available in shallow, medium and deep-diving models making them among the most useful of all crankbait profiles. Like minnow divers, shad bodies can be trolled at a wide variety of speeds.

The action produced by shad bodies is a little more aggressive than that of diving minnows. Most shad baits combine a top-to-bottom roll with a little side-to-side tail wobble. The combination of actions is one that walleyes seem to appreciate because shad bodies account for staggering numbers of fish each year.

FAT-BODIES

Crankbaits that feature a round or thick body profile are often lumped into a category known as fat-bodies or high-action baits. The lip and body shape of these baits gives them an aggressive side-to-side wobble in the water. Like stickbaits, many of these lures got their start as bass fishing lures.

Fat-body baits are most productive when trolled at moderate to fast trolling speeds. Summer is the best time to use high-action cranks. In warm water conditions walleyes feed actively and don't hesitate to chase down fast-moving prey.

A few of the most popular fat bodies include the Storm Hot n' Tot family and Wiggle Wart series, Bagley Killer B II, Luhr Jensen Hot Lips series, Mann's Plus series and Rapala Fat Rap.

For open-water cranking anglers will need an assortment of stickbaits, minnow divers, shad bodies and fat-body lures.

JOINTED CRANKBAITS

Jointed cranks are different enough that a few words should be dedicated to them. Putting a joint in a crankbait allows the lure to have significant action at slow speeds. Early and late in the year when the water is cold, jointed cranks can be amazingly effective. Some good selections include the Rebel Fastrac, Rapala Floating Jointed Minnow and Storm Jointed ThunderStick.

JUDGING CRANKBAIT DEPTH

It doesn't take much time on the water trolling crankbaits to realize the depth levels various baits achieve plays a major role in fishing success. The lip size, line diameter and lead length are the three factors that most influence crankbait diving depth.

The book *Precision Trolling* is the authoritative guide to crankbait diving depths. Much of the data provided in *Precision Trolling* is offered in a chart known as a "dive curve." A dive curve shows how deep a crankbait will run on various lead lengths. In other words, anglers can target lures to run at the exact depth fish are marked on the sonar. With this information cranks can be presented close to but not on the bottom or set to run just over the top of submerged weeds or brush.

The book also contains approximately 40 pages of trolling tips relating to planer boards,

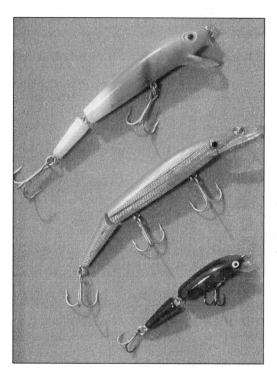

Jointed crankbaits like these are good choices when trolling at slow speeds. Jointed baits have more action at slow speed than solid body cranks.

snap weights, lead-core line, downriggers and diving planers.

As you have come to appreciate, trolling crankbaits in open water is a multi-faceted presentation that depends on a wealth of fishing knowledge. Granted, trolling crankbaits is one of the more complicated forms of walleye fishing, but it's also the most productive both in numbers and size of fish produced.

The real frontier of walleye fishing is taking place on open water. Fishing tools such as quality sonar, GPS units and planer boards make it practical to find and stay on walleyes living in the wide-open spaces. Crankbaits, and the ability to present these lures accurately, combine to develop an angling method that can only be described as a fish-harvesting system!

In the next chapter we'll explore crankbait casting and how this presentation can be put to work catching more walleyes.

CHAPTER 20
CASTING CRANKBAITS

Crankbaits are powerful fish-catching lures. Ask anyone who trolls and you will find out cranks are the answer to producing big catches and big fish. Crankbaits can also be cast into position. Bass anglers routinely cast crankbaits as a method for locating fish. This fast-paced presentation eats up water quickly, making it one of the best ways to search for active fish.

Despite the obvious benefits, you'll find few dedicated crankbait casters among those who fish frequently for walleyes. So why do bass anglers seemingly recognize the benefits of casting cranks, while walleye anglers favor other methods?

I can offer no logical explanation except to say, in general, anglers are followers, not leaders. Fishermen learn by example. Those who are learning to fish for walleyes imitate what they see on the water and read about in magazines. The headlines usually go to the big three: jigging, rigging and trolling.

Think for a moment back to the many walleye fishing articles you've read in various outdoor magazines. Can you remember reading anything about casting crankbaits for walleyes? Chances are you haven't come across this topic all too often.

Sometimes anglers have to break away from what's considered normal and explore other fishing methods. Casting cranks ranks as one of the best methods for locating fish-holding cover or structure.

Because of the way a crankbait dives into the water, these lures are a valuable tool for literally bumping into fish-holding spots that might otherwise be missed. When a crankbait slams into an isolated rock pile, a clump of weeds or stump, important information about potential fish location is gained.

Keep in mind that casting crankbaits is most useful in water 15 feet deep or less. In deeper water, trolling is usually a more efficient method of fishing crankbaits.

It's also important to note that crankbaits are most effective when fished in contact with some type of cover such as submerged weeds, sunken wood or rocks. In many cases the bottom holds fish and to be effective the crankbait must occasionally make contact with the bottom.

Casting crankbaits can be an effective way to pattern walleyes. Ironically, few anglers have discovered how effective casting cranks can be.

Obviously, a crankbait has lots of hooks. To avoid costly and annoying snags, anglers must select lures that dive to the desired depth and no deeper. Imagine a 10-foot flat with cabbage weeds growing up off the bottom approximately 6 feet. The ideal crankbait would be one that dives 3 to 4 feet on a normal retrieve. Deeper diving baits will spend most of the time snagged in the weed cover. If the bait doesn't dive deep enough, the lure may not pass close enough to fish to tempt a strike.

In addition to monitoring how deep various lures dive, the shape or profile of crankbaits can make a difference in fishing success. Selecting lures that closely resemble local forage species is the best place to start. Fly fishermen refer to this process as matching the hatch, but in walleye fishing it's not always easy to tell what fish may be feeding on.

It often helps to match up crankbait shapes to forage species found in a body of water. In this instance shad-shaped lures have been selected because gizzard shad are a primary forage.

Some fishing maps, such as those produced by Fishing Hot Spots, indicate the common forage species present on specific waters. This information can also be acquired by placing a call to a local fisheries biologist who's familiar with the water you plan to fish. Of course the best way to match the hatch is to catch a fish, clean it and examine the stomach contents.

As a general rule I recommend taking this step any time you plan on keeping some fish. With walleyes, this is most of the time. Examining the stomach contents of walleyes has led me to some surprises over the years.

A lake near my northern Michigan home is a good example. Almost every fish taken from this fishery has a belly full of small bluegills. Despite the fact that everything I've read about walleyes suggests that bluegills aren't a likely forage for this species, the proof in this instance is undisputed. All I can figure is walleyes feed on young bluegills because they are locally abundant.

Ironically, the lake in question has an equally abundant population of yellow perch that are considered a more traditional walleye forage. Apparently perch are tougher to catch than bluegills or perhaps there is a less obvious reason why, in this case, walleyes favor bluegills over perch.

Regardless of the reasons why walleyes favor one forage over another, in this example it stands to reason that a crankbait closely resembling a bluegill is likely to be more productive that those that look like a perch.

Not all bodies of water have the same types of forage species, but matching the hatch with cranks that look the part isn't difficult. There's a crankbait on the market that looks like just about everything that swims or comes near the water.

If spottail shiners, fatheads, emerald shiners or other slender minnows are abundant, stickbaits or diving minnow baits are likely to be the best producers. A few lures that fall into this profile category include the Storm ThunderStick and Deep ThunderStick Jr., Bomber Long A, Bomber 24 A, Bagley Bang-O-Lure, Reef Runner Rip Stick, Rapala Husky Jerk and Rebel Fastrac.

If perch are a frequent item in the walleyes' diet, crankbaits including the Cotton Cordell Wally Diver, Rapala Risto Rap, Luhr Jensen Rockwalker and Fingerling are tough to beat.

On waters where shad are the primary forage, try the Storm Rattlin' ThinFin, Rapala Shad Rap, Excalibur Fat Free Shad or Mann's Wally-Trac. If crayfish are a mainstay in the diet, Storm's Wiggle Wart and Bill Norman's Walleye Magnet are good bets.

Some baits such as balsa stickbaits or other small lures are simply too light to be cast any distance. Other more compact lures cast like bullets.

The farther a crankbait can be cast, the more water it covers and the more fish it potentially can contact. Also, since crankbaits must be retrieved relatively quickly to bring out their action, active or aggressively feeding fish are the ones most likely to strike. When casting cranks keep another rod handy with a jig tied on. When a fish is taken on a crankbait, try several more casts in the same area. If no additional fish are taken, try tossing the jig into the same areas working it slowly along the bottom.

Using this one-two punch is a good way to milk out an extra fish or two. The lesson is that not every fish present in a spot is going to strike at a crankbait. Fish that, for whatever reason, are not actively feeding aren't likely to chase down and

Sometimes crankbaits and jigs make a perfect combination. If a fish is taken in an area on a crank and several more casts don't produce additional fish, try tossing a jig into the same area. Sometimes the slower presentation of a jig is just the ticket.

strike a crankbait. But a jig bounced right in front of their nose is often more than they can refuse.

We've already discussed that casting cranks is a presentation that produces best in rather shallow water. We also know that the most productive areas are going to feature some type of cover or structure that attracts fish. To expand on the "where" aspect of crankbait casting imagine how a pack of walleyes feeds.

Unlike a bass that usually lays in ambush, walleyes hunt by slowly cruising while searching for something good to eat. Undoubtedly you've witnessed minnows jumping out of the water because predators such as walleyes were forcing the minnows to the surface.

To walleyes the surface is a barrier that's a vital part of their hunting technique. Walleyes use the surface film like a wall they can herd minnows against to prevent their escape. Walleyes also use walls that are vertical in the water in much the same way. Instead of trapping the minnows against the surface, the vertical edge serves to prevent minnows from darting away from walleyes that dog their every move.

Channel edges, sea walls, rip rap banks, dense weed edges, piers and fast-sloping breaks along points or shoreline contours are just some of the vertical walls that walleyes use while hunting. It matters little whether the wall is natural or manmade. The water depth or height of the wall doesn't have to be significant to attract fish.

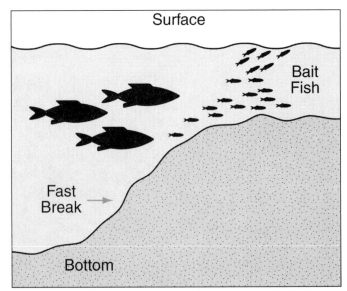

Walleyes herd baitfish against the surface like a barrier. Some of the best places to cast for walleyes are areas where walleyes can trap baitfish between the bank and the surface.

Numerous times I've taken fish by casting crankbaits into only 2 or 3 feet of water.

Walleyes tend to avoid places where the bottom gradually slopes to deep water, such as sandy beaches. Instinctively walleyes seem to know that baitfish can escape by simply swimming into water too shallow for these predators to follow.

WEED STRATEGIES

Pulling these bits and pieces of walleye know-how together is a good way to develop a strategy for casting crankbaits. Emerging weed beds are one of the most common areas where casting cranks can be productive. This dependable spring pattern works almost anywhere walleyes and weeds are found together.

Walleyes cruise among the loose groups or patches of weed cover in search of unsuspecting baitfish and other small fish. Depending on the type of weed cover the water may be only a few feet or up to 15 feet deep.

Certain weeds such as coontail usually grow best in rather shallow water, while common pond weed and smart weed often grow in deeper water. Regardless of the water depth, the trick is to select a crankbait that will dive down to the tops of the weeds.

For shallow water situations stickbaits, sometimes called jerkbaits, are among the best choice.

On a steady retrieve most of these baits will dive three or four feet. A little extra depth can be achieved from these lures by placing a small weight on the treble hooks or the split rings.

Soft lead wire wrapped around the shank of the treble hook is one way to add weight to a stickbait. Another method is to purchase special weights made to clip onto the split ring. These weights resemble miniature bell sinkers and they come in 1/32- and 1/16- ounce sizes. Clipped onto the split ring of the lure they cause stickbaits to slowly sink, increasing the running depth a few feet.

Don't bother looking for these products in the walleye tackle section of your favorite retailer. You're more likely to find them where bass fishing tackle is sold. Bass anglers frequently weight jerkbaits to get a little more mileage from these lures.

Lures can also be weighted by drilling holes in the baits and filling the holes with lead shot or water, then sealing the hole shut with epoxy glue. I'm not a fan of modifying crankbaits by drilling holes in them. Too often this practice has left me with ruined lures.

A steady retrieve may be effective but, not unlike bass fishing, the most productive retrieve is a twitching motion that causes the bait to dart back and forth.

A few years ago I watched Randy VanDam, the brother of B.A.S.S. superstar Kevin VanDam, smoke walleyes using a weighted jerkbait. I first

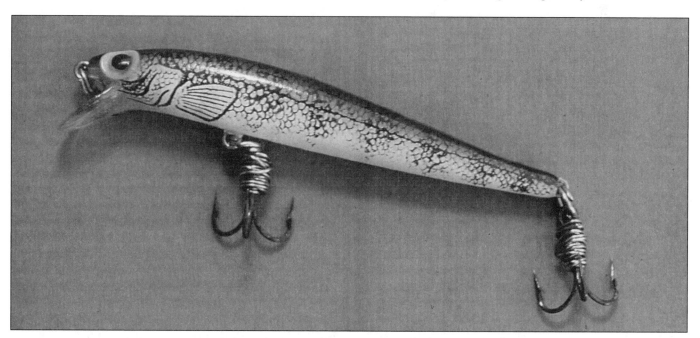

Adding weights to cranks to increase their diving depth is a trick that can be used to expand the effective depth range of many lures. Here lead wire has been wrapped around the hook shank to add weight.

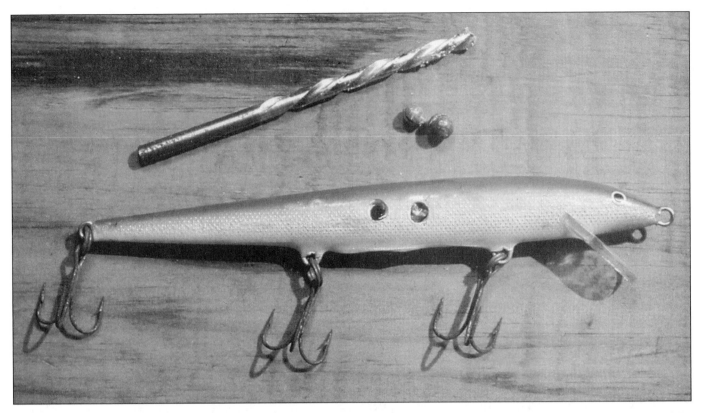

Crankbaits can also be weighted by drilling holes and filling them with lead shot. The holes are then filled with epoxy glue. Be careful however, this method of modifying baits ruins lures as often as it catches fish.

spotted the action from a distance. Naturally I eased closer to see who was catching all the fish and more importantly what technique was so productive.

When I got close enough to recognize the angler as my friend Randy, I parked my boat a few yards away and watched the show. Cast after cast, Randy hooked 16- to 18-inch walleyes as if they were waiting in line to get caught.

Randy's retrieve was simple. He would cast beyond his intended target, a submerged weed bed, and crank the bait hard a few turns of the reel handle to get the lure down to necessary depth. Once the bait was in position he stopped the retrieve and switched to a rod tip in a short jerking motion.

Apparently the bait must have been irresistible, because nearly every cast produced a fish. In the span of 10 minutes Randy caught and released as many fish. Eventually the spot burned out. Randy responded by moving down the weed bed a few boat lengths and starting the whole process all over again.

In the situation just described the weeds were thick enough that it was necessary to fish over the top of the weeds. In some instances the weeds

grow in clumps or loose groups that a crankbait can be threaded through with few snags.

Scattered weeds can be fished with jerkbaits and some diving cranks, but lipless lures like the famous Bill Lewis Rat-L-Trap are designed for this kind of fishing. Because the lure has no lip to catch on weed cover, these baits snake through weeds with amazing efficiency. When the bait catches on a weed stalk, a quick snap of the rod tip usually frees the lure and leaves the bait free of debris.

Most lipless cranks are count-down versions. You achieve the desired depth by allowing the bait to sink a few seconds before starting the retrieve. Normally a steady retrieve produces the best, but a stop and go or twitching action can also be deadly.

A third and equally common weed fishing situation occurs where weed edges are well defined. This situation often occurs where a flat drops off sharply into deeper water. Weeds grow right up to the edge of the break, making for a meandering wall of weeds. Walleyes will often cruise along the edge of the weeds or just inside the weed edge.

A rather deep diving crankbait that dives down near the bottom is usually required to tempt these fish into biting. Diving minnow or shad

Lipless cranks are among the best choices for casting into scattered weeds. These lures pick up less weed debris than models with diving lips.

cranks are the logical choice. Since the weed edge is defined and rather easy to avoid, diving style cranks can be used without fouling on weed cover.

Position the boat with an electric motor and cast parallel to the weed edge. Move along at a steady pace casting in front of the boat so the bait is always contacting new water.

CASTING SHORELINES

Some of my most enjoyable walleye fishing memories have taken place while casting crankbaits to rocky shorelines. Many natural lakes and reservoirs located in Canada and along the northern tier of the United States feature rock outcroppings along the shoreline. Often the water near shore is deep creating an ideal set up for walleyes to herd minnows against the rocks.

The problem is there are usually miles of potentially productive shoreline to explore. Casting a jig to these edges could eat up an entire vacation. A crankbait on the other hand can be cast and retrieved quickly, covering water almost as fast as trolling.

Because the water is often deep near shore, a crankbait that dives quickly is required. A number of crankbaits have small weights in the lip that cause the bait to rest in the water with the lip pointed almost straight down. This feature enables these lures to dive down at a sharp angle, achieving maximum depth with just a few turns of the reel handle.

Most crankbaits remain horizontal in the water with the lip parallel to the surface. These baits dive gradually, making them less suitable for fishing deep water edges.

A few of the baits that feature weighted lips include the Cotton Cordell Wally Diver, Rebel Wee-R Double Deep and Wally Demon. Other baits that dive quickly include the Storm Hot n' Tot family and the Luhr Jensen Baby Hot Lips.

It's best to position the boat a moderate cast away from the rocks and throw the baits right up to the edge of the rocks. Many of the strikes will occur as soon as the bait starts diving.

I recommend putting the electric motor on the continuous setting and adjusting the speed so the boat moves slowly along the shoreline. Cast ahead of the boat and towards shore. Use a quick retrieve and concentrate on covering water.

When a fish strikes, slow down and work the area more thoroughly. Anglers working together can cover a shoreline in short order.

CASTING RIVERS

Casting cranks in rivers also makes sense. Normally the water in rivers is somewhat turbid or off color. Because crankbaits are large, colorful and they make a considerable amount of noise, these lures are a perfect match for flowing water.

It's important to note however that crankbaits won't dive as deeply in flowing water as in still water. The flowing water creates resistance on both the line and lure. Depending on the speed of the current, the diving depth of popular baits can be cut in half.

Large crankbaits that are very buoyant and poor producers in current. Instead look for compact baits that feature a good-sized diving lip. Some excellent models to try include the Storm Wiggle Wart, Rebel Wee-R Double Deep, Luhr Jensen Baby Hot Lips, Bomber 6A and Cotton Cordell Wally Diver.

Search for walleyes in spots where the water is fairly deep right up to the bank. Steep sloping banks, sea walls, rip rap banks and the edges of bridge pilings are just a few of the places to try.

Flats can also be great places to cast crankbaits for river walleyes. Walleyes often spread out on flats featuring 4 to 8 feet of water. This is especially true in late spring when fish that entered the river to spawn start dropping back to their summer haunts. Male walleyes ranging from 15 to 20 inches are often slow to leave the river. Perhaps these fish are hoping that more females will come up to spawn or maybe the abundant forage rivers typically offer holds them for weeks after the spawning season.

One of the best ways to attack flats is to drift downstream with the current and cast perpendicular to the current flow. Retrieve the lure fairly quickly until it can be felt hitting bottom, then slow up the retrieve. As the boat moves downstream the lure will swing slightly upstream. Many times the strike comes as the bait changes direction to come directly towards the boat.

There's nothing subtle about the strike of a walleye hitting a crankbait. These fish slash at

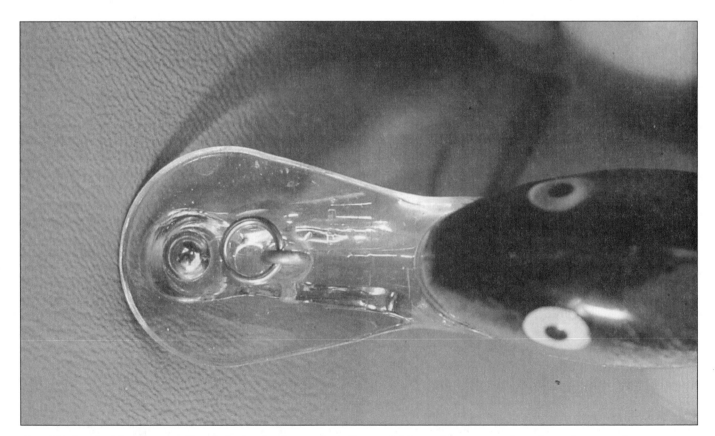

Crankbaits that have a small weight in the lip tend to dive quickly and are a good option when casting to areas with deep water close to the bank.

passing crankbaits often engulfing the bait deep into their mouth.

Rivers that feature wing dams are another situation where casting crankbaits makes sense. A wing dam is a pile of rocks placed perpendicular to the current. The rocks start at the shore and stretch out into the main river current.

The location of the wing dam is given away by turbulence on the surface sometimes called a slick. The wing dam is actually located just upstream of the slick.

The purpose of wing dams is to increase current flow in the center of the river so shipping channels don't silt in as quickly. Normally wing dams are only found on rivers with significant shipping traffic. Places where you'll find lots of wing dams include the Mississippi, St. Croix, Missouri and Illinois rivers.

Wing dams aren't built to attract walleyes, but they certainly do. Current striking the front face of the wing dam creates a swirling of water much like an eddy. Walleyes and other fish often tuck in tight to the face of the wing dam where the current is broken and they can lay in wait for minnows and other foods washed down by the current.

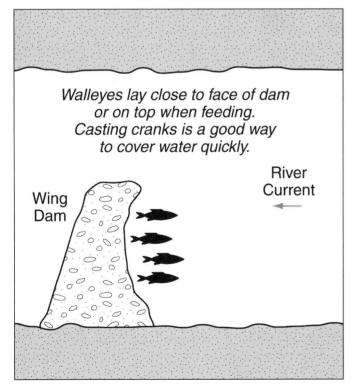

Wing dams are a good place to cast crankbaits. Active fish are most likely to be located on top of the dam or along the front face where the rocks meet the bottom.

Walleyes also feed on the top of the wing dam where a few feet of water rushes over the rocks. On the back side of the wing dam a hole, known as the scour hole, develops. Fish will hold here as well, but usually the most active fish are found on the front face of the wing dam or on top.

Fishing the front face of the wing dam requires precise boat control. Most anglers opt to anchor well above the wing dam, then let out enough rope to position the boat within casting distance of the face. A strong electric motor or gasoline kicker motor can also be used to hold the boat in the current.

When fishing the front face of a wing dam remember that most of the fish will be located near the point where the rocks make contact with the bottom. If the wing dam has some irregularity such as a hole in the dam or an arm that juts out at an angle, these places are going to collect the most fish.

Presenting a crankbait in these narrow strike zones is no easy task. To make contact with the face, cast parallel to the dam and a few yards upstream. Crank the bait down to the bottom immediately and then slow up the retrieve. The current will wash the bait downstream and at some point in the retrieve the bait will come in contact with the rocks.

Should the bait snag in the rocks give some slack line and, with a little luck, the current will wash the bait free. If the bait snags securely there's nearly no hope of recovering the lure.

It takes dozens of casts to thoroughly fish the face of a wing dam. The boat may also need to be moved a couple times to reach all the water that potentially holds fish.

When fishing the top of the wing dam quarter cast downstream and retrieve the bait right over the top of the dam. Make sure the bait is diving deep enough to contact the rocks. As in fishing the face, it takes a lot of casts to completely cover the top of a wing dam.

Compact cranks that are built to take abuse are the best choice for fishing wing dams. Two lures including the Storm Wiggle Wart and Bomber family of baits are head and shoulders the prime picks. Bright colors such as firetiger, chartreuse, clown and fluorescent red tend to be the best producers.

Not all wing dams attract fish. Large dams that stretch well out into the river are usually prime spots to locate walleyes. Also, if a dam has a break in it, or a substantial feature such as a log jam or dog leg, it's more likely to hold fish. Lastly, wing dams that are located on the outside bend of rivers routinely hold fish. Current is constantly washing into these dams making them prime feeding spots for walleyes and other fish. If several dams are located along a short stretch of river, the first or second dams the current contacts are usually the best fishing spots.

A word of caution regarding wing dams. The water passing over the top of a wing dam is often shallow enough that the boat's outboard or even the hull can hit the rocks. It's never a good idea to pass over the top of a wing dam.

EQUIPMENT NEEDS

The equipment needed to cast cranks is modest. Most anglers already own both rods and reels suitable for casting cranks. A 6-foot medium-

Unless you're comfortable with baitcasting tackle, a spinning combination is usually the best tool for casting cranks. Spinning tackle is also better able to throw light or small lures.

action spinning rod equipped with a quality spinning reel and 6- to 8-pound test monofilament line is the ideal tool for casting cranks. The rod should be a lightweight graphite model because it may require hundreds of casts per day to locate fish.

Spinning rods are the ideal choice because the average angler can use this equipment easily. Light lures can be cast with ease and the problem of tangles is all but eliminated.

Baitcasting gear can also be used for casting cranks, but I wouldn't advise those who are unfamiliar with baitcasting gear to try it. Backlashes are a reality of baitcasting equipment, even among those who use this gear frequently. Also, baitcasters aren't designed to handle the smaller line sizes needed to cast light lures.

A small cross-lock style snap is the best way to attach crankbaits to the line. These snaps allow baits freedom to wiggle, yet it's easy to change baits when needed. Snap swivels are not an option. Many snap swivels are heavy enough to throw off the balance of a crankbait and make the baits tough to tune.

TUNING AND TWEEKING CRANKS

Crankbaits are wonderful fish-catching tools, but to perform properly they must be tuned to dive and run straight as they are retrieved. Contrary to manufacturer claims, most cranks are not perfectly tuned when they come out of the package.

If a bait isn't tuned properly it may run on its side, flip over and come to the surface or simply not reach its maximum depth. Tuning a crankbait is a simple process, but it requires a little time and know-how.

Some baits are easier to tune than others. Baits with long wire eye-tie attachments such as those on the Hot n' Tot family of lures are very easy to tune. If the bait runs a little left when retrieved, simply bend the wire arm a little to the right. After each adjustment cast the bait, point the rod straight at the lure and retrieve it to see how it runs. Trial and error is the only way to achieve a bait that runs straight down in the water.

Baits with screw eyes or wire loops that function as line ties need to be adjusted with a pair of needle nose pliers. The same tuning principles apply, but a little adjustment goes a long way.

When tuning a crankbait never bend or try to adjust the lip of the lure. If the lip is damaged or bent, chances are the bait will be ruined.

The orientation or way a crankbait rests in the water can also be changed. Storm Lures produces two products known as SuspenDots and SuspenStrips that are lead tape with an adhesive back. The dots are lighter and are usually placed along the bottom of the lure to make the bait neutrally buoyant. The strips weigh a little more and can be used on the lip to cause a bait to rest nose down in the water.

When using these dots or strips remember the balance of the bait must be maintained. If the bait tilts on its side, the running depth and tune of the lure will be lost. Several strips or dots can be placed one on top of the other if necessary. To remove these weights simply take a knife blade and peel them off.

Casting cranks may not be featured in every outdoor magazine, but this presentation is hard to beat when it comes to finding fish. A fun and easy way to catch walleyes, think of crankbaits as little search and destroy missiles.

In the next chapter the focus switches from crankbaits to jigging spoons. Often pigeon-holed as ice fishing lures, jigging spoons have a lot more to offer walleye anglers.

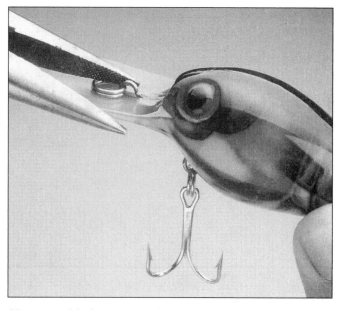

Most crankbaits need to be tuned to get the best performance. If the bait runs left of center, the line tie or screw eye must be bent in the opposite direction using a needle-nose pliers. Go easy, a little adjustment goes a long way.

Storm SuspenStrips or Dots can be used to change the orientation of a crankbait in the water. By placing a couple strips along the lip of the lure, baits can be made to dive at a steeper angle. These adhesive-backed strips and dots can also be used to create neutrally buoyant cranks.

CHAPTER 21

CASTING, SWIMMING AND JIGGING SPOONS

Imagine a walleye fishing lure than can be used in shallow or deep water. A lure that can be cast away from the boat or jigged straight down below. This same lure has fish-catching flash, action and can be tipped with live bait.

Now imagine how frustrated you might be if this versatile and effective lure was only available at a certain time of year. Jigging spoons aren't seasonal lures, but judging by the way anglers use them it seems that way.

Jigging spoons are popular ice fishing lures, but sadly they don't get much exposure during the open-water season. Simply jigging them up and down in an ice fishing hole doesn't do these baits justice.

My own experience with jigging spoons was limited to ice fishing until I started competing in walleye tournaments during the mid 1980s. The one thing about tournament anglers is they aren't afraid to experiment and stretch the limits of what's considered normal.

As I recall, I took my first serious look at jigging spoons soon after suffering some lumps on a Saginaw Bay tournament. Normally this body of water is noted as being a spinner or crankbait trolling fishery, but this particular tournament was won by a pair of anglers fishing jigging spoons on a well-known series of humps near the mouth of the Saginaw River.

The successful anglers used no live bait, but instead jigged the spoons vertically in 18 to 22 feet of water. I distinctively remember the trolling bite being tough. I struggled to catch a limit of small fish and ended up with much less weight than normal for a Saginaw Bay event.

Meanwhile the anglers using jigging spoons popped easy limits and were able to cull up to winning weights. What's even more impressive is all the fish were taken from an area no larger than a football field.

Jigging spoons like the one that took this fish are powerful walleye baits that don't get the attention they deserve. An alternative to casting jigs or cranks, jigging spoons are yet another way to trigger strikes.

There's something about a jigging spoon that seems to make walleyes bite when jigs, rigs, crankbaits and other traditional tackle fails. I can't claim to know what trips a walleye's trigger, but I suspect in the case of jigging spoons the strikes generated are reactionary.

Over the years I've become convinced that walleyes often follow trolled baits such as spinners or crankbaits for a considerable distance. The consistent action and speed of these lures often doesn't trigger a strike response, but rather one of curiosity. However, the moment the lure changes direction, slows or speeds up, the walleye's action is definite.

Jigging spoons create a fluttering, wobbling and flashing action that's never the same twice. Sometimes these lures seemingly have the power to tempt strikes from fish that will not bite other lures and presentations.

If walleyes think a potential meal is about to get away, a slamming strike occurs. Because of the unpredictable action of jigging spoons and the way these lures are often fished, I feel they generate a reactionary strike response more often then other lures.

When a jigging spoon is free falling on a slack line, the bait wobbles, flashes and glides towards the bottom. No two jigging strokes produce exactly the same action. On the same note, no two models of jigging spoons wobble or flash in exactly the same way.

A fish that spots a spoon wobbling at a distance is attracted to take a closer look. About that time, the angler snaps the spoon to life by jigging it up off the bottom and the rest is history. A reactionary strike is stimulated and the fish is hooked before it knows what happened.

SORTING OUT SPOON OPTIONS

When it comes to models, sizes and colors of jigging spoons there are more than a few decisions to be made. In recent years a number of new spoons have popped up on the market and many of these have promising finishes, shapes or actions.

The models of jigging spoons that have proven themselves over the years include the Hopkins Shorty, Luhr Jensen Crippled Herring and Krocodile, Little Bay de Noc Swedish Pimple, Acme Kastmaster and Mann's Mann-O-Lure. Some of the promising newcomers include Rapala's Minnow Spoon, Cabela's Real Image, Bait Rigs Willow Spoon, Northland Buck Shot Spoon, Dardevle's Cop-E-Cat, Wolverine Tackle's Cobra and the Mepps Cyclops.

Many of these spoons are available in sizes ranging from 1/4 to 1-1/2 ounces. The most popular sizes for walleyes are the 3/8-, 1/2-, 3/4- and 1-ounce versions.

The finishes and colors offered on jigging spoons are mind-boggling. Models are available in several combinations of painted, plated, hammered and flash tape finishes.

All jigging spoons function in much the same way, but the shape of these lures gives them vastly different actions. For example, the Swedish Pimple is a triangular spoon that sinks quickly and features a subtle wobble. The Krocodile spoon is wider, has a more pronounced wobble and it sinks more slowly than most spoons.

When building a collection of jigging spoons, make sure to select an assortment of sizes, shapes and colors.

When selecting jigging spoons note that some models are streamlined and sink rather quickly, while others are wider and have a more pronounced wobble.

EQUIPMENT REQUIREMENTS

Two basic rod and reel combinations will be needed to fish jigging spoons. Light spoons ranging from 1/4 to 1/2 ounce are best served with a medium-action spinning rod and reel combination. Load the reel with monofilament line in 8-pound test.

For working heavier spoons select a medium or medium/heavy action triggerstick from between 6-1/2 and 7 feet long. This rod should be equipped with a baitcasting reel. Line ranging from 10- to 17-pound test monofilament works best.

The only other gear that's needed for fishing jigging spoons are a few sturdy snaps that make it easy to change lures.

CASTING TIPS

Jigging spoons don't get much use in open water, and they see even less action as casting lures. These baits are usually favored for jigging near the bottom in fairly deep water.

As an excellent alternative to jigs or crankbaits, casting jigging spoons requires a little different approach. First off, when casting crankbaits a steady retrieve is normally used. On a steady retrieve a jigging spoon has little more action than

a bell sinker. Jigging spoons must be allowed to fall on a slack line to bring out their action.

Jigs on the other hand are often hopped along the bottom using short pops of the rod tip. Spoons need a more aggressive jigging stroke to lift the bait and allow it to flutter and wobble back to the bottom.

When casting spoons, pitch the bait to the target and allow it to sink straight to the bottom. Once the bait hits bottom, reel up the slack line

Baitcasting tackle is favored for fishing jigging spoons because these lures are often rather heavy. Line ranging from 10- to 17-pound test is best.

until the weight of the spoon can be felt in the rod tip. Using a fairly aggressive snap of the wrist, pop the rod tip lifting the spoon a couple feet off the bottom. Let the spoon fall back to the bottom, reel up the slack line and repeat this process until the bait has been worked all the way back to the boat.

The flashing and wobbling action of the spoon as it flutters towards the bottom is what makes these lures work. Don't make the mistake of trying to fish a spoon with a subtle hop or jumping action when casting these lures.

On the average, jigging spoons are somewhat heavier than lead-heads. This fact allows spoons to be fished faster making them a good choice for covering water fast.

When casting it's best to fish spoons clean. The aggressive jigging stroke will tear live bait from the hooks. A piece of pork rind or a plastic grub body will be tough enough to survive this type of fishing. But adding these trailers slows down the drop time of the lure and can change the action.

Casting jigging spoons can be a shallow- or deep-water presentation. Normally these spoons are cast to specific targets such as the tip of a point, a hump, rock pile or saddle between islands. Casting can also be an excellent way to cover large flats where walleyes are scattered.

VERTICAL JIGGING TIPS

Jigging spoons were designed with vertical jigging in mind. The ideal choice for fishing near the bottom in deep water, a jigging spoon is tough to beat when fishing isolated cover or structure such as rock piles, the tops of sunken islands, sunken cribs or fish-attracting structures and submerged wood.

The best way to fish these spots is to sit on top of them using an electric motor to hold the boat in position. If the spot to be fished is large enough a short yet precise drift is another excellent way to control the boat.

The region of northern Michigan where I live has a long history of logging that has an influence on modern walleye fishing. All the natural lakes in the region had, at one time or another, major saw mill operations. When trees were cut into lumber the bark and a little wood were sawed away before the logs could be cut into boards. At the time there was no market for these slabs, so they were bundled up and slid out onto the ice of local lakes during the winter. When the ice melted, the piles of slab wood sank to the bottom where they were out of sight and mind.

Those slab wood piles have become fish magnets attracting walleyes and a wealth of other species. No one knows for sure how many slab wood piles were sunk in the waters of Michigan, Wisconsin, Minnesota, Ontario and other popular logging regions. One thing is for sure, jigging spoons are a deadly way to fish these unique spots.

To reduce problems with snags many anglers remove the treble hook that comes on the spoon and replace it with a single Aberdeen hook. The wire in an Aberdeen hook is soft enough that the hook can be bent out and the spoon recovered if it snags the wood. For other applications the treble hook that comes on the spoon is the best choice.

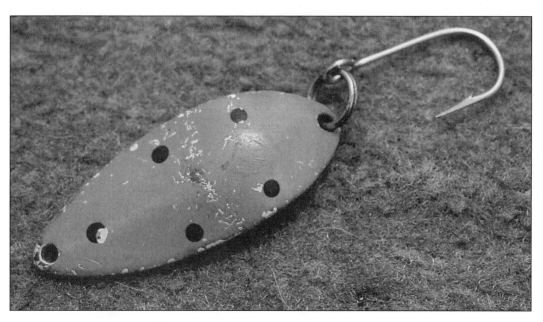

When snags are a problem, the treble hook on spoons can be replaced with a single hook.

Vertical jigging is also a great way to fish spoons in rivers. Used as a supplement to lead-heads, jigging spoons offer another dimension to vertical jigging. In addition to the flash and wobble spoons deliver, they are also larger than lead-heads making them more visible in darker water.

Two different jigging strokes are suited to river jigging. The first method involves lifting the spoon a couple feet off the bottom, then dropping the rod tip and allowing the lure to flutter freely back to the bottom.

This jigging method is simply a variation of tight-line jigging often practiced with lead-head jigs. The difference is the spoon is allowed to fall back to the bottom on a slack line. The spoon may be fished clean or tipped with a minnow or piece of nightcrawler to add more enticement.

The second jigging stroke is a little more aggressive. Start with the spoon resting on the bottom and, using a sharp snap of the wrist, pop the spoon up off the bottom a foot or two and allow the lure to flutter back to the bottom. If minnows are used with this jigging method, hook the bait through both lips then take a piece of soft plastic from a grub body and thread it over the hook point. The plastic acts like a washer and prevents the bait from being snapped off the hook.

Crawlers are a poor choice for this jigging technique. The jigging motion causes the bait to quickly ball up on the hook. After only a few jigging strokes the crawler will look like it was tied onto the treble hooks.

Also, I don't recommend dragging jigging spoons equipped with treble hooks. The bottom of a river is a snag waiting to happen. Unlike jigs that cost only a few cents each, jigging spoons rival the cost of crankbaits.

BLADE BAITS

Blade baits are one of those lures that are hard to categorize. Technically blade baits aren't jigging spoons and they aren't jigs either. They can be cast and retrieved like a crankbait, but these lures aren't part of the crankbait family.

One thing is for sure, blade baits are versatile lures that are every bit as effective as spoons, jigs or crankbaits. Of these three lure groups, blade baits probably fit in closest to the jigging spoon.

Blade baits are often fished using an aggressive jigging action similar to that used with spoons. They are also a common choice when fishing near the bottom in deep water with precise structure. Blade baits generate reactionary strikes much the same as jig-

Blade baits are similar to jigging spoons in that these lures also are strike triggering tools.

ging spoons. Flash and vibration are the fish-attracting powers of both blade baits and spoons.

Not exactly new lures, blade baits have been around for years, but the introduction of the Reef Runner Cicada a few years ago stimulated a whole new love affair with this lure type. The Cicada was originally developed as a deep-water lure for springtime walleyes and smallmouth bass.

"What makes the Cicada unique is the cupped blade used for the body," says lure designer Scott Stecher. "Other blade baits have to be fished aggressively to bring out the vibration of the lure. The Cicada can be fished slower and still produce strike-provoking vibration."

Some of the other blade baits to choose from include the Heddon Gay Blade and Sonar, Luhr Jensen's Ripple Tail, Bass Pro Shops Silver Buddy and Cabela's Zounder. All of these models are sim-ilar in construction. The body is made from a thin piece of metal with a weighted head molded onto one end. A treble hook is mounted on both the front and back of the lure and the line tie is located midway on the back of the lure. Usually more than one line tie attachment is provided to give anglers with an option that changes the lure's orientation in the water.

Some blade baits come with a snap that serves as a line tie. Others simply have holes drilled into the metal body. Attaching the fishing line directly to the hole in the metal body isn't a good idea. Blade baits are often fished using an aggressive jigging action. In order to insure the line doesn't fail, a snap must be used to attach the lure.

"I prefer to fish small blade baits on light line," says Stecher. "I catch most of my fish with a 1/4-ounce lure and 6-pound test monofilament. The

The Cicada is among the most unique of blade baits. The cupped body causes this lure to have vibration when moved slowly in the water. Other blade baits must be fished aggressively to get the desired vibration.

trick is to watch the line closely for any sign a fish has hit the falling lure. When lifting the lure off bottom, be ready and set the hook if you feel any weight."

The advice that Stecher offers echoes that of successful jig fishermen. Not surprisingly, blade baits seem to produce best when hopped or bounced along the bottom. Dragging or scooting the bait doesn't seem to deliver the right combination of vibration and flash.

One of the most common ways of fishing blade baits is to cast them downwind of a drifting boat. Flip the bait a short distance downwind of the boat and allow the lure to sink to the bottom. Hop the bait back towards the boat a few times using a snap of the rod tip. When the bait is directly beneath the boat, vertical jig it a couple times then reel it up and cast downwind again.

Early in the spring when walleyes are concentrated along the deep water edges of spawning reefs, this technique is deadly and often produces better than jigs or jigging spoons. A lure without a clear category, blade baits share a lot of the properties of spoons and these lures can, in most cases, be used in the same situations.

Both jigging spoons and blade baits have earned a niche in the world of walleye fishing. Often looked upon as seasonal baits, the truth is this form of heavy metal can be used to take walleyes at any season.

In the next chapter another overlooked presentation will be highlighted. Floats are often considered to be for kids, but they are also serious walleye fishing tools. We will look at how floats can be used to fish waters that other presentations can't touch.

CHAPTER 22

POPPING THE CORK

I'm constantly amazed at how fishing techniques become popular in some areas while not in others. Float fishing is a good example. On certain waters in Minnesota and Wisconsin, floats are the most popular way to catch walleyes. Anglers dedicated to this method of fishing anchor the boat and use the wind to drift the bait over nearby reefs, weed flats and a wealth of other spots that routinely hold walleyes.

It's not hard to see why floats are so effective. The use of floats allows the bait to be positioned at the exact depth where fish are most likely to spot it. Snags are all but eliminated. It's also easy to see when a bite occurs and water is covered thoroughly. In addition, floats can be fished during the day or at night. Most of all float fishing is fun and a technique that anglers young or old can master.

To say that float fishing works on walleyes is a major understatement. A recent tournament I fished in was won by a pair of anglers who cast slip bobbers baited with leeches to isolated patches of cabbage weeds. This presentation proved the perfect way to deal with dense weed growth that so often makes fishing similar areas with other techniques troublesome.

Despite the obvious virtues of float fishing, these fishing aids are often considered kids toys instead of serious gear. Make no mistake, float fishing for walleyes is light years ahead of those round plastic clip-on bobbers we all used as kids. In fact, serious floats designed for serious fishing make this overlooked presentation more productive and enjoyable than ever before.

BECOMING FAMILIAR WITH FLOATS

There's not much in the way of sport fishing gear that isn't new or improved. Floats are no exception. You might ask what could be done to improve the basic function of a bobber? The answer is lots. The service that floats provide is simple, but the way these fishing aids function is rather complex.

Just as an example there are tall floats, short floats, fat floats and thin floats. Weighted floats, slip floats, European floats and lighted floats. If that's not enough, consider floats made of cork, plastic, foam and balsa. You get the picture.

Fortunately for walleye anglers, there's no need to purchase every type of float produced. Slip bobbers are the most useful design for wall-

It's easy to see why floats are so effective at catching walleyes. What's hard to understand is why this method of fishing is not more widespread.

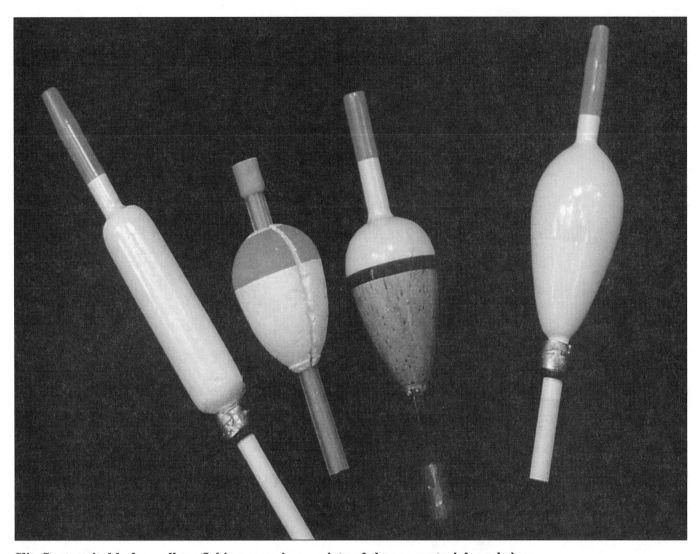

Slip floats suitable for walleye fishing come in a variety of shapes, materials and sizes.

eye fishing. Designed to slide on the line, a hole barely bigger than the fishing line runs completely through the float.

Rigging is easy. A stop made of soft rubber, plastic or thread is placed on the line ahead of the float. Every float angler has his or her favorite type of bobber stop. I favor the cloth knot style stop because they can be slid up and down on the line many times without damaging the line or the stop.

The stop is used to set the fishing depth. Next, a small plastic bead is threaded onto the line to prevent the stop from passing through the hole in the float.

At the terminal end anglers have two popular options from which to select. A small jig is often used to provide both a hook and weight to hold the bait in position. Normally a 1/64-, 1/32-, 1/16- or 1/8-ounce jig is selected.

With smaller jig sizes it can be difficult to find hooks big enough for walleyes. Most small jigs are built to catch panfish. A few companies produce jigs especially for use with slip bobbers. The Angle Jig produced by Freshwater Tackle of Deerwood, Minnesota is a unique jig shape that's concave on the bottom. Even the smallest sizes have hooks suitable for walleye fishing.

A single hook with a split shot or two positioned a few inches above the hook also works well. A number of hooks are used on slip bobber rigs, but wide bend or kahle hooks are the best choice. These hooks are thin wire, extra sharp and the wide hook gap provides added holding power when fishing floats.

Wide-gap hooks run a little larger than other hook sizes. Plan on using a hook one size smaller than normal. For example, if you normally use a

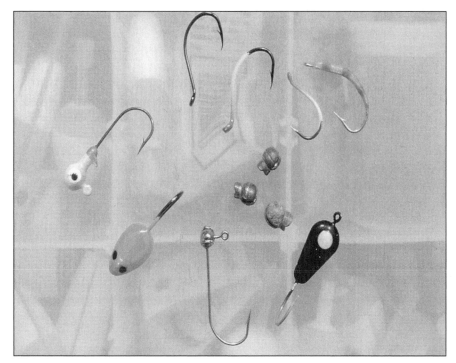

At the business end of a slip float a number of jig styles and hooks can be used. These examples represent some excellent choices.

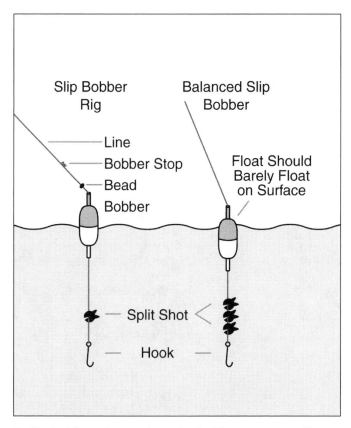

Slip Bobber Rig

Balanced Slip Bobber

Line

Bobber Stop

Float Should Barely Float on Surface

Bead

Bobber

Split Shot

Hook

A slip bobber rig consists of a bobber stop, small bead, float, split shot and hook. A slip float must be balanced so the slightest strike causes the float to sink. This illustration shows a float that's not weighted enough and one that's just right.

No. 4 hook for live bait fishing a No. 6 wide-gap is the right choice.

BALANCING A SLIP FLOAT

The object when fishing floats is to present the bait so when a walleye takes it, the fish feels little or no resistance. A float that's too buoyant provides unnatural resistance that can cause the fish to drop the bait.

Small weights are added on the line until only the stem and a small amount of the brightly painted top can be seen resting above the water. Known as balancing a float, this practice insures that the slightest strike will cause the float to react.

Some floats have weights attached to the lower stem. The weight helps to balance the float and make it easier to cast in windy conditions. On Thill brand floats the weights can be added or removed as required by using an O-ring to hold the weight in place. Extra weights and O-rings are sold separately.

Some anglers favor unweighted floats. Should a fish pick up the bait and move upwards with it, an unweighted float will react by tipping. If the float is weighted, this telltale message isn't telegraphed.

Small lead shot pinched onto the line is the most practical way to balance a slip float. Place the weight about 6 inches above the hook. Keep adding weight until 2/3 of the bobber is under water.

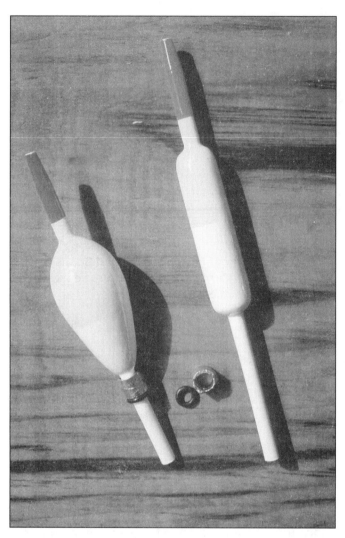

Some floats have weights on the stem to make them easier to cast. Thill offers a float weight that can be put on or taken off as desired.

FLOAT DESIGNS

Floats also come in a wide variety of shapes designed to offer the least amount of resistance. Thin pencil-shaped floats have the least buoyancy followed by cigar-shaped models and standard or oval-shaped floats. The difference in buoyancy among float designs is one of inches not miles. The important step is to insure each float is balanced correctly.

A unique slip bobber known as the Easy-On does not require the line to be threaded through the bobber like other floats. Instead a slot is cut in the stem and body of the float. The fishing line is laid into this slot then the stem is twisted slightly to close off the slot and create a slip bobber. An

optional cap is available that slips over the end of the float, making the hole the line passes through smaller so the stop doesn't stick in the end of the bobber.

Produced by Freshwater Tackle Company, the Easy-On bobber is the fastest way yet to rig a slip float for walleyes. These floats are sold two in a package or you can buy them in a walleye kit that includes a float, bobber stop, counter balance weight and four sizes of Angle Jigs.

Floats are made from a number of different materials. The highest quality floats are hand-built from balsa wood that's painstakingly stained, dipped in colorful paint and covered with a clear coat for lasting durability. Some of these floats are works of art, but frankly it's hard to tell the difference in performance compared to less expensive foam or plastic models. Some folks drive a Chevy

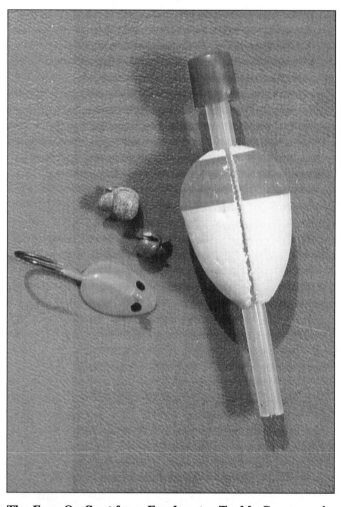

The Easy-On float from Freshwater Tackle Company is a sliding float that doesn't have to be threaded onto the line. The unique design allows the float to be added or removed as needed without cutting the line.

and others a Cadillac. Both are dependable forms of transportation.

TACKLE SUITABLE FOR SLIP BOBBERS

Slip bobbers are most often used on spinning rods ranging from 6 to 7 feet long. The rod should feature a medium or medium/light action. Expensive graphite models aren't required since the rod doesn't telegraph the bite. Less expensive fiberglass or graphite/fiberglass composite rods are a good choice for slip bobber fishing.

Equip this rod with a matching spinning reel loaded with either 6- or 8-pound test premium monofilament. A limp monofilament is the best choice. Some excellent choices include Stren's Easy Cast and Magna Thin, Berkley's Trilene Pro Select, Super Silver Thread and Spiderwire Super Monofilament.

BEGINNING WITH BASICS

Slip bobbers work best when used from a fixed position such as an anchored boat or casting from shore. This very fact suggests that slip bobbers aren't a good method to try when it's necessary to search for fish. Floats are most useful for fishing known structure, cover or a school of fish that has been located using another technique.

Float fishing is also a presentation that requires anglers to work with and not against the wind. Anchor upwind of the area fish are expected to be. The boat should be positioned with the bow pointed into the wind. Working out of the back of the boat, cast the float rigs quartering into the wind and let them drift naturally into position.

When the float reaches the end of the drift, reel it up and make another cast. In states where more than one line may be used at a time, casting a second line provides welcome double coverage.

After making several casts and drifts in an area, let a little more anchor line out and make several more casts. This style of fishing requires a lot of anchor line and patience to work water thoroughly. Plan on having at least 100 to 150 feet of sturdy line available. To prevent tangles store this rope on a plastic yoke intended for wrapping extension cords.

Braided or twisted nylon lines are soft to the touch and easier on the hands than less expensive poly ropes. Expect to pay around 50 cents per foot for quality anchor lines.

A WORD ON ANCHORS

An anchor that holds fast in windy conditions is an absolute must when slip bobber fishing. Depending on the size of the boat used and the type of bottom that must be anchored on a variety of anchors are suitable. I strongly recommend two styles of anchors for use with walleye boats ranging in size from 17 to 20 feet.

Lightweight fluke style anchors such as the famous Water Spike, Chene or Hooker designs

An anchor heavy enough for the job, plus lots of anchor rope is needed for slip float fishing.

This angler is using a float to fish small openings in weed cover. Short and precise casts are made to visible openings.

hold exceptionally well in all bottom types and these anchors are easy to dislodge from rocks and other debris on the bottom. Two pointed flukes made from steel dig into the bottom giving a firm grip on just about any bottom type. When it's time to pull anchor and head for home, simply pull from the opposite direction to release the grip on the bottom.

These anchors hold by digging into the bottom instead of using weight. Because this style of anchor is light it is easier to handle.

The traditional Navy style anchor is another excellent choice. Navy anchors use two flukes that dig into the bottom, but the flukes are made from heavy cast iron. The extra weight of these anchors makes them bite the bottom quickly and hold a little better in soft bottoms. They are available in weights ranging from 8 to 20 pounds. I use an 18-

pound anchor to hold my Fisher FX DV that's 18.5 feet long and approximately 1,500 pounds.

Most anchors aren't designed to hold on firm bottoms or in difficult conditions. Mushroom and grapple style anchors are for holding row boats, not a full-fledged walleye boat in a biting wind.

Nothing is more frustrating than carefully positioning the boat and setting the anchor only to find the anchor is inadequate to hold the boat. My advice is to buy a good quality anchor that's more than capable of holding whatever you plan to fish from. Match this anchor up with at least 100 to 150 feet of quality nylon line.

There are electric anchor winches on the market that deploy and retrieve anchors, but I can't

Floats are a good way to fish snag-filled rivers. It's best to fish from an anchored position or while casting from shore.

say I've used one. The bow of a walleye boat takes a terrible pounding and I'm reluctant to mount anything except an electric motor and graph on the bow of my boats. However, anglers who fish slip bobbers frequently, may find the convenience of an electric anchor winch a useful accessory.

BOBBERS BEYOND THE BASICS

Slip floats are most often used to drift live bait to structure or cover that holds fish, but there are lots of other applications for floats in walleye fishing. A technique I call pocket hopping is useful when fishing dense weed cover that has small openings or pockets of open water among the dense growth.

Instead of anchoring the boat in one position and casting, an electric motor is used to slip quietly along while watching for openings in the weed cover. When a likely looking opening is spotted a slip bobber rig is flipped into position. Because the openings are generally small, a cast or two covers the area. If no fish are contacted, the boat is moved along until another opening is located.

The best strategy is to keep moving and checking openings until you find fish. There's no need to sit and fish a small opening for a long time. If a spot has fish the bite occurs quickly. Normally these small spots are only large enough to support a fish or two, so there's no need to camp out after catching a fish.

This same method of fishing can also be applied to submerged tree tops from blow downs or stump fields. I've also used it to fish the brush piles beavers store in front of their lodges as a winter food source. When fishing near wood, I'd recommend using at least eight-pound test line so hooked fish can be wrestled free from the cover quickly.

When fishing around submerged wood precise bait placement is critical. Long steelhead-style spinning rods are handy for reaching out away from the boat and making short casts or flips to hit intended targets. Good sunglasses are also a must for these methods of slip bobber fishing. Without sunglasses it's difficult to spot the weed

openings or wood in the water required to make accurate bait presentations.

Another little known slip bobber fishing technique is deadly when fishing snag-filled rivers. Lots of rivers hold walleyes, but the bottom is often littered with snags that eat up jigs and other bottom fishing gear.

A slip bobber with the bait set to ride about 12 inches off the bottom is the ideal way to present bait in the strike zone while reducing the chances of snags. For best results the water depth should be approximately the same along the entire drift. Deep holes, flats and lazy runs are some of the best places to try slip bobbers. It's also important to use enough weight to sink the bait in the swift current. Normally an oval shaped slip float with a 1/8- or 1/4-ounce lead-head jig is ideal. Tip the jig with a lively leech, minnow or nightcrawler.

Fishing floats in rivers must be conducted from a fixed position. Anglers can get in on the action from an anchored boat, standing on shore or wading. The trick is to position yourself so you can cast quartering upstream, then let the current wash the float and bait downstream naturally.

Watch the float closely as it drifts downstream. Set the hook immediately if the float hesitates, tips or plunges under water. Again, long steelhead style rods are an advantage for this style of fishing because casting distance is increased with longer rods. Also, the longer rod makes it easier to raise the monofilament up out of the water as the float drifts along. Keeping the line up out of the water allows the float to drift naturally and increases the reaction time when setting the hook.

These are just some of the ways that floats can be used to catch walleyes. Float fishing is popular in some areas and not in others, but this method of bait presentation is effective no matter where walleyes are found. An overlooked way to catch more walleyes, floats are an essential part of the walleye game.

In the next chapter a couple big-water trolling tactics are outlined. Trolling diving planers and downriggers got its start in the Great Lakes, but anglers coast to coast can use these methods to take open-water walleyes.

CHAPTER 23

DIVERS AND DOWNRIGGERS

Downriggers and diving planers are fishing tools normally associated with salmon and trout fishing. Despite the fact that these fishing aids were designed for deep-water trout fishing, they are just as effective on walleyes.

This is especially true in the Great Lakes region where walleyes are frequently taken suspended in open water.

"At times this popular species favors deep water, frequently living 50, 60 or 70 feet below the surface," says Bruce DeShano of Riviera Downrigger Corp. "In some isolated cases walleyes have been taken from water as deep as 100 feet."

Downriggers and diving planers are the answer to deep-water fishing situations, yet use of these products is not limited to deep water. Both of these trolling aids are also beneficial for trolling the moderate depths ranging from 20-40 feet. Also, downriggers and divers aren't limited to the Great Lakes. These methods can be used to catch walleyes just about anywhere this species is found suspended in the water column.

How deep walleyes are likely to turn up is the important question. The answer lies in the types of forages available and the habitat requirements of these species.

Walleyes that feed on free-roaming schools of pelagic baitfish, such as smelt, alewives, shad, ciscoes and emerald shiners are forced to locate at the depth level these baitfish prefer. You could say that walleyes are prisoners to their food. Certain species of baitfish live in deep water, while others find the elements they need to survive higher up in the water column.

Smelt, alewives and ciscoes are temperature-sensitive fish that are forced to live in deep water most of the year. Shad and emerald shiners can tolerate the warmer water found near the surface. If a body of water has an abundance of shad or emerald shiners, walleyes can find all the food they need in the top 40 feet. However, if smelt, alewives or ciscoes are the primary forage, walleyes are certain to appear in deep water.

EQUIPMENT NEEDS

The idea of using downriggers and divers is foreign to many hard-core walleye anglers. After all, for most anglers walleye fishing is about jigs, rigs, light line and sensitive rods. Downrigger and

Bruce DeShano of Riviera Downrigger Corporation used a rigger to dredge up this deep-water walleye. Downriggers are the most accurate method of fishing spoons, spinners and crankbaits at depths below 40 feet.

Rods designed for fishing diving planers are considerably heavier and usually a little longer than downrigger rods. Large diving planers such as the Luhr Jensen Dipsy Diver generate a lot of drag in the water when trolled at 2-3 miles per hour. A stout rod is needed to take this abuse. These rods are usually 9 to 10 feet long to gain a little extra outward lure coverage. Smaller diving planers can be fished nicely using a standard downrigger rod.

As in other trolling presentations, lead length can be a critical element of success with downriggers and diving planers. Line-counter style reels are the only logical choice to match up with downrigger and diver rods. The same size and brand of reels outlined in Chapter 5 are suitable for these fishing presentations.

For most walleye trolling situations 10-pound test monofilament is considered the bench mark. With downriggers and divers however, somewhat heavier line is welcome. For downrigger fishing 12- to 17-pound test is an excellent choice. The same holds true for the smaller diving planers. When fishing the larger divers 17- to 25-pound test line is recommended.

Downrigger and diver fishing requires rods designed for the purpose. Fiberglass or fiberglass/graphite composite models are good choices.

diver fishing requires completely different kinds of rods, reels, lines and terminal tackle. The ways this gear is fished and the types of water targeted is also vastly different from what most walleye anglers would consider normal.

Downriggers and diving planers are specialized products that require the use of specialized rods, reels and lines. A number of manufacturers produce rods especially designed for downrigger fishing. A baitcasting style rod from 7 to 8-1/2 feet long with a medium or medium/light action is ideal.

Most downrigger rods are built from fiberglass or a fiberglass/graphite composite that delivers the ideal combination of strength and stiffness. These same rods double nicely as planer board rods.

Braided lines have a niche when fishing divers. The thin diameter of these lines enables anglers to reach deeper depths with shorter lead lengths.

The braided super lines enjoy a welcome niche in diver fishing, especially when fishing long lead lengths. The thin diameter of these lines creates less resistance in the water that allows the diver to achieve significantly deeper depths. Another benefit of braided lines is they have little stretch, making it easier to trip the diver when checking or resetting lines. Braided line sizes ranging from 20- to 40-pound test are best for fishing divers.

Several sizes and types of divers are suitable for walleyes. The most popular styles are round disks that feature a weight on the bottom that can be adjusted to make the diver run to the left or right of the boat. Directional divers are useful for fishing out away from the boat, but they don't provide as much outward coverage as planer boards.

The famous Luhr Jensen Dipsy Diver is the leader in this category. The Dipsy is available in three sizes including the Size O, 1 and Mini Dipsy.

The Size O and 1 Dipsy Divers feature a triggering mechanism that when set causes the device to dive, then release when a fish is hooked. The trigger amounts to a metal arm that is pressed into a plastic slot that uses a screw for adjusting the triggering tension.

The main line is attached to the arm, the arm is pressed into the slot and a leader with a spoon, spinner or stickbait is attached to the back of the diver. When placed in the water and trolled, water rushing against the face of the diver forces it down. The more trolling lead that's let out the deeper the diver will fish below the surface.

Obviously, larger divers can be used to fish deeper than smaller divers. A plastic ring can also be snapped onto the outside edge of the diver to increase surface area and cause the diver to achieve greater depths.

In addition to the popular Dipsy, some other useful products are also worth noting. A unique product called the Slide-Diver enables long leads to be fished with a diver. With most divers the lead length must be limited to the length of the rod.

The Slide-Diver works by threading the line through the trip arm and a hole in the middle of the diver. The lure is attached using a snap or swivel and the desired amount of lead length played out into the water. The trip arm is then set by folding it against the face of the diver. The line is held firmly in place while the diver is being trolled. When a fish strikes, the trip arm releases allowing the diver to slide down the line while the angler fights the fish.

Like the Dipsy, the Slide-Diver is weighted to make it directional and plastic rings can be added to increase the surface area of the diver. Produced in two different sizes, this new product is designed to function using monofilament lines.

A number of different divers are suitable for walleye fishing. These are among the most popular styles and brands.

The author feels that manual downriggers are adequate for the needs of most walleyes anglers. Here, he prepares to mount a manual unit with attached swivel base.

A downrigger is only as good as its weakest link. A quality downrigger line release is critical to this style of fishing. The author has enjoyed excellent success with these pinch-pad style releases.

Another diver that offers something unique is the Kastaway Diver. Instead of a trip arm that fits into a slot, the Kastaway Diver uses a magnet to hold the trip arm closed. If the diver is tripped by a fish, but the fish isn't hooked, the diver can be reset by simply giving some slack line. Like the Dipsy and Slide-Diver the Kastaway is available in several sizes, and is directional.

Diving disks are also available that are small enough to be used in combination with planer boards. The Big Jon Diver Disks come in two sizes, one that reaches a maximum depth of approximately 22 feet and a larger one that runs up to 38 feet when trolled on 10-pound test line. The Luhr Jensen Mini-Dipsy is similar to the largest size Big Jon Diver Disk.

The Luhr Jensen Jet Diver is another type of diver that, unlike other divers, floats at rest and dives like a crankbait when pulled. The smaller sizes of the Jet Diver are often used in combination with planer boards to take lures both down and out to the side. Larger Jet Divers are fished as flat lines. The Jet Diver is not a directional diver.

With the exception of the Slide-Diver all other divers require a short leader to be attached to the back of the diver. The lures used at the terminal end must have minimal drag in the water to allow the diver to function properly. Typically, trolling spoons, worm harnesses and stickbaits are the most commonly used lures behind divers.

When it comes to downriggers, anglers can choose from manual or electric models. Manual units require the angler to turn a handle to lower and raise the downrigger weights. Electric units take care of this function automatically.

Aside from the convenience of electric downriggers, both units accomplish the same goals. Manual units are recommended for anglers who expect to fish two downrigger lines. Anglers who plan to use four or more riggers are wise to invest in the convenience of electrics.

Only a handful of companies produce downriggers. Some of the most popular names include Riviera, Cannon, Walker, Penn, Scotty and Big Jon. Each of these companies produce both manual and electric models suitable for walleye fishing.

Downriggers generally aren't sold with weights. A 10-pound downrigger ball will need to be purchased for each rigger. It's also a good idea to purchase at least one extra downrigger weight and an extra cable termination kit should a weight become snagged on the bottom and lost.

A dependable line release will also need to be purchased for each downrigger. I recommend the pinch-pad style releases produced by Off Shore Tackle. The OR-4 Light Tension Downrigger Release was designed especially for the needs of big water walleye anglers.

USING DOWNRIGGERS

To the casual observer, a downrigger may seem like a lot of trouble to catch a few fish. Actually, downrigger fishing is easy to master and the ultimate in depth-control fishing. Only a few basic rules need to be followed to enjoy success with this technique of trolling.

The first step in fishing downriggers is to set the lure a desired distance behind the boat. Next attach the line into the pinch-pad line release. Place the line near the back of the rubber pads to insure the release has a firm grip on the line.

When lowering the downrigger weight to the desired depth, open the reel bail and engage the line clicker feature on the reel. The line clicker fea-

ture allows line to slip off the reel without causing a backlash.

When the downrigger weight reaches the desired depth, close the reel bail and reel up slack line until the rod bends over double. Place the rod in a conveniently located rod holder and you're ready to troll.

When a fish strikes, the resistance of the struggling fish sets the hook and pulls the line free of the release. If the tension setting on the line release is too light, fish that strike may not be hooked securely. To insure a solid hook set, the release tension must be firm.

Should a fish strike and the line not pop free of the release, the angler can easily trigger the release. Remove the rod from the holder and give a sharp upwards snap of the rod tip. This triggers the line release and picks up some of the slack line at the same time.

Often a walleye is hooked and doesn't trip the line release. If the anglers don't watch the rod tips closely for signs of a strike, fish may be dragged

A variety of trolling spoons are productive on walleyes. Small to medium-sized baits are the best producers.

along without knowing it. To avoid this, watch the rod tips closely for signs of a strike and check lines frequently to be sure a small fish hasn't been hooked.

All the common trolling lures may be used with downriggers, but spoons are among the most trusted lures. When fishing lightweight trolling spoons, relatively short lead lengths produce the best results. Leads ranging from 10-30 feet insure that the trailing spoon has the maximum amount of kick or wobble. If longer leads are used, the action of many spoons begins to go flat.

Heavy casting spoons such as the Luhr Jensen Krocodile or Acme Little Cleo are the exception to this rule. These spoons may be run on longer leads without sacrificing action.

A surprisingly small number of trolling spoons have become popular for walleyes. The Wolverine Silver Streak, Michigan Stinger, Pro Spoon, Northern King and Diamond King are the leaders in this arena.

Stickbaits, diving crankbaits and spinner harnesses are also useful lures for downrigger trolling. A few of the popular stickbaits include the Storm ThunderStick and ThunderStick Jr., Bomber Long A, Smithwick Rattlin' Rogues, Reef Runner Rip Stick, Bagley Bang-O-Lure, Excalibur Minnow and Rapala Husky Jerk.

These shallow diving lures are most often set 50 to 100 feet behind the downrigger weight. The extra lead length enables the bait to dive a few feet below the weight.

The same is true of diving crankbaits. When these lures are combined with downriggers they can be fished at depths much greater than their normal diving depth. Some of the most popular choices for Great Lakes trolling include the Bomber 25A, Storm Deep. ThunderStick Jr, Deep ThunderStick and Rattle Tot, Smithwick Deep Rogue, Reef Runner Deep Runner, Rapala Shad Rap series, Luhr Jensen Power Dive Minnow and Hot Lips, Mann's Stretch series and Cotton Cordell Wally Diver.

When using diving crankbaits the downrigger weight is set several feet above the level at which fish are being marked. The lures are then set using leads long enough to dive down to the depth at which walleyes are holding.

Snelled spinners also see lots of use with downriggers. But the spinners normally used on bottom bouncers aren't suited for serious downrigger trolling. Most spinner rigs are tied using two No. 4 single hooks. These hooks simply aren't up to the chore of hauling big fish from deep water.

Open-water trolling calls for harnesses tied using a single hook on the front and treble on the back, or two treble hooks. The treble hooks should be No. 6 or No. 4. Only a couple of manufacturers commercially produce such a harness. Walleye Stopper, Bait Rigs and Quick Change Systems each produce spinners designed with big-water trolling in mind.

In addition to offering treble hooks on the harness, these rigs also come with large Colorado

Stickbaits are another common lure used with downriggers. Often longer leads, out to 100 feet, are used with these baits.

blades. Fishing in deep water calls for more flash than can be generated with the small blades normally used on spinner rigs. Size 4, 5, 6, and 7 blades are the most productive in deep water. Indiana and willow leaf blades can also be used with good success.

When fishing these harnesses it's also important to use a quality ball bearing swivel to avoid problems with line twist. The extra dollar or two these swivels cost is minor compared to the problems line twist can cause in lost fishing time.

Downriggers are also frequently used to run more than one lure per line. Known as sliders and add-a-lines, this practice allows a second lure to be fished above the main line on a short leader.

Sliders are an easy way to add a second lure to a downrigger set-up. Simply take a 6-foot length of monofilament and attach a snap swivel to both ends. On one end attach a spoon, spinner or stickbait, then take the other snap and clip it over the main line. When the lure is tossed into the water it works its way down the main line.

The forward movement of the boat in the water causes a bow to form in the line between the rod tip and the downrigger release. The slider travels down the line until it reaches this bow. When a fish is hooked, the slider works its way down to the main lure.

Add-a-lines function in the same way except they are secured at a particular depth. Using a fixed add-a-line enables the angler to select the exact depth at which the lure will run and pro-

vides enough resistance that when fish strike they are hooked solidly.

To make an add-a-line take a 6-foot length of monofilament and tie a snap swivel on one end and add the desired lure. Next thread an Off Shore Tackle OR-12 planer board release onto the line using the hole at the end of the release. Finish the add-a-line by tying on a snap swivel at the other end.

Setting an add-a-line goes like this. After the main line is attached to the release on the downrigger weight, lower the weight approximately 10 feet into the water. Take the add-a-line and clip the free snap swivel over the main line, then open the OR-12 release and place the downrigger cable into the rubber pads. Toss the lure over the side and lower the downrigger weight to the desired depth.

The add-a-line is held in place on the downrigger cable at the desired distance above the main line. When a fish strikes, the release provides enough tension to insure a solid hook set. Normally an add-a-line is set to fish 5 or 10 feet above the main line.

A second rod can also be fished from a downrigger. To use a second rod a stacker release must be used. A stacker release is two downrigger-style releases connected together with a short and long length of plastic coated wire and a heavy snap.

Like the add-a-line, a stacker is set to fish 5 to 10 feet above the main line. Before a second rod and stacker can be set the main line has to be set. Once the lure on the main line is set the desired distance behind the boat and the line placed in the

Spinners used with downriggers are often heavy-duty models made from heavy monofilament or coated wire. Often these spinners are equipped with multiple blades or big blades.

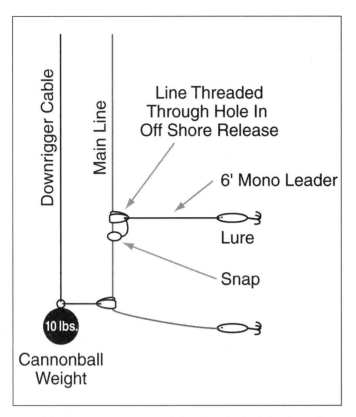

Downrigger Cable

Main Line

Line Threaded Through Hole In Off Shore Release

6' Mono Leader

Lure

Snap

10 lbs.

Cannonball Weight

An add-a-line works like a slider but the bait is pinned to a particular depth. Also the release on the add-a-line provides enough resistance that the hook set is improved.

release on the downrigger weight, lower the weight a few feet into the water.

Next take a second rod equipped with the desired lure and let out a lead that's either shorter or longer than the lead on the main line. If the leads on both rods are the same length, the chances of them tangling is greatly increased.

When the desired lead has been established for the second rod, take the stacker and clip the heavy snap over the downrigger cable. Open the release on the short wire and place the downrigger cable between the rubber jaws. Finish the stacker rigging by placing the line from the second rod into the release on the long wire lead.

The downrigger weight is then lowered to the desired depth. One rod is attached to the release on the downrigger weight and the second rod is connected to the stacker release. To use stacker releases a second rod holder must be added to the downrigger or nearby.

All this talk of sliders, stackers and add-a-lines is confusing and difficult to describe, but using these trolling aids is not difficult. The beauty of these downrigger accessories is they put more lures in the water. In most states up to two lures can be run on one line. However before using sliders, add-a-lines it's best to check with local fishing regulations.

Stacker releases such as these allow two rods to be fished from a single downrigger. The stacker is secured to the downrigger cable and positioned 5 to 10 feet above the main line.

USING DIVING PLANERS

Because there are so many different types of divers on the market, we'll divide them into two categories roughly described as disk-divers and full-sized divers. Disk-divers include the small divers that are often used to achieve modest depths in combination with planer boards. Full-sized divers are designed for deeper depths and are fished as flat lines.

In the big picture, disk-divers are the new kids on the block. Only in the last few years have these products made an impact on the walleye trolling game. The small size of these divers makes them ideal for fishing the top 30 feet of the water col-

Small disk divers are often used in combination with planer boards. Here an in-line planer, disk diver and crawler harness combined to take this fish.

umn. Because they have only a moderate pull in the water compared to full-sized divers these products can also be used nicely with 10- to 12-pound test line.

Matching these products up with planer boards is a great way to achieve the required depth and outward lure coverage. Both in-line boards and catamaran-style ski systems can be used to fish these divers. However, some in-line boards aren't suitable for this chore. The smaller in-line boards simply can't overcome the resistance these divers have in the water. The Off Shore Tackle Side-Planer is the ideal in-line board for fishing disk-divers.

Because of their modest size disk-divers are best suited to trolling spoons, small stickbaits and spinner rigs. These lures are fished on 6- to 8-foot leaders attached behind the diver.

The depth range of these divers and full-sized divers is determined by how much trolling lead is let out. The book *Precision Trolling* provides detailed depth diving information for all the popular disk and full-sized divers.

Full-sized divers are a different animal from disk-divers. These divers are much larger, dive deeper and require heavier tackle. These trolling aids are most often used as a supplement to planer board and downrigger fishing. Think of divers as the in-between lines set to cover the water between planer boards and downriggers.

Planer boards, diving planers and downriggers are used together to completely cover the water column from top to bottom. Imagine the water column as three equal parts. Planer boards are used to cover the upper third, divers the middle third and downriggers the bottom third.

The directional feature on most divers allows them to have a modest outward coverage. At the "0" setting the diver pulls straight down and achieves the maximum diving depth. At the "1", "2" and "3" settings the diver planes progressively more to the side, forgiving a little diving depth at each step in the process.

Actually the small amount of water coverage this directional feature provides is probably more important to separating lines and avoiding tangles than contacting or catching fish.

Like disk-divers, full-sized divers function best when used with lures that have modest drag in the water such as spoons, stickbaits and spinners. The lead length these lures are fished behind the diver should not exceed the rod length.

Both disk-divers and full-sized divers may be trolled at a wide range of speeds ranging from 1 to

3 miles per hour. Normally divers and downriggers are used during the summer months when warm water temperatures permit anglers to troll at the fast end of the speed spectrum. However, when fishing spinner rigs it's usually necessary to slow down a bit to prevent the line on the harnesses from twisting.

A trick I learned from a Lake Erie charter captain has made my diver fishing more productive. As with downriggers, sometimes it tough to tell when a fish has been hooked on a diver.

To deal with this situation, Ron Levitan the owner of R&D Sportfishing Charters watches the angle of the line going down into the water. When the diver is set, the line angles sharply down into the water. If a fish is hooked but doesn't trip the diver, the weight of the fish being dragged causes the line to swing back a little towards the back of the boat. This subtle but effective trick for detecting bites makes diver fishing a more productive adventure. With a little experience, it's easy to tell if a diver is dragging a fish.

Downriggers and divers aren't required to catch walleye in all bodies of water, just the deeper areas. In the Great Lakes these trolling aids bring in countless fish. In other areas they may not be used as often.

In the next chapter we'll examine how tournaments impact on the sport of fishing for walleye.

Full-sized divers are most often used on large boats such as this Sportcraft heading to fishing grounds on Lake Erie, but these trolling aids can be used on any size boat.

CHAPTER 24

TOURNAMENTS AND WALLEYE FISHING

Walleye fishing tournaments are one of those issues that most anglers either support completely or not at all. Unfortunately, tournaments often become a wedge separating sportfishing interests. On one side you have the fishing tackle

Tournament anglers live a love/hate situation. Many anglers love to fish these events, but in some cases local anglers hate to see tournaments held on their waters.

and marine manufacturers who support tournaments because they are a good vehicle for spotlighting products and new techniques that generate product sales. On the other side, there are lots of anglers who believe fishing should not be a competitive venture, but rather a recreational one.

Caught in the middle are those undecided soles who haven't formulated a clear decision one way or another. Perhaps the easiest way to evaluate tournaments and the controversy they create is to look at the facts of how tournaments are conducted.

It's a fact that tournament anglers purchase fishing licenses and are entitled to fish and keep a legal limit of fish just like other anglers. Tournament anglers must abide by all the laws of the state in which they are fishing. In most cases the fish kept for the weigh-in amount to less than the legal daily limit.

Organized tournaments must apply for special permits to hold events on public waters. Usually the local Fish and Game Department is responsible for monitoring tournaments including inspection of permits, the size and numbers of fish caught and those fish released.

Most of the fish caught at tournaments are released after being weighed. A small percentage of the fish brought to the scales die. These fish are normally cleaned and the meat donated to agencies such as senior citizen homes, soup kitchens and other community centers.

Some states don't allow major tournaments to be held on public waters during peak weekends. In these situations tournament anglers compete during the week when fishing pressure and traffic at boat launches is modest.

In some instances biologists from local Game and Fish Departments collect biological data at tournament sites by measuring and weighing fish, taking scale samples and installing jaw tags. On

forth at tournaments benefits walleye tournament anglers and recreational anglers alike.

In fairness to those who have specific problems with tournaments, not everything about these events is positive. The most common complaint stems from competition for fishing spots on prime weekends. Most tournaments are held on weekends when local anglers must compete with tournament anglers for a place to fish. To some, so many boats on the water ruins what might have otherwise been an enjoyable day of fishing.

The age old issue of jealousy also comes into play. Local anglers are often jealous of tournament anglers who roll into town with fancy boats and an attitude that sometimes suggests they know

Many tournaments require contestants to pay a conservation fee in addition to their entry fee. This money is used to support local stocking efforts, fish management plans and other worthy programs.

the Illinois River, the Masters Walleye Council tournament held each spring provides spawn laden walleyes and sauger that are stripped of their eggs and milt to raise more fish for an ongoing stocking program.

Some tournament circuits charge contestants a conservation fee in addition to their entry fee. Money raised through these conservation fees is used to support fish stocking efforts, maintain boat launches, fund fisheries research projects, sponsor youth fishing events and a wealth of other beneficial programs.

Most tournament anglers are eager to share their knowledge of a particular body of water with others. The fishing information passed back and

Most of the fish caught in tournaments are released alive. Those fish that do die are cleaned and donated to charity.

In Ohio the Game and Fish Department recently decided to kill all the walleyes caught during a major contest held on Lake Erie. In recent years the Lake Erie quota for sport harvested walleyes hasn't been met by local and non-resident anglers. Rather than release these fish caught using sport fishing methods, the officials in charge elected to kill the fish and donate the meat to charity. More than a few eyebrows were raised at this decision on both sides of the issue.

Some anglers also note that tournaments focus attention and ultimately fishing pressure on waters that might otherwise go unnoticed. After a tournament is held on a particular body of water, a significant increase in fishing pressure often follows.

Mike Norris of St. Charles, Illinois was the author's first tournament partner. Together they learned the walleye game from square one.

everything there is to know about fishing. Blame for this situation goes both ways.

In some rare cases, fish that are released as alive, later die and turn up on local beaches. Several years ago a major die-off occurred after a nationally sponsored tournament on a Great Lakes fishery. The weather was exceptionally hot, the water temperatures warm and to make matters worse a strong wind caused heavy seas. Many seriously stressed walleyes were brought into the weigh-in. Some of these marginal fish were released only to die later and drift up on beaches. Livid local anglers made an example of the situation creating a wealth of bad publicity in newspapers, television and radio.

Tournaments have given the author credibility and the background to write hundreds of magazine features on walleye fishing. Tournament experience has also helped pave the way for him to develop long-lasting relationships with a number of major tackle manufacturers.

Anglers armed with information gleaned from the tournament are well-equipped to go out and catch fish in areas they may never have fished before. This phenomenon is especially true of walleyes because this species is in such great demand.

For the most part, tournaments are positive activities that stimulate interest in fishing, foster sportsmanship and share angling information with tournament and non-competitive fans of walleyes alike.

I became involved in tournament fishing during the early 1980s because I was anxious to learn more about walleye fishing. At the time my home state of Michigan was becoming involved in a number of experimental walleye stocking efforts. The success of these reclamation efforts led to a series of fisheries management projects aimed at introducing walleyes in a variety of waters. These projects have become so successful that neighboring states are modeling similar programs.

My timing couldn't have been better. Not only did I learn more about walleyes and how to catch them, I got involved at a time when the fishing and marine industries were getting serious about developing products suited to walleye fishing.

For more than 10 years I fished nearly every tournament I could find. Along the way I traveled to just about everywhere walleyes are caught and fished using a wide variety of methods.

Despite that I no longer fish tournaments professionally, I continue to fish a few events each year to keep close to the action and make sure my edge remains sharp. For me the learning curve has never leveled out and I hope it never does.

IS COMPETITIVE FISHING FOR YOU?

From the outside looking in, competitive fishing is an exciting, appealing and glamorous occupation. The idea of traveling from community to community fishing for a living is a romantic passion that countless anglers dream about. Who wouldn't want to go fishing for a living?

Unfortunately, the glamorous light is clouded by reality that's more work-like than you might expect. A typical day of pre-fishing starts at 5 a.m. and lasts until 5 p.m. Most days are spent fishing alone because it's hard to find folks who can get time off during the week to fish. If you're lucky, the weather cooperates, but just as often wind, heavy seas, rain and cold make the experience uncomfortable at best and down right miserable at times.

Normally the first few days pre-fishing are spent running and gunning trying to check spots quickly in hopes of locating fish. Often it takes several days of fishing to develop a pattern and another day or two to refine these patterns.

At each event tournament anglers collect an enormous amount of information that pertains to the fishery. This information comes from bait shops, conservation officers, other anglers or just about anyone who will talk. The difficulty comes when it's time to decide what information is useful and what information amounts to a waste of time. Some tournament anglers are better at making these decisions than others.

After fishing a few days most tournament anglers get a sense for what's happening on the water. At the same time it starts to become clear whether this event will be one where it's a struggle to catch fish or a coveted tournament where success awaits.

No matter how skilled you are as an angler, there are days when stepping on stage is a painful admission of failure. In fact, there are more days when your tournament catch is average or below than there are days when the basket weighs heavy and a check rewards your work.

Weather and equipment failures are the primary concerns of a tournament angler. A change in weather frequently wipes the slate clean and nullifies several days of pre-fishing. If a critical piece of equipment such as a GPS unit or kicker motor fails at the worst moment, you have little choice but to play the hand as it was dealt.

The problem with tournament fishing is there are no excuses. When it's your turn to walk across the stage you either caught fish or you didn't.

To some anglers competitive fishing is like a drug. Once these individuals taste the excitement and fanfare that tournaments generate, the habit can be tough to kick. Sadly, I've witnessed a number of individuals take tournaments to the extreme. The results when anglers don't keep tournaments in perspective can be devastating. Divorce, financial ruin and lost friendships are just some of the fallout associated with tournament anglers who's desire to fish is not kept in check by common sense.

Tournaments are a form of gambling. You pay your entry fee and take your chances that in the end you'll come out ahead. As for coming out ahead financially, tournaments are no different than any other form of gambling. Most participants lose, so that a few can strike it rich.

Very few tournament anglers are actually professional fishermen. Anglers such as Ted Takasaki survive not by tournament winnings, but by conducting seminars, writing articles, producing videos and representing a select group of tackle and marine manufacturers.

It's safe to say that many anglers are addicted to tournament fishing, but the addiction is not always unhealthy. The love of fishing is a primary factor that attracts anglers to competitive fishing in the first place. Very few of the tournament anglers I've known have grown tired of fishing as the years pass. Fishing with these men and women is a passion that grows with each passing year.

Like other competitive sports, the road to the top is a long and winding route. Only a select few ever achieve any notoriety as a walleye angler. Ironically, it's not raw fishing talent or the checks cashed at tournaments that enables these select few to survive and thrive. It's business skills and the ability to help manufacturers market their

products. Most anglers don't realize that the leading walleye tournament pros rarely win enough money per year to pay their expenses, let alone enough to live on.

This fact alone is what separates the run-of-the-mill tournament angler from those exceptional individuals who can be called professional anglers. Professional anglers have the skills required to teach fishing and communicate their knowledge in a friendly and interesting way. These are the individuals you see doing seminars at the major outdoor shows or in-store promotions at popular sporting goods outlets.

Professional anglers become acquainted and work frequently with the most successful outdoor writers. As a result, they are often quoted in articles that appear in fishing magazines, newspapers and books. Professional anglers also frequently turn up on outdoor television programs and radio call-in shows to share their knowledge. It's little wonder that marine and fishing tackle manufacturers seek out these individuals to help promote and market their products.

The wealth of fishing knowledge professional fishermen have to offer is staggering. The average tournament angler, on the other hand, is not as valuable a commodity to the fishing industry.

UNDERSTANDING SPONSORS

It doesn't take long to discover that it's difficult to win enough money in tournaments to support a career as a professional angler. Simply breaking even is a major accomplishment. Sponsors and the cash and or product they provide in exchange for becoming a spokesperson is the logical way that anglers attack the financial struggle to survive.

"Unfortunately, there are far more tournament anglers interested in sponsorships than promotional dollars available within the fishing and marine industries," says Bruce DeShano owner of Off Shore Tackle Company. "This classic supply and demand situation enables manufacturers to be picky as to who they select to represent them in the public eye. The same environment also creates a situation where the wages willing to be paid are modest."

Manufacturers simply can't justify the salary it takes to be the sole support of a professional angler. Therefore, most pros align themselves with several non-competitive companies. In other words, you can't represent Lund and Tracker at the same time, but you can represent Tracker and

It's better to have a small but loyal group of sponsors, than to have a relationship with lots of manufacturers who feel your value is diluted.

Storm Lures because these companies do not compete with one another.

Attracting several sponsors is how professional anglers parlay enough cash to pay entry fees, travel and other related expenses. Obviously the more companies an angler represents the more money that can be made. However, a point is quickly reached where the time commitment made to each company begins to suffer.

Sometimes less is more. It's better to have a small group of loyal sponsors than a relationship with lots of manufacturers that feel your value is diluted.

The manufacturers who are approached by tournament anglers the most include those who produce boats, outboard motors, props, electric

motors, terminal tackle, electronics, rods, reels, scent products and tackle boxes. These bread and butter items are an important part of any tournament angler's core of sponsors.

Outside of these traditional sponsors the sky is the limit. Companies that don't produce fishing or marine goods, but who's products are often used by anglers and boaters are good candidates. This list could include but is not limited to, motel and gasoline chains, soft drinks, tobacco companies, car manufacturers, candy, snacks, bottled water, batteries and a wealth of other products.

Making contact with perspective sponsors and selling them on your value as a professional angler is the tough part. As mentioned, many of the major

Mike Brendenhall and his partner Todd Conner were able to negotiate a nice sponsorship with a spring water company. Non-industry sponsors are an area where a select group of professional fishermen can find financial reward.

fishing and marine manufacturers are hit with dozens of requests for pro-staff positions daily.

Developing a resume is a good place to start. This resume doesn't need to be long, but it should highlight some personal information, the types and number of tournaments fished, successes achieved, how many seminars are conducted annually and how your skills as a professional angler can benefit the sponsor. Make sure to include a good quality photograph with the resume.

Call the prospective sponsor and try to determine exactly to whom the resume should be forwarded. Large companies such as Zebco have full-time staff members who select pro-staffers and coordinate their field activities. Smaller companies often pass this responsibility on to a staff member working in the marketing department.

After forwarding your resume to the person most likely to be given the job of reviewing it, place a call and introduce yourself. Keep the call short and offer your services in a friendly and sincere manner. Getting the door open far enough to prove yourself may take a little creativity.

When I first started as a tournament fisherman, I offered to work sports shows for various manufacturers free of charge as a sign of good faith. My goal was simply to establish a relationship and show off my communication skills and work ethics.

In-store promotions are another good way to prove to a potential sponsor your willingness to work hard and understanding of how promotions are conducted. In-store promotions not only provide a link to manufactures and their efforts to sell products, they involve the pro staffer with retailers who are the middlemen in the fishing tackle business.

Try sharing a favorite fishing presentation with an outdoor writer. Work together to build a feature story around a particular method of catching walleyes. When the article comes out, send a tear sheet to manufacturers who's products were mentioned as part of the article.

If you're handy at writing, pen a short feature about walleye fishing and submit it to a local or regional outdoor newspaper. When the piece is published, be sure to send tear sheets immediately to manufacturers mentioned in the copy or who's products appear in the photographs.

"The biggest mistake most tournament anglers make when approaching sponsors is not having something to offer," says DeShano. "Don't open the conversation by saying you've won this or that tournament. Concentrate on finding ways that you can help the manufacturer expose and sell more product."

Landing sponsors is about the beneficial services you have to offer, not how many patches are on your shirt or the stickers in the windows of your truck.

TRENDS IN TOURNAMENTS

The trend in tournament fishing is towards pro-am events where a professional angler pairs up with an amateur. At the end of the day, both anglers share the weight caught. The pro provides the equipment and makes the decisions. The amateur benefits from the experience of the pro.

A win/win situation for everyone, pro-am events are becoming popular wherever walleye tournaments are held. Unfortunately, pro-am events are expensive with entry fees that range up to $1,000 for the pro and $500 for the amateur. Pro-am events are not a good place for a young tournament angler to break into the business.

Team events are the logical place to cut your teeth on fishing tournaments. In a team event two anglers split a modest entry fee. During the practice period each angler normally fishes from his or her own boat to cover more water. During the tournament both anglers fish together in one boat and combine their daily weight.

Most team events are two-day tournaments, but a few last just one day. Entry fees on these events normally run from $100 to $300.

The nice thing about team events is you have someone in the boat to bounce ideas off of. During any tournament there are times when decisions have to be made and it's always easier to make these decisions when two anglers share the burden. In a pro-am, the pro has no one to brainstorm with and decisions can become much more difficult to make. Also, when you make the wrong decision, there's no one to share the blame.

A number of excellent tournament circuits are available for those who are interested in taking the plunge. My advice is to start with small club tournaments, move up to state team events, then national team events and eventually pro-am events.

Also, anyone serious about tournament fishing should consider joining the National Professional Anglers Association. Based out of Pierre, South Dakota the NPAA was formed by a dedicated group of professional walleye anglers whose vision is to raise the level of professional conduct and ethics among all tournament anglers. The NPAA offers three membership categories including Associate, Registered and Professional. For details write NPAA, POB 7048, Pierre, SD 57501 or call 605-223-2136.

A WORD ON TOURNAMENT ETHICS

The driving spirit of competition is not always a good thing. When the desire to succeed outweighs the rules of sportsmanship, tournaments sometimes explode into bitter debates. I've seen anglers on the verge of a fist fight because one angler moved in on the spot another was fishing.

Having ethics is a lot like having a conscience. The difference between right and wrong is in most cases as clear as black and white. Those who are honest with themselves normally have no problem telling the difference between right and wrong.

Making ethical decisions on the water is simply a matter of treating other anglers as you would like to be treated yourself. In life, in church or in tournament fishing the same simple rules apply.

Despite these cut-and-dried facts regarding ethics, disputes at tournaments are common. Many of the problems stem from the fact that walleyes are gregarious fish that are often found in sprawling schools. It's not uncommon for several tournament boats to fish over the same school of fish.

If the fish are spread out and the fishing is good, a number of boats can work an area with few problems. However, the tougher the fishing becomes the more likely you'll find anglers playing bumper boats and casting angry glances. Human nature such as it is, contestants tend to concentrate on the areas that are producing the best results, even if this means crowding.

Now the stage is set for some serious disputes. Piling too many tournament boats into a small space is like watching a busy night at the drunk tank in a local police station. Sooner or later, something will happen and words will be exchanged.

The solution to this problem is simply to leave the area, but that also would mean leaving an area where fish are being caught. It's easy to see why conflicts occur.

Unfortunately, money is the fuel that makes these disputes burn brighter. Larger events with significant cash tend to generate some of the most outrageous disputes. Unfortunately, the level of ethics shown doesn't necessarily rise with the level of competition.

Keeping a cool head and plenty of space between boats is the best way to avoid disputes on the water.

SUMMING IT UP

I have mixed feelings about tournaments, but mostly I believe they are a beneficial part of sportfishing. When conducted in a professional manner, there's no better way to learn the sport of walleye fishing than by competing against anglers who take the sport seriously. Tournament fishing is also a great vehicle for exposing fishing products and to help communities show off their fishing resources.

Like any sport, competitive fishing is a good thing so long as the contestants play by the rules. For those anglers who aren't sold on tournament fishing, that's fine, too. That's the great thing about fishing for walleyes, tournament experience is not a prerequisite.

In the next chapter some of the nation's leading experts on walleye fishing share their tips on finding and catching more fish.

CHAPTER 25

SECRETS OF THE PROS

Professional anglers spend countless hours on the water developing new products, honing fishing skills and refining presentations. The desire these men and women have to catch more and bigger walleyes drives them to become efficient in every aspect of the sport.

In the case of the individuals who have shared tips and techniques in this book, walleye fishing is not just a matter of life or death; it's more important than that. Walleye fishing is a passion that these anglers can't satisfy.

Like any pursuit, the learning curve in walleye fishing begins with a steep incline. At first there's lots to learn. Anglers must start by building a foundation of knowledge rooted firmly in the basics.

Learning the lure types and where they are most useful, becoming familiar with the types of rods and reels used in walleye fishing, developing skills for locating fish and practicing boat control skills are just some of the topics anglers focus on early in the game. Gradually as an angler's knowledge, experience and skill levels improve the learning curve starts to level out.

Professional anglers are always pushing to raise the bar and keep the learning curve moving upwards. Even though these individuals are at the top of their field, most are not satisfied to simply reap the benefits of what they have learned.

The desire to learn more and become better never ends. People are motivated for a lot of reasons. In the case of professional anglers, the promise of fame and fortune are strong motivational forces. Who wouldn't want to be a famous and successful angler?

Despite this obvious appetite for recognition, it's not greed or vanity that drives people to fish 200 or more days a year. A more pure form of motivation keeps professional anglers coming back for more. Love of fishing and the desire to share their knowledge with others is why these anglers work to obsession.

The basics of walleye fishing can be learned in amazingly little time. Books, videos, magazines and television programs all speed up the learning process. However, once an angler masters the basics, it's the details and fine points that can take a lifetime to master. Those who love walleye fishing wouldn't have it any other way.

SPINNERS ON THE SURFACE

Bruce DeShano is a touring professional on the In-Fisherman Professional Walleye Trail and the

Bruce DeShano is a top PWT pro and owner of Off Shore Tackle Company which produces some of the leading trolling hardware designed for walleye fishing.

owner of both Off Shore Tackle and Riviera Downrigger Company. A master at the art of trolling, Bruce has spent an entire career developing and refining fishing tackle. Just some of the trolling aids Bruce has built and marketed include various pinch-pad line releases, dual planer boards, in-line planer boards, in-line trolling weights, planer board masts, stacker releases and many other items.

"My favorite way to fish walleyes is by trolling spinners near the surface," admits DeShano. "The most overlooked trolling bite takes place right under our noses. Walleyes frequently feed on the surface. Because fish this high in the water column aren't readily marked on the graph, anglers don't realize the fish are there."

When fishing spinners or other lures near the surface, planer boards are critical to trolling suc-

Dr. Steve Holt is the co-author of *Precision Trolling* and *Precision Casting* and the tournament partner of the author.

cess. Not only do boards spread out lures to increase trolling coverage, they reach out to encounter fish undisturbed by the passing boat.

"Snap Weights are in-line trolling weights that are a popular tool for presenting spinners and other shallow-running lures below the surface," says DeShano. "The hidden value of these unique trolling sinkers is that they allow the weight to be placed well away from the lure. Separating the bait and weight allows spinners and other lures to run at a more consistent depth."

Most anglers use light Snap Weights when fishing near the surface. The 50/50 rigging system is often employed with the spinner set 50 feet behind the boat then a Snap Weight placed on the line and 50 more feet of lead let out.

"The 50/50 system works well, but at spinner speeds even light 1/2- or 3/4-ounce Snap Weights can run too deep to catch walleyes feeding right on the surface," explains DeShano. "Instead of using the 50/50 system I let my spinner out 100 feet behind the boat, then pinch on a rather heavy 2-ounce Snap Weight. A Side-Planer in-line board is attached to the line either 5, 7 or 10 feet behind the Snap Weight."

The heavy Snap Weight runs at a steep angle down into the water, making it easier to control the depth level of the trailing spinner. The leader can be shortened to 50 feet to add even more control over this presentation for making tight turns on small schools of fish.

THE WHEEL AND DEAL

Dr. Steve Holt is a tournament pro and co-author of the books *Precision Trolling* and *Precision Casting*. Trolling crankbaits is one of Steve's favorite ways to fish for walleyes.

"When trolling it's common to encounter small pods of walleyes," says Holt. "Most anglers troll through these fish, hook one and then make a wide turn before coming back through the area for another pass. The wide turn is made to prevent tangling lines. Unfortunately, many of these schools are so small the boat must be trolled back into exactly the same area to trigger additional strikes."

The time it takes to make a wide turn is suffered in lost fishing minutes. Also, once the boat has been turned in a wide arc it's hard to navigate the boat precisely back to the spot holding fish.

"The best way to get the boat into position quickly and accurately is to pull the lines from one

Mark Brumbaugh is a past PWT Champion and one of the leading minds in walleye fishing.

STRIKE-TRIGGERING LURES

Mark Brumbaugh is a past Professional Walleye Trail Champion and one of the leading money winners on the pro circuit. A resident of Ohio, Mark frequently fishes in Lake Erie where he finds deepwater walleyes that aren't always willing to bite.

"When I mark fish but I can't make them bite a crankbait, spinner or jig, I'll tie on a blade bait and make short drifts through the fish," suggests Brumbaugh. "If the water is calm an electric motor is used to slowly drag the boat along while I fish a blade bait by letting it free fall to bottom then jigging it up a few feet off bottom."

Of the many blade baits on the market Mark favors the Reef Runner Cicada because this lure

Todd Conners is a Michigan Walleye Tour Champion and a top stick on the MWC circuit.

side of the boat, then spin the boat quickly and head directly back into the fish," advises Holt. "Save an icon on the GPS unit for reference and reset the lines as quickly as possible. When resetting the lines use shorter leads so that the boat can be turned sharply without fear of tangles."

Using a loose figure eight as a trolling route, circle the area making short and very precise trolling runs.

"I also like to speed up when wheeling and dealing," says Holt. "Often these schools of fish are actively feeding. Trolling faster simply increases the number of times your lures can be run through the school before the fish spook or move off."

features a cupped body that vibrates even when jigged slowly.

"I believe that blade baits are triggering lures, explains Brumbaugh. "Perhaps it's the vibration, the flash or the darting action that walleyes like, but I'm convinced that these baits stimulate strikes when other lures don't."

The water can be cold or warm when fishing blade baits. Water temperature doesn't seem to matter, but in cold water it usually works better to fish the lure slowly. In warm water, experiment with progressively more aggressive jigging strokes.

TUBE-TYPE ROD HOLDERS

In a walleye boat there never seems to be enough room. Rods that get laid down on the deck quickly tangle with other rods and run the risk of getting broken. Putting the rods away in the rod locker isn't practical when simply running from one fishing site to another.

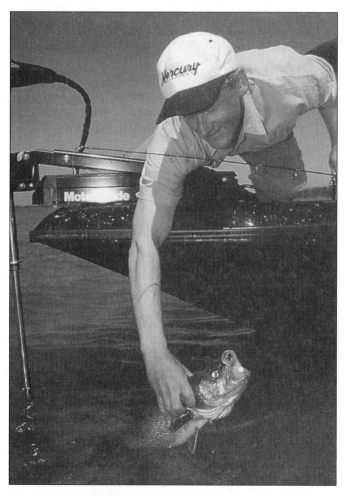

Jon Bondy catches more walleyes in April than most anglers do in several seasons. A guide on the Detroit River, Bondy is an expert river fisherman.

Todd Conner is a past Michigan Walleye Tour Champion who uses tube-type rod holders mounted at strategic spots in his boat. "Vertical rod tubes are ideal for storing rods while running from one location to another," says Conner. "Rods stay organized, tangle-free and are safe from being stepped on."

Conner recommends a series of four or six vertical rod tubes positioned along the back of the boat. "When tube type rod holders are mounted at the back of the boat, they serve double duty as holders when running from one spot to another and they can also be used as rod holders when fishing planer boards."

RIVER JIGGING TRICKS

Jon Bondy is a Canadian guide and tournament angler who specializes in spring walleye trips on the Detroit River. Sometimes it's the little things that can make a big difference in fishing success.

"Keeping bait on the hook is one of the biggest problems when jigging for river walleyes," says Bondy. "It's critical to use lively minnows when jigging early in the season. To keep the bait wiggling the minnow must be hooked lightly through both lips. Unfortunately, the constant up and down movement of the jig tears a hole and allows the hook to back out."

When using heavy jigs and fishing in deep water it's hard to tell if the minnow falls off. Some anglers simply reel up and check their bait every couple of minutes, but Bondy has a better solution.

"After I hook a minnow through both lips, I take a small waffer of plastic from a grub tail and press the plastic over the hook point and past the barb," says Bondy. "The plastic acts like a washer preventing the hook from backing out and insuring that bait is on the hook even while jigging aggressively."

Walleye Stopper Lures produces a product known as Bait Bumpers specially designed to help keep bait on a jig. In a pinch take a pair of scissors and cut small pieces from the body of a plastic grub.

Early in the season Bondy uses live minnows on a plain jig head, but after the spawn is done he feels using minnows is unnecessary. "After the spawn walleyes are aggressive and will readily hit a jig tipped with plastic," comments Bondy. "Most anglers use twister tails, but I've had better luck using a small plastic worm threaded onto the jig. I jig using an aggressive pop of the rod tip that lifts

Rick LaCourse is a past PWT Champion and a trolling specialist.

the jig off bottom. As the jig is falling, I catch the jig and lower it back to bottom on a tight line."

A fairly stiff rod and 6-pound test monofilament works best for this style of jigging. Most anglers use spinning tackle, but Bondy feels a baitcasting outfit produces less line twist problems.

If line twist becomes a problem, Bondy recommends tying a small barrel swivel in-line about 12 inches above the jig.

BOARD TROLLING AFTER DARK

Trolling after dark has long been a method for taking monster walleyes. Most anglers troll using an electric motor and fish crankbaits on flatlines out the back of the boat.

Rick LaCourse a past Professional Walleye Trail Champion takes a different approach. "Wall-

eyes that may be living in the weeds or tucked up tight to the bottom during the daytime, prowl open water at night," says LaCourse. "The cover of darkness enables these fish to hunt for minnows near the surface, along shore or anywhere they can find an easy meal."

LaCourse fishes after dark primarily with shallow diving stickbaits such as the Smithwick Super Rogue, Rebel Minnow and Excalibur Minnow. Instead of fishing these baits on flat lines he uses in-line planer boards to gain more trolling coverage and to reduce the chances of tangles when fishing multiple lines.

"Planer boards work great after dark, but you have to be able to see your boards to know when a fish has been hooked," says LaCourse. "I use small flashing lights called Night Lights produced by Off Shore Tackle that clip onto the board's flag. These blinking lights allow me to easily see my boards even on the darkest nights."

LaCourse rigs his boat for night fishing comfort. Flood lights are mounted at strategic loca-

Mike McClelland is a member of the Fresh Water Fishing Hall of Fame and one of the leading money winners on the walleye tournament trail.

tions so he has plenty of light to tie on lures or land fish. When trolling he turns the lights off and fishes using only a small bow and stern light.

"It's important to keep your boat clutter free and organized when fishing after dark," advises LaCourse. "A crankbait left laying on the deck is almost sure to get stepped on, caught in the net or otherwise cause problems. Items like pliers should be stored in a specific spot and put back after being used. Only have out the rods you are actually fishing with to reduce clutter in the boat."

SELECTING BLADES FOR SPINNER RIGS

Mike McClelland has been fishing walleyes as long as he can remember. One of the leading money winners on the Professional Walleye Trail, Mike was inducted into the Fresh Water Fishing Hall of Fame for his significant contributions to the sportfishing industry.

"I enjoy fishing spinners for walleyes," says McClelland. "Day-in and day-out it's hard to beat a bottom bouncer armed with a spinner for both locating and catching walleyes."

Keith Kavajecz is a past NAWA Angler-of-the-Year and threat to win any tournament.

The size, color and shape of the blades used on these spinner rigs can make a big difference in how walleyes respond to them. Also some blades function better at slower speeds, while others can be trolled faster with good success.

"The major blade styles are Colorado, Indiana and willow," states McClelland. "Of these blades Colorado spin at the slowest speeds and are usually the best option for most situations. Indiana blades also spin easily, but offer a slightly different look and vibration than Colorado blades. Willow blades spin at an acute angle to the leader and must be pulled rather quickly to get good blade rotation."

Blades used for walleye fishing range in size from No. 1 to no. 7.

"I like to use small blades when walleyes are inactive and progressively larger blades on active fish," recommends McClelland. "Because I change blades frequently, I use a Quick Change clevis that allows blades to be snapped on and off the harness in seconds. Many harnesses produced by the major tackle manufacturers feature the Quick Change clevis. These clevises can also be purchased as components and used to tie custom made spinners."

Blade color is another concern when fishing spinners. Metallic finishes such as nickel, silver plate, brass, palladium, copper and gold plate are some of the best finishes in clear water. McClelland recommends using brightly painted blades in waters that range from murky to muddy.

NETTING FISH

More walleyes are lost at the net than any other time during the fight. Keith Kavajecz is a tournament pro whose living depends on successfully landing walleyes.

"The problem with landing fish is everyone involved is excited and on edge," says Kavajecz. The angler fighting the fish is pumped and sometimes puts too much pressure on the fish. The person running the net is full of anxiety that can cause him or her to stab at a fish before it's ready to be netted."

Landing a walleye is a team effort. Both members of the team need to communicate so no confusion occurs at the moment of truth. The angler fighting the fish should be calling the play by play, so the net man knows where the fish is located, how big it might be, when the fish is getting close and when the fish can be felt getting tired.

"If you're trolling when a fish is hooked, take the boat out of gear after the fish is hooked solidly and coming towards the boat," advises Kavajecz. "Taking the boat out of gear reduces the amount of pressure on the fish and helps to keep the walleye down in the water. If the boat continues to move forward, the fish is often forced to the surface where it can thrash around outside of net range and tear free."

It's also important not to pump a fish when fighting it. "Most anglers make a serious mistake when fighting walleyes," says Kavajecz. "They fight the fish by pulling the rod and fish towards the boat. When the rod has been pulled back to the 11 or 12 o'clock position, they are forced to drop the tip back towards the fish to get more leverage. Pumping the rod for any reason is asking to lose the fish. Hold the rod up and reel slowly and smoothly. The trick is to maintain steady pressure on the fish."

Trying to net a walleye that isn't ready is another leading cause of losing fish.

"A walleye can only be netted effectively when the fish is being led head-first into the net," cautions Kavajecz. "The net man should be posi-

tioned in front of the angler where he can see the fish clearly and remain at ready. Usually when a fish sees the boat for the first time it will turn and make a strong run."

Don't try to prevent the fish from making a run. Let the fish wear itself out. Eventually the angler should be able to feel the fish getting tired.

"When the fish is exhausted, the angler has to let the net man know to get ready," says Kavajecz. "The angler leads the fish to a spot where the net man can easily get at it. The moment the fish hits the surface the net man scoops up the fish in one smooth motion."

Long handle nets are a real advantage. It also helps to have a net with a large hoop and to try to lead the fish to a corner of the boat if possible.

When fishing in rough seas it may be necessary to put the boat in reverse to take off some of the strain on the fish. This trick enables the angler to gain line without putting too much stress on the line, lure or fish.

PICKING IN-LINE PLANER BOARDS

Gary Parsons is a tournament professional, book author, popular seminar speaker and host of the *Outdoor World* television series. In addition, Parsons is a pioneer in the use and design of in-line planer boards.

"In the past decade the market has been flooded with new in-line planer boards," says Parsons. "These mini-skis are valuable tools for trolling, but not all boards have the features required to make them excellent products for walleye fishing."

Ballast is a critical factor of in-line boards used for walleye trolling. Because walleyes are often fished using slow trolling speeds, boards must be weighted to ride upright in the water. A board that's weighted properly has bite in the water and will track to the side better. Also, boards with ballast are less likely to roll or dive when fishing in heavy seas.

"In addition to ballast, an in-line planer board should be easy to put on and take off the line," says Parsons. "The Side-Planer board produced by Off Shore Tackle is among the easiest boards to use. A pinch-pad style line release is mounted on the tow arm and at the back of the board. To put the board on the line the angler only needs to pinch open these clips and place the line between the rubber jaws. These same clips make it easy to remove the board when fighting fish."

Because in-line boards are often used in rough water conditions, it helps to have a board equipped

Gary Parsons is a two-time PWT Angler-of-the-Year and trolling pioneer.

with a brightly colored flag. A flag may seem like a minor accessory, but they make it much easier to keep track of the boards while trolling.

"The size of an in-line board is another consideration," says Parsons. "In-line boards range widely in size. Small boards are limited in the amount of weight they can handle. The larger

Ted Takasaki is the 1998 PWT Champion, a past Top Gun award winner and a live-bait fishing specialist.

models are best equipped to handle various trolling gear such as in-line weights, Snap Weights, deep-diving crankbaits and lead-core line."

SIX STEPS TO JIGGING SUCCESS

Ted Takasaki is the 1998 Pro Walleye Trail Champion, a past PWT Top Gun and one of the leading personalities on the pro circuit. A confessed jig fishing fanatic, Takasaki's strategy for using jigs can help anyone become a more successful walleye angler.

"The first step and golden rule in jig fishing is to always use enough weight to maintain contact with the bottom," says Takasaki. "I tell folks to select jigs that are heavy enough to easily feel the bottom. If you can't readily feel the bottom chances are the jig isn't on the bottom."

Where jigs are the most beneficial depends on how fish are relating to bottom structure. "Jigging works best when fish are concentrated in select

spots, such as the tip of a point, rock pile, weed edges or other features," advises Takasaki. "Flats or other places where fish are usually scattered are better fished using other methods."

Selecting the jig style that suits the situation is also an important aspect of walleye fishing. "I use hydrodynamic jigs when fishing in strong current. The Jumbo Fuzz-E-Grub is shaped to help it cut through the water and maintain contact with bottom. Jigs that are pointed and have the eye coming out the front of the jig are excellent for casting into weed cover. Round-head jigs are a good choice for casting and vertical jigging in rivers. Propeller-style jigs such as the Lindy Hummer are a good choice for casting and swimming jigs along bottom."

Anglers should also concentrate on varying the action of the jig. "Most anglers only use one jigging motion," explains Takasaki. "I like to start with an aggressive jigging style, then if that doesn't produce I'll slow down and try more subtle actions. Spend some time experimenting with the jig by hopping, swimming and dragging it along bottom."

Varying the color of the jig and grub body can help refine jigging even further. "I depend on brightly colored jigs when fishing in dingy water," said Takasaki. "Fluorescent colors such as chartreuse, orange, green, red or pink and combinations of these are good choices when water clarity is limited. In clear water, dark colors and natural shades are the way to go."

The same applies to grub bodies. A brightly colored grub body makes a jig more visible in dirty water. Adding a grub also makes the jig more buoyant and slows down the rate at which the lure will sink.

The last rule of jig fishing is to always keep hooks sharp and use healthy live bait. "Much of the time jigs are in contact with rocks, sand, gravel and boulders," warns Takasaki. "A file should be standard equipment for all jig fishermen. Keep a close watch on the tip of the hook and file it as needed to maintain a needle-like point."

Live bait is a component of jig fishing that shouldn't be taken lightly. "Many times I've seen live bait make the difference between getting bites and getting skunked," says Takasaki. "Sometimes one type of bait such as leeches or minnows will work better than another. Generally, I feel that minnows are best in the spring and fall, leeches work good during the summer months and nightcrawlers catch walleyes at all times of year."

In the next chapter we'll take a different approach to walleye fishing. Most walleyes are caught with the help of a boat, but fishing from shore can be a productive way to catch more walleyes.

CHAPTER 26

STUCK ON SHORE

Throughout my youth, college days and young adult life, fishing was a pursuit conducted from shore. Hardly a lake, stream, dock or pier was safe from my appetite for fish and fishing adventure. My rod, tackle box and a pair of waders had a permanent home in my truck. Like most anglers, I started fishing from shore through necessity. As my skill levels increased, I discovered that fishing from the bank didn't have to be a handicap. In fact, shore fishing is an excellent way to target walleyes in a wealth of situations.

I was 22 years old when I purchased my first boat. Though modest, it did have an outboard motor, swivel seats, a livewell, electric motor and sonar. Compared to the boat I currently own, this first introduction in the world of boating didn't turn heads. Over the past 15 years I've owned many boats and frankly lost track of my shore fishing roots. It wasn't until my own sons grew large enough to develop an interest in fishing that shore fishing found its way back into my life.

Few things are more perfectly matched than kids and fishing. I'm a firm believer that anyone introduced to fishing at a young age will never completely grow up. There's something magical about fishing that stirs the soul of those who are young and young-at-heart.

As this copy is being written, my boys, Zackery and Jacob, are 6 and 4, respectively. Their first experiences with fishing came at a trout pond in a sport show. Next they graduated to farm ponds full of panfish and not long ago both boys caught their first walleyes in a northern Michigan lake.

While the boys are still young I plan to spend as much time as possible fishing with them from shore. The lessons I learned as a young angler prowling around every pond, lake and stream with a fishing rod strapped to my bike have served me well in adult life. Many of those lessons had little to do with fishing. Suffice to say that there are much worse things for a young boy or girl to be doing than fishing and enjoying the outdoors.

Fishing from the shore is the ideal way to introduce children to our sport and build a lifelong love affair with the natural world. Despite the fact that I own a beautiful and fully rigged walleye fishing boat, I have chosen to introduce my kids to fishing using a more simple environment. Kids, like many of us, have a terrible trait of not appreciating things that come too easily.

This weakness of human nature has me convinced it's best to let my kids appreciate the virtues of shore fishing before moving on to the

The author's oldest son, Zackery, has helped his dad regain the fun and pleasure of bank fishing. Most anglers start their angling careers fishing from shore and some never leave these roots.

This young man could be riding off to worse places than a favorite fishing hole.

adventures of fishing from a boat. Fortunately, my wife, Mari, and I are having no problems introducing this learn-from-the-basics strategy. Like most kids, our boys don't care where or how they fish.

Another reason I've selected shore fishing as a foundation for the boys' fishing careers, relates to the experiences a kid can have on shore. Patience is a small commodity with kids. Fishing from shore allows them to take breaks from the main attraction to explore the shoreline, throw stones, catch frogs, climb trees and get involved in a dozen other activities. None of these diversions are possible in the cramped quarters of a fishing boat.

When a kid gets bored in a fishing boat, it's time to cut the trip short or risk turning the child off to fishing completely. From a selfish point of view, fishing from shore allows me to continue wetting a line even after the boys get bored and move on to other activities. The rules are simple. Life vests are mandatory where deep water is

located close to shore. When not actually fishing the boys can amuse themselves along the shore, so long as they are within sight of mom or dad.

What might have been an hour-long fishing trip in a boat, turns into a half- or all-day adventure on shore. Mix in a few sandwiches, some cold pop and snacks and you've got the makings of a great day outdoors.

Both kids and adults enjoy fishing from shore, but to be honest most anglers don't target walleyes. Given the proper equipment and knowledge, fishing from shore can be a very productive way to catch walleyes. In fact, in some situations fishing from the bank can be more productive than having access to a boat.

SHORE FISHING RIVERS

Rivers are a great place to shore fish for walleyes. The prime times of the year are early in the spring when spawning fish fill the rivers and again during the late fall when fish attracted by rising currents and abundant baitfish pile into these flowing waters to put on the feed bag.

Rivers are productive places to fish from shore in spring and fall. Some rivers such as the Mississippi offer good fishing all year.

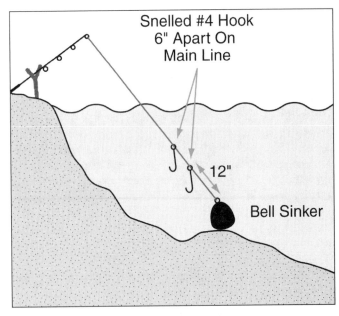

Snelled #4 Hook
6" Apart On
Main Line

12"

Bell Sinker

A simple bottom rig is a good way to fish in swift waters below dams.

Some rivers provide year-round action for walleyes. The Mississippi River is a prime example. Some excellent fishing takes place along the Mississippi in Minnesota, Wisconsin and Iowa throughout the spring, summer and fall seasons. At certain locations, good walleye fishing can be found even during the dead of winter.

On big rivers such as the Mississippi, Illinois and Missouri, much of the shore fishing takes place below dams where walleyes concentrate prior to the spawning season. The rip-rap-covered banks stretching for miles below dams are also prime spots to fish for walleyes.

Wing dams can also be fished readily from shore. Both casting and still-fishing methods can be employed to take walleyes.

Despite the number of fish supported by large rivers, smaller flows can be more productive for the shore fisherman. In big waters walleyes can be just about anywhere and locating them is often a

Trees that have fallen into the water are prime spots to find walleyes. Fishing wood requires a little heavier line than normal and weedless-style jigs.

difficult chore when limited to the water within casting or wading distance of shore.

In small rivers, walleyes tend to be located in obvious areas such as deep holes, turbulent water below dams, near the mouth of in-flowing tributaries and other spots where the water is relatively deep near shore. Walleyes can also be taken by wading and casting flats where fish often scatter to feed on minnows and crayfish.

The types of places where walleyes are found in rivers determines the best fishing methods. Below dams with strong turbulent current a simple bottom rig is hard to beat. Tie a snap swivel onto the end of the line and attach a bell sinker. Approximately 18 inches above the sinker tie a loop in the line using two overhand knots. To this loop attach a No. 4 Aberdeen snell hook.

This rig can be baited with a minnow, leech or crawler and cast into position. Allow the sinker to pull the bait to the bottom, then reel up the slack line until the weight of the sinker can be felt. Let the sinker rest on bottom for a few moments. If no bite occurs, reel the sinker in a couple feet and wait again. Repeat this process until the rig has been retrieved and is ready to be cast into a new spot.

Use just enough weight to keep the bait on bottom. Spinning tackle and 6- to 8- pound test monofilament line enables this rig to be cast long distances.

Steelhead-style rods are ideal when it's necessary to make long casts. The extra length of these rods can significantly increase casting distance. If you don't believe me, try a little experiment. Pick up a small apple from beneath a tree and see how far you can throw it. Then take a pocket knife and cut a small limb about 3 or 4 feet long from the apple tree. Trim off any limbs or leaves and sharpen the small end to accept a small apple.

Using the stick, fling the apple as hard as you can. You'll be amazed how far an apple can be tossed using this simple principle of leverage. A fishing rod uses the same benefits of leverage. Longer rods, being bigger levers, are capable of casting lures much greater distances.

Casting distance is important when working from shore. Long casts help to cover water and contact fish that would otherwise be out of reach to the shore fisherman.

Jigs are another lure that are well-suited to fishing from shore in rivers. Select a jig that's heavy enough to reach bottom. Normally for most casting situations a 1/16-, 1/8- or 1/4-ounce jig is ideal.

Tip the jig with a minnow, leech or half a nightcrawler and cast quartering upstream and across the current. Jigs may also be dressed using an action tail grub. Allow the jig to sink to the bottom and then reel up the slack line. Once the slack has been picked up, use the rod tip to lift the jig slightly off the bottom and allow the current to sweep it downstream.

The current will sweep the jig a couple feet downstream before it comes to rest again on the bottom. Reel up the slack line and repeat the process over and over again until the jig is directly downstream. At this point reel up and make another cast.

If too heavy a jig is used the current won't be able to sweep the bait naturally downstream. If too light a jig is used the current simply washes the lure and bait quickly downstream.

Jig casting is an excellent way to fish deep holes, runs with moderate current flow and flats with a lazy current speed.

Slip bobbers are another river fishing trick that works especially well on deep river holes or stretches where the bottom is snag-filled. Set up the slip bobber rig as outlined in Chapter 22 using a jig on the terminal end. Set the bobber stop so the jig is positioned a few inches off bottom and cast this rig quartering upstream and across the current.

Let the bobber float freely with the current using the rod to keep the line up out of the water. When the bobber is directly downstream reel up and make another cast.

Crankbaits are another lure that can be cast with good success from the bank. It's important to select a model that dives deep enough to make contact with the bottom, but not a model that dives so deeply the bait dredges the bottom and increases the chances of snags.

Like jigs and slip bobbers, it's best to cast cranks quartering upstream. Use a slow but steady retrieve and be ready for a smashing strike. Walleyes often hit with amazing vigor the crankbaits worked in rivers.

SHORE FISHING NATURAL LAKES

Natural lakes are a more challenging atmosphere for the shore fisherman targeting walleyes. While these popular game fish are often found near the shore, this species spends much of its time beyond the reach of shore casters. The situation is not hopeless however. A number of

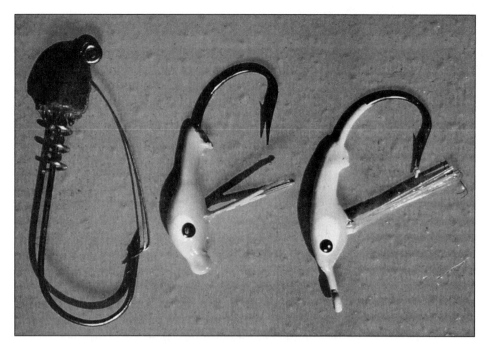

These weedless jigs are ideal for casting into sunken tree tops.

situations enable shore-bound anglers to get in on the action.

Unlike rivers where walleye fishing is often very seasonal, walleyes in natural lakes are likely to be found in shallow water and near the bank during spring, summer and fall.

The first crack at this fish comes immediately after spawning. Walleyes put on the feed bag and shallow water is the first place many of these fish head. In most natural lakes the highest concentrations of forage fish are located near shore. Schools of spottail shiners, fatheads, emerald shiners, small perch and other baitfish roam the shoreline usually along the weed edges or the first contour where the bottom drops off into deeper water.

If the shoreline has washed away the roots of trees and allowed this timber to topple into the water, a golden opportunity to find walleyes close to shore exists. This is especially true if the timber falls where there is deep water near shore. Minnows are attracted to the submerged timber and walleyes don't hesitate to help themselves.

A little wind that pushes waves into the shoreline makes for the best fishing conditions. Wave action turns the water murky along shore making it easier for walleyes to slip in and grab a meal.

A 1/16- or 1/8-ounce weedless jig tipped with a minnow is a great way to work in and around this wood cover. Normally 6-pound test line is advised for this style of fishing, but the shore fisherman is better equipped with slightly heavier 8-pound test. The heavier line comes in handy when struggling with the snags that will be impossible to avoid.

Slip bobber rigs are another great way to fish shoreline timber. Cast the bobber rig outside the timber and let the wind and waves drift the bait naturally into position.

A similar situation occurs in natural lakes when wave action pushes baitfish up along rocky shorelines or points. The combination of bait and murky water is more than walleyes can resist.

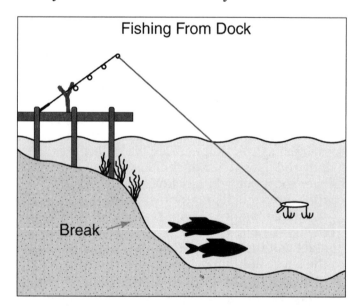

Docks that stretch out towards a breakline or weed edge can be great places to cast for walleyes. Some of the best dock fishing takes place after dark.

Both jigs and slip bobber rigs are good options, but don't overlook the option of casting a shallow-running crankbait.

Walleyes feeding in shallow water often hit anything that moves. Crankbaits are a good way to cover water quickly and many of these lures can be cast long distances.

Another situation to look for in natural lakes takes place after dark. In many clear-water fisheries walleyes make a move towards shallow shorelines once the sun sets. It could be weeds, sunken timber or boulders that attracts baitfish and, in turn, walleyes.

On many lakes cottage owners build docks that stretch out away from the shoreline. These docks can be an excellent place to target walleyes, especially if the dock ends within casting distance of a weed edge or sharp drop in the bottom contour.

The best docks are those that have lights mounted on them. Light attracts baitfish and walleyes aren't far behind. Similar situations can be found around boat landings and marinas where lights attract baitfish and lure walleyes close to shore.

Another spot to locate night walleyes is anywhere current comes into a lake. A river that flows in or a channel between lakes is enough current to attract baitfish and walleyes.

Two lakes near my home have a channel that connects them. The channel was dug to float logs from lake to lake, but is now used for fishing and recreational traffic. Despite lots of traffic in the area, walleyes are often taken by anglers wading along the shoreline and casting jigs tipped with minnows or crankbaits near the channel mouth.

SHORE FISHING THE GREAT LAKES

Piers jutting out into the Great Lakes are a prime hot spot for walleyes after dark, and the chances of catching big fish are excellent. This night fishing pattern seems to produce best during the late summer and runs into late fall.

Every fall I take a trip to Lake Erie to fish walleyes at night along the shore from Cleveland to Port Clinton. Schools of gizzard shad move shallow at this time of year where walleyes chase them into water less than knee deep.

Lipless cranks like these are some of the most popular baits among pier casters. These lures can be cast great distances and the rattle chambers help fish find these lures.

On the quiet evenings you can hear walleyes splashing as they slash into schools of shad and force them to the surface. You can imagine the drama going on below the surface.

Many anglers have great success casting crankbaits from piers, docks, boat landings, boat slips and any place else where they can gain access to the water. So effective is this style of fishing that the Ohio state record on walleyes has been broken twice in recent years by anglers casting crankbaits from shore.

Most any crankbait can be used, but the hard-core shore anglers have learned that baits which can be cast long distances are the best choice. A favorite is the famous Bill Lewis Rat-L-Trap. Designed to both look and sound like a shad, these baits are responsible for countless fish each fall. Other good lipless style cranks to try include the Rapala Rattlin' Rap, Excalibur Super Spot and Luhr Jensen Sugar Shad.

A wealth of floating/diving style crankbaits can also be used. Blade baits are another casting bait that are productive when casting at night.

For me the Lake Erie night bite is so good it's tough to go anywhere else, but a number of other fisheries in the Great Lakes region offer opportunities for shore-bound anglers. Inland lakes that drain into the Great Lakes are prime examples. Most of these lakes feature a channel that connects the two bodies of water. Generally this channel is protected from wave action with large boulders. Walking along the channel edge and casting crankbaits is a popular way to fish for walleyes.

SHORE FISHING EQUIPMENT

No special equipment is required to tap into shore fishing opportunities for walleyes, but a few items can make fishing more enjoyable.

The spinning rods used for jigging, slip sinkers and slip bobbers can be used to fish from shore. However, where kids are concerned I recommend using spincasting or closed-face equipment. These reels are less expensive and better able to handle the abuse kids dish out.

A backpack is a great way to carry fishing gear when hiking to a favorite spot. Tackle, waders, bait, lunch and everything else needed for a day of fishing can be carried comfortably on your back.

For instance, if a child drops your favorite spinning reel in the sand you're in trouble. It will take a visit to the closest reel repair center to put the smooth back into this model. Closed face reels are just more trouble-free than spinning gear when in the hands of young anglers.

Long steelhead rods are a good investment for anglers who need to cast maximum distances. Many of these rods come packaged in a plastic tube that's ideal for transporting the rod into the field.

Also, because shore anglers are always on the move, a traditional tackle box isn't very practical. A fly fisherman's vest is the answer to carrying lots of different fishing tackle. Buy a model that features an inflatable life vest with a CO2 cylinder and you'll never have to worry about stepping in over your head.

Waders help shore fishermen reach more walleyes. In warm weather thin nylon waders are the best choice, especially if a considerable amount of walking is required. Be sure when purchasing waders to get the correct size. A pair of waders that binds in the groin is not only uncomfortable, it can be dangerous. Waders come sized in short, medium and tall models. Select the length that fits both in the foot size and inseam.

In cold weather you can't beat the comfort of neoprene waders. Neoprene stretches making them very comfortable for walking. However, neoprene waders can be too warm to walk long distances. In cold weather plan on packing in the waders and putting them on once you're ready to fish.

Lights are another important item if you plan on fishing after dark. Lights that strap onto your head or cap are an excellent way to direct light where you need it most, such as when tying on lures or landing fish. For general purposes a gasoline-powered Coleman lantern is tough to beat. Not only do these lights give off a reassuring glow, they generate enough heat to take the chill away from stiff fingers.

A landing net is just as important to a shore fisherman as to one who fishes from a boat. Models with both collapsible handles and hoops are handy for trips that require packing gear in a considerable distance. Otherwise select a net with an extension handle that makes it easier to reach out and land fish.

Carrying bait is often a problem associated with shore fishing. It's hard to carry bait buckets any distance. I've discovered that soft-sided coolers are a great way to carry minnows without fear of spilling. Put a couple inches of water in the bottom of a soft-sided cooler and add your minnows. When you get to the place you plan on fishing add a little more water to keep the bait frisky.

If you plan on hauling a lot of gear such as bait, food, drinks, tackle, waders and a landing net, consider loading everything into a backpack. There's no easier way to carry a load than letting your leg and back muscles carry the majority of the burden.

Fishing for walleyes from shore isn't the kind of stuff you read about in the major outdoor magazines, but this species can be taken readily without the benefit of a boat. The key to success is knowing where, when and how to get in on the action.

In the next chapter ice fishing for walleyes takes center stage. Like fishing from shore, ice fishing requires only a modest amount of equipment to reap impressive benefits.

CHAPTER 27

WALLEYES ON ICE

Just about everywhere walleyes are found, anglers anxiously await the season to open. Crowds of anglers flock to popular waters. Lines form at boat launches, bait shops run out of minnows and convenience stores can't keep enough cold pop and snacks on the shelves.

Many of these dedicated anglers don't waste a minute of potential fishing time. The most committed souls launch their boats in the middle of the night, so they can be on the water and ready to fish when the season officially opens at 12:01 a.m.

Few other fish species stimulate so much excitement among the ranks of anglers. Walleyes are unique in that they are abundant, challenging to catch, they grow to a good size and their table fare is legendary. It's little wonder that anglers so anxiously await opening day.

In the northern parts of the walleye's range, first ice is almost as important an event as opening day. Few other species are pursued as relentlessly during the winter as walleyes. The interest in winter walleye fishing is so intense, many states are forced to close the fishing season from late February through April to prevent anglers from over-harvesting fish on the spawning grounds.

Late winter and early spring is the one time of year that the whereabouts of walleyes is no mystery. Thousands upon thousands of fish show up on wind-swept reefs, rocky shorelines and tributary streams in preparation for the annual spawn. If the fishing season remained open throughout this period, the walleye population in most waters would be seriously reduced.

Only a handful of waters can support year-round walleye angling pressure. Most of these fisheries are either sprawling bodies of water with enormous populations of fish such as Lake Erie, or remote areas that see little fishing pressure such as the reservoirs of the Dakotas.

First ice is like having a second opening day for those who take the sport of walleye fishing seriously. Once the ice is safe enough to walk on, an explosion of fishing interest that can only be compared to opening day occurs.

There are several reasons why first ice attracts so many anglers. In most of the northern areas first ice comes along with the holiday season. Many workers are off on vacation and kids are enjoying a break from school.

Secondly, ice fishing enables those anglers who don't own boats to get in on the action. Some modest equipment, a little bait, warm clothes and the willingness to brave the elements are all that's needed to enjoy winter fishing.

First ice is almost as important to walleye anglers as opening day. The author's wife took this fish with a jigging spoon.

Thirdly, walleyes bite actively throughout the winter. Unlike many species that become dormant or inactive in icy water, walleyes can be caught using a number of presentations from first ice until the season closes in late winter.

Quality winter clothing is another reason ice fishing has risen in popularity. Garments developed for snowmobiling first gave ice fishermen the duds to stay outside for long periods in freezing conditions. Later high-tech big game hunting clothing came onto the scene providing anglers with garments that are lightweight, windproof, waterproof, breathable and warm.

Add up these factors and ice fishing for walleyes takes on an importance far greater than many anglers realize. A major percentage of the fishing tackle industry survives by developing and selling nothing but ice fishing tackle, clothing, shelters and accessories.

Walleyes are one of the most popular fish targeted by ice fishermen. Not surprisingly a wealth of gear and gadgets suitable for chasing winter walleyes awaits anglers at their favorite sports shop.

GEARING UP

A good ice auger, spud and ice scoop are mandatory items on every ice fishing trip. For walleyes an auger with an 8- to 10-inch blade ranks as the best choice. On first ice a hand-auger will get the job done nicely, but later in the season when the ice thickness grows, serious fishing calls for the convenience of a power auger.

No angler should ever walk onto the ice without a spud handy. A spud is the best tool for testing both the thickness and hardness of the ice. Safety should be your first concern when ice fishing. Use the spud to test the quality of the ice every few yards.

Not so many years ago commercially produced ice fishing rods were mostly targeted at the panfishing market. Finding a rod suitable for winter walleye jigging was downright difficult.

I can remember when I first became serious about walleye fishing in the early 1980s. Graphite rods for open-water fishing were just becoming

When walleyes are biting there's usually no shortage of anglers willing to brave the cold.

popular, but shorter versions suitable for ice fishing simply didn't exist.

Along with many of my friends, I got involved in rod building because that was the only way to get quality equipment. We built custom jigging sticks made from graphite rod blanks cut to the desired length. Several fly rod stripper guides were added along with a few cork handle disks glued together and sanded into shape. The rods we crafted ranged in length from 24 to 48 inches, suitable for both shanty work and open air fishing.

It took a number of failures before we discovered that a rod with too light an action was easily broken. Thin wall graphite rods are delicate, especially in bitter cold fishing conditions. Gradually we settled on graphite/fiberglass composite blanks that were sensitive yet more durable and flexible enough to handle big fish.

Along the way we also learned that fly rod stripper guides iced up too quickly. These guides were replaced with oversized Fuji ceramic guides and tip tops that allowed us to fish without the line icing up.

Our hand-made rods were dressed with a small spinning reel positioned on the handle using tightly wrapped electrical tape. Ironically the materials alone required to build these rods cost more than the higher quality commercially prepared rods available today. Back then however price wasn't an issue. We were interested in rods that met our ice fishing needs. Commercial rods of the time just didn't measure up.

Today a wealth of manufacturers produce outstanding ice fishing rods suitable for winter walleyes fishing. These rods are functional, reasonably priced and durable. Anglers need only be concerned with length and action.

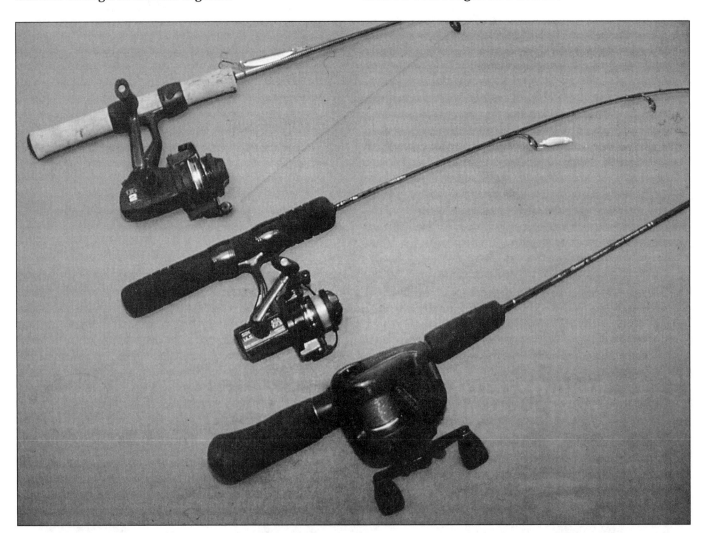

Quality ice fishing rods are currently available from a number of manufacturers. Most anglers favor spinning tackle, but baitcasting gear can also be used.

Most of the commercially produced rods are less than 36 inches long, making them suitable for fishing in both a spacious shanty or in the open air. The quarters in some shelters are tight enough that a 24-inch rod is required for comfortable fishing.

Personally, I own two sets of ice fishing rods. A short set of spinning rods measuring 24 inches is used for shanty fishing. A second set of longer rods are put into action when fishing outside the shanty. In my mind, longer rods are a clear advantage. Not only do these longer jigging sticks enable the angler to enjoy more control of hooked fish, the shock absorbing effect helps to insure against lost fish. Anglers using longer rods can get away with lighter line and lures.

I prefer spinning rods for ice fishing. Lightweight and easy to use, spinning gear functions flawlessly in cold fishing conditions.

Baitcasting style rods and reels can also be used for ice fishing. Some anglers favor this gear arguing that the drag systems are much better than that of most spinning reels.

Avoid using spincasting or closed face reels when ice fishing. This style of reel freezes up readily. Spincast gear may be used however if the weather is above freezing or these reels are used in a heated shanty.

For most winter jigging situations monofilament is the best line choice. Select a line that's limp and has little memory. Eight-pound test is a good choice for winter walleye jigging. Some exceptions do exist however. In areas where big fish are present, heavier 10- or 12-pound test is recommended.

Ice fishermen on Saginaw Bay in central Michigan frequently jig with 12-pound test line. The average fish taken here during the winter weighs more than 5 pounds and brutes ranging from 10 to 13 pounds are common. When a big fish is thrashing just below the jagged edge of the ice hole, the heavier line is welcome insurance.

Some anglers even use a heavier line such as 17-pound test as a leader. Once the fish is near the hole, the angler grabs the leader and drops the rod. The strong line makes it possible to man-handle the fish into the ice hole and onto the surface.

This method for landing winter walleyes makes more sense than gaffing the fish. Many walleyes have been lost while the angler farted around trying to find the gaff or waited for a clear shot with the gaff. Also, if the fish is to be released, using a gaff is out of the question.

Braided super lines also have a place in ice fishing. When walleyes are located in deep water, using braided line provide anglers more sensitivity to detect light strikes. The low-stretch characteristics of these lines makes them the clear choice in deep water situations.

Tip-ups are fish traps for walleyes. In some states such as Pennsylvania several tip-ups can be set per angler. Most states allow two tip-ups.

Jigging lures near the bottom is the most popular way to catch winter walleyes, but set lines known as tip-ups are another good way to fish for walleyes. Tip-ups are used to dangle a minnow below the ice. A spool of line attached to a wooden or plastic frame rests below the water surface where it won't freeze. A trigger holds the line at the desired depth until a fish strikes. When a fish strikes and pulls out line, a trip flag signals the bite.

A tip-up could be described as a fish-trap for walleyes. Some states allow two, three or more tip-ups to be set per angler, making them the ideal way to spread out and cover water.

Tip-ups are one area of ice fishing equipment that have enjoyed significant improvements. Most notable are the various brands of round tip-ups that cover the ice hole preventing the water from freezing and blocking light from entering. Several of these tip-ups can be stacked inside a standard 5-gallon pail for transport.

Super braids are useful for deep water jigging, but don't make the mistake of spooling tip-ups with these lines. The thin diameter and slick nature of these lines makes them hard to handle while landing fish. If a fish makes a powerful run, the line passing through your fingers can cut skin like a knife. Monofilament line in 8- or 10-pound test is ideal for spooling tip-ups, but many anglers continue to use the old-fashioned black braided nylon line.

The terminal tackle required for tip-ups is rather simple. An assortment of split shot is required to hold the bait at the desired depth. A No. 6 or 8 treble hook is tied directly to the line. Premium quality treble hooks such as the Heddon Excalibur, Mustad Triple Grip, VMC Barbarian and Eagle Claw Wide Gap are built from thin wire to make them penetrate and bite with the least amount of force.

The terminal tackle used for jigging winter walleyes is modest enough to carry in a pocket-sized utility box. Heading the list are a few jigs ranging in size from 1/8 to 3/8 ounce. The jigs suitable for vertical jigging outlined in Chapter 13 are a good starting point. For best results the jig should be tied directly to the monofilament and rest horizontal in the water. Both long shank and short shank live bait style jigs can be used successfully.

Jigging spoons also rank as must-have items in a winter tackle box. Dozens of different brands and models can be used, but the more popular choices include the Bay de Noc Swedish Pimple, Hopkins Shorty, Mepps Scyclops, Luhr Jensen Krocodile, Rapala Minnow Spoon, Bait Rigs Willow Spoon, Mann's Mann-O-Lure and Northland Fire-Eye Minnow.

A selection of spoons ranging in size from 1/4 to 1 ounce will cover winter walleye fishing needs. It's also a good idea to select a number of different

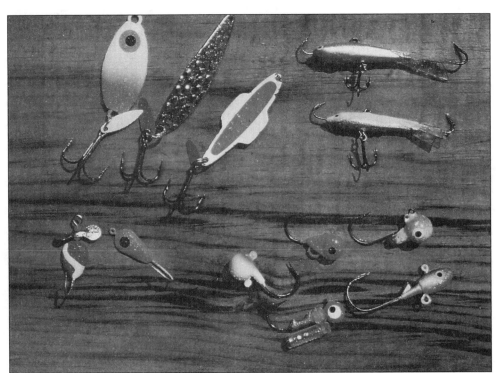

Lures for winter walleye fishing fall into three simple categories including lead-heads, jigging spoons and jigging/swimming lures.

color patterns including models with flash tape, painted and plated finishes.

I refer to the third winter lure group as jigging/swimming lures. The Jigging Rapala is the most famous of these baits. These minnow shaped lures feature a single hook on the nose and tail and a small treble hook on the bottom. A fin at the back of the bait causes the lure to swim and glide when jigged then allowed to fall on a slack line.

Nils Master produces a similar bait that is equally deadly on winter walleyes. You might also include blade baits such as the Reef Runner Cicada in this category. These jigging lures vibrate when lifted and wobble and glide to the bottom when dropped on a slack line.

TRICKS FOR FISHING JIGS

The methods for jigging up winter walleyes isn't much different than those used on open water. The primary difference is that during the winter months the jigging action should be subdued somewhat. This is especially true when using a lead-head jig and minnow combination.

Normally the most productive jigging stroke is the tight lining method. Allow the jig to free fall to bottom then reel up the slack line and hold the jig a few inches from bottom. Using a slow upwards movement lift the rod tip 12-18 inches off bottom then slowly lower the jig until it hits bottom. Moving the rod slowly up and slowly down keeps the line taunt all the time.

Spend a lot of time pausing the jig a few inches off the bottom. Some subtle hops can be incorporated to give the jig a little more action between lift and drop strokes.

When the minnow starts to die, replace it with a lively candidate. Set the hook the instant a bite is detected.

Where legal it helps to fish two lines. Both jigs can be lifted and dropped at the same time, or one rod can be positioned on the ice in a rod holder so the jig and minnow is suspended a few inches from the bottom.

Often it's the jigging action that attracts walleyes into the area, but the stationary jig that gets bit. The same thing can be accomplished by jigging one rod and setting a tip-up nearby.

USING JIGGING SPOONS

Jigging spoons must be fished more aggressively than lead-heads to bring out their natural action. Two jigging methods bring these lures to life.

The first method involves lifting the spoon approximately 24 inches off the bottom using a slow steady lift, then dropping the rod tip and allowing the spoon to wobble and free fall back to bottom.

The second method uses a moderate snap of the wrist to pop the jigging spoon 12 to 24 inches off bottom. The spoon is allowed to wobble and flash its way back to bottom. Between jigging

This selection of jigging spoons includes some that are narrow and fast-sinking and others that are wider with a more pronounced wobble.

This photo shows how to modify a jigging/swimming lure by placing a larger treble hook on the bottom.

strokes hold the spoon suspended a few inches off bottom for a couple seconds.

Spoons can be fished clean or tipped with a piece of minnow or small live minnow. If too large a minnow is used, the natural action of the spoon is lost. I like to tip spoons using small fathead minnows. These minnows are tough enough to stay on the hook, yet they live for a considerable time.

As with lead-heads, set the hook immediately when a strike is detected. Spoons should not be tied directly to the fishing line. Use a small snap to attach spoons. The snap makes it easy to change lures or colors, also a snap is a stronger connection point than tying directly.

When using spoons keep in mind that some models sink rather quickly, while others are wider and fall more slowly and with a more pronounced wobble. When fishing two rods I like to equip one rod with a fast-sinking spoon and the other with a spoon that features a pronounced wobble. This gives approaching fish two different looks to consider.

WORKING JIGGING/SWIMMING LURES

Jigging/swimming lures such as the Jigging Rapala and Nils Master are aggressive fishing lures. Lifting and dropping these lures slowly takes away their natural swimming action.

Start the jigging stroke with the bait suspended an inch or two off bottom. Using a sharp snapping motion of the rod tip, hop the bait 12 to 24 inches off bottom and allow the lure to free fall back to bottom. This quick hopping motion causes the lure to dart in a different direction each time. On the fall the bait glides out away from the center of the hole then swings in like a pendulum, eventually coming to rest in the center of the hole.

If the bait is allowed to crash into bottom some of the swimming action is lost. Concentrate on catching the falling lure before it hits bottom and allow it to swim naturally.

Two schools of thought exist on how to use jigging/swimming lures. One school feels that adding bait to these lures reduces their natural swimming action. A second school suggests that a small minnow hooked on the bottom treble hook adds scent, flash and action.

I believe these lures catch more fish when baited with a small minnow. The key is to use a perch-sized minnow hooked through both lips. The minnow doesn't have to be alive, but it should be shorter than the lure used. If too big a minnow is used the swimming action is reduced considerably.

The treble hook that comes on these lures must be replaced with a hook one size larger. This simple step insures that fish will be hooked more securely. Unfortunately, it also increases the chances that a walleye will catch the hook on the ice at the moment the fish is about to be landed.

For walleye fishing the size No. 5 and 7 lures are the best sizes. In deep water it may be necessary to use the No. 9 size.

These jigging/swimming lures have a clear advantage when used in flowing water. A number of popular walleye rivers develop safe ice during the winter. The minnow shape of these baits causes them to track naturally into the current. Jigs and spoons have a tendency to spin when fished in river current, causing problems with line twist.

Blade baits are fished in much the same way as jigging/swimming lures. An aggressive jigging motion is required to bring these lures to life. Normally these baits are fished clean, but a small minnow can be hooked to the back treble.

Ice fishing is the one time of year when using scent products makes the most sense. Anglers are forced to fish directly below them, reducing the amount of lure coverage considerably. Using scent products can help attract walleyes close enough that they spot lures or baits.

There are more scent products on the market than places to fish them. Most can be broken down into two categories: natural scents and cover scents. Cover scents tend to be strong smelling oils such as anise or garlic. Natural scents are extracts from real forage species such as shad, crayfish or nightcrawlers.

Both types of scents seem to work, but I have a strong preference towards those that smell like something a walleye naturally eats. Those that I have the most faith in are the Kodiak Paste scents. These products are made from freeze-dried baitfish, nightcrawlers, etc., and come packaged in a soft plastic tube that makes it easy to spread a small amount of paste on bait or lure. Oils, pumps and sprays just make a mess of everything they come near.

The Kodiak Walleye Formula works well and I've had excellent results with the Nightcrawler Formula as well.

SLIP BOBBERING

Slip bobbers are a good way to tempt winter walleyes. Problems with the line freezing to the bobber limits their use to days when the mercury is above 32 or when fishing in a heated shanty.

Select a float that's just big enough to suspend a small split shot and lively minnow. Set the bobber stop so the bait is positioned approximately 12 inches above bottom.

A slip bobber rig is a good way to put a second line in the water while fishing jigs, spoons or jigging lures. Make sure the holes are far enough apart that a jigging/swimming lure won't swim over and foul the bobber line.

Scent products are popular among ice fishermen. Products that smell like something a walleye would eat are the author's favorites.

A WORD ON ICE SHELTERS

Sooner or later every winter walleye angler ends up needing a shelter. The problem with most shelters designed for ice fishing is they are not mobile enough. When ice fishing for walleyes, it's often necessary to move several times before fish are located. If the shelter being used is tough to set up, take down or too heavy to move easily, chances are the owner will sit tight instead of moving to locate fish.

For my money the only shelters worth investing in are those that can be pulled along over the ice. Some of the most functional models are the popular Fish Trap and Frabill's new Ranger. Both are similar in that they feature a polyethylene base that acts as a sled. A canvas cover is supported by poles that allow the cover to be flipped over the top of the angler's head and closed or opened to act as a wind break in a matter of seconds.

Gear is stored inside the base and when it's time to move the cover is simply folded back. The unit can be towed by hand or pulled along using a snowmobile or all-terrain vehicle When a new fishing site is reached, holes are punched, the shelter slid into position, anglers get inside and sit down and finally the cover is flipped closed. The whole process takes less time than it takes to read about it. There's no faster way to enjoy the warmth and comfort of a shelter while ice fishing.

The disadvantage of this type of fishing shelter is they are designed for one or two anglers. Tent style shelters are more roomy and better suited to fishing with groups of anglers.

TRANSPORTATION ON THE ICE

Most of the lakes where walleyes are found are large enough that walking to the action is not practical. In the far north, the ice is usually thick enough to support trucks. Lodges that cater to winter fishermen often plow roads out onto the ice so their customers can drive right to the fishing waters.

Snowmobiles and four-wheel-drive all-terrain vehicles are also popular options for getting to and from fishing sites. If you can't decide which of these vehicles is best for ice fishing, snowmobiles have more power to haul shanties and other heavy gear, but all-terrain vehicles roll over the ice with less noise and disturbance. The transporta-tion trend among ice fishermen is towards all-terrain vehicles. These vehicles are not only useful for ice fishing, they come in handy on hunting trips or for working around the yard.

One of the most unusual vehicles I've ever seen for transporting ice fishermen is found on Lake Winnibigoshish in northern Minnesota. Owned by Ron Hunter of Judd's Resort, a full-sized van has been mounted on a cleated track. Like a cross between a tour bus and a bulldozer, this unlikely vehicle does an excellent job of shuttling anglers on and off the ice.

At Put-in-Bay, Ohio, Lake Erie walleye guide Pat Chrysler often uses an air boat to transport his clients across bad ice and open water in route to more secure ice. Pat built the boat because he was frustrated with the unstable ice conditions this region is known for. The air boat allows Pat and his clients to cross unsafe ice without fear. The air boat is also used to vertical jig from open pockets of water.

These home-made solutions aimed at getting to the fish stands as proof that there's little anglers won't do to make winter walleye fishing more productive. Winter is the one time of year anglers can walk on water. Who could turn down such an opportunity. Besides, there are worse ways to survive winter than hovered over a hole in the ice.

In the next chapter we'll leave the ice and cold behind to discuss the future of walleye fishing. A number of issues threaten to change walleye angling as we currently know it.

The Juddsmobile is one of the most unusual vehicles designed to carry ice fishermen to the fishing grounds.

CHAPTER 28

MANAGING THE FUTURE OF WALLEYE FISHING

W alleyes are one of the few sportfishing species that are more plentiful today than they were a decade ago. This is a remarkable statement considering that walleyes are among the best tasting fish that swims. Despite the fact that walleyes

Walleyes are actually more plentiful today than they were a decade ago. Stocking efforts on many waters have made fish like this possible where a few years ago no one dreamed of catching walleyes.

are more likely to be kept and eaten than other fish, the population of this popular species is on the rise in many areas.

Insuring that walleye populations continue to expand in both range and numbers is a major challenge for fisheries managers. Bass maintain their populations in part because of catch-and-release practices. The same is true of muskies, northern pike and trout. In the case of walleyes, their populations require special regulations and in some cases stocking efforts to insure there's enough fish to go around.

Most walleyes are not released to fight again, especially if the fish are between 15 to 20 inches long. Ironically, adult walleyes are more likely to be released than young ones. With most game fish, the large specimens are kept as trophies and the small ones returned to grow. With walleyes, the small fish are considered prime table fare and the larger fish less desirable.

Because walleyes are sought for both their eating and sporting qualities a different set of "rules" apply to this species. Most anglers don't look at large walleyes as providing a larger slice of tasty meat. Instead they consider the smaller fish to be the prime cuts and larger fish to be chopped steak.

Many anglers feel that as walleyes grow larger they develop a "fishy" flavor. Smaller specimens have the mild flavor that walleyes are famous for. This phenomenon is most noticeable in waters where walleyes feed on oil-rich forage species such as gizzard shad, alewives or ciscoes.

Of course not all adult walleyes are going to be released, mild-tasting or otherwise. When a trophy walleye is caught, the taxidermist's phone soon rings. Lots of adult walleyes are also kept for the table, but a significant number of anglers practice a self-imposed form of selective harvest that rivals the catch-and-release ethics made popular by bass and trout fishermen.

When practicing selective harvest, small fish are harvested for the table, adult fish in the 4- to 8-pound range are released and the occasional trophy fish is kept for mounting. This method of selectively removing certain fish benefits both the angler and the fish.

Young walleyes are more abundant in the population than adult or trophy fish. This age-class of fish are best able to support a moderate harvest. If some of these fish aren't removed from the population, food resources sometimes become limited and growth rates slow down as a result.

Adult fish from 4 to 8 pounds are the primary spawning stock. These fish make up only a moderate percentage of the total population, yet they are critical to the annual population recruitment. Only a small number of fish from this age-class can be harvested before spawning production is influenced.

Large trophy class fish make up the smallest percentage of the total population. While these fish are desirable to have in the population for their sporting and trophy characteristics, their role is like that of an old whitetail buck. A buck that has survived for several seasons has fathered

Trophy walleyes like this one on the author's office wall represent a minor part of the total population. These fish are also past their prime, having spawned many seasons.

countless fawns. As cruel as it may sound, fish or deer that reach trophy size have already made their primary contribution to the species. The value of trophy fish to the welfare of the overall population is not significant.

Compared to species that benefit from catch-and-release management plans, balancing a walleye population is more complex. Because walleyes are routinely kept for food, biologists must compensate by setting conservative creel limits and seasons. Regulations such as minimum size length, creel limits, possession limits, slot limits and season limits are the tools biologists use to insure the walleye population enjoys a balanced number of young, adult and trophy fish.

Small walleyes like this one caught by the author's father-in-law, Don Parsons, are prime candidates for the frying pan. Many anglers prefer to eat small walleyes and release the larger ones.

MINIMUM SIZE LIMITS

In most bodies of water walleyes must reach a minimum size limit before they can be kept. The purpose of this regulation is to protect the fish until they reach sexual maturity. In the case of

Minimum size limits are a fact of life in most walleye fisheries. Most states set 15 inches as the minimum.

walleyes this minimum size limit is usually around 15 inches. Depending on the body of water, growth rate, forage base, sex and a number of other factors, 15-inch walleyes may or may not be sexually mature.

Still, setting a minimum size helps to preserve a significant number of fish that would otherwise be kept and lost to the population. In many bodies of water you can tell the minimum size limit based on the size of fish routinely caught. In my home state of Michigan the minimum size is 15 inches on most waters. When fishing popular lakes it's common to catch four or five sub-legal fish for every legal fish.

The comment is often made that next year the fishing is going to be great when these 14-inch fish grow up to 16 or 17 inches. It sounds good in theory and makes great conversation around the bait shop, but the bonanza never comes. Each year more sub-legal fish than legal fish are caught.

The reason so many "short" fish are caught compared to the number of legal fish is a direct effect of fish harvest. When fish achieve the 15-inch minimum, they are caught and kept. Only a small percentage of fish survive to grow to a larger size. This explains why in most bodies of water walleyes usually range in size from 15 to 18 inches. Few fish above 20 inches are caught as a rule.

The exception to this rule is of course the Great Lakes where walleyes have so much space to live they can avoid fishing pressure. Unlimited food supplies also allow walleyes to grow at the fastest possible rate, further increasing the chances of catching a larger average size fish.

Some remote lakes also support populations of larger than average sized walleyes. The lack of fishing pressure and or special harvest regulations enables this delicate balance to survive.

It's interesting to note that raising the minimum size limit can help improve the average size of fish caught. On lakes where the minimum size limit is raised to 16 inches, within one year the majority of the fish caught will again be just short of the legal size limit. The number of legal size fish doesn't necessarily increase, but the average size of fish caught goes up.

The bottom line is that there are only so many walleyes in any body of water. If these fish are not protected using minimum size limits over-harvest can easily occur.

Only a handful of fisheries can function with no minimum size limits. On Lake Erie there are no minimum size limits because the natural reproduction far exceeds the annual sport fishing harvest. In fact, the sport harvest of walleyes on Lake Erie has not yet met a projected quota established by the adjoining states. The limit was even raised from six to 10 fish per day a couple years ago to stimulate an increase in the harvest.

The possession limit was also dropped in Ohio waters in an attempt to increase the sport fishing harvest. None of these measures has significantly

This fish is being released because it is bigger than a slot limit set to protect adult spawning stocks. Slot limits are a valuable walleye management tool.

increased the sport fishing harvest in Lake Erie. This body of water is unique in that it has near perfect spawning habitat. The enormous population of fish found in these waters easily produces more offspring each year than anglers can catch.

In the big picture, few waters can claim such a feat. Size minimums are a necessary part of species management.

SLOT LIMITS

A growing number of states are using what are known as slot limits to manage walleye populations. A slot limit establishes a range of sizes from which fish may be harvested.

Slot limits can be used in a wealth of ways to protect delicate spawning stocks. Some slot limits

are simple size regulations and others are part of a more complex management plan.

A slot limit is most often used to protect adult fish from over-harvest. A typical slot limit is established so smaller fish may be harvested abundantly, but the harvest on larger fish is limited or prohibited.

A common slot limit allows fish from 15 to 20 inches to be harvested. Fish over 20 inches must be returned to the water. This slot is often adjusted to allow a certain number of fish per day, with only one fish more than 20 inches allowed in the bag.

The size requirements of the slot limit vary depending on the individual fishery. Again, the goal of these restrictions is to provide a degree of protection to fish that might otherwise be in danger of over-harvest.

Not only do slot limits protect a particular year-class of fish, they focus harvest on more abundant segments of the population. Slot limits are not in place everywhere walleyes are common. However, as the demand for walleyes continues to expand, fisheries managers will likely be forced to use this management tool more often.

SEASON LIMITS

In the same way that minimum size limits are necessary, most areas must live with a limited fishing season to protect walleyes. In most states walleye season opens near the end of April or early May and closes in late February or early March. The closed season closely corresponds to the spawning season when walleyes are concentrated in small areas.

It's easy to see how walleyes could be overharvested when an entire population of fish is often located in one or two small areas. Walleyes that spawn in rivers often stack up below dams that prevent upstream migration. Sometimes tens of thousands of fish spawn in a few acres of water. Walleyes that spawn on isolated reefs are just as susceptible to angling pressure.

Protecting walleyes during the spawning season makes sense in most areas. There are fisheries where a year-round season poses no serious threat to walleye populations. In the reservoir systems of the Dakotas walleyes often spawn in not one or two locations, but rather a number of different creek arms. Many of these areas are extremely remote and receive only a limited amount of fishing pressure.

In much of the Great Lakes, walleyes may be fished year-round, however most of the tributary streams dumping into these waters have highly regulated seasons. During the spawning season many walleyes enter tributary streams where they are protected. Those fish that do spawn in the lakes are spread out over a large area making them less susceptible to fishing pressure.

Of course there's also Lake Erie, which breaks every rule in the book. No closed season is required in Lake Erie simply because the water area is so large and the population so huge that angling pressure has little impact on the fish population.

The spawning season has become an important fishing period for the charter boat industry on Lake Erie. Anglers flock to the spawning reefs because it's one of the few times of year when the whereabouts of walleyes is no mystery. Fleets of charter boats fish the spawning reefs daily and when conditions are right countless fish are taken.

Despite the potential for a heavy harvest, weather conditions usually make it impossible to fish enough days to have any real impact. Also, most of the fish taken are smaller males. The larger females don't spend as much time on the spawning reefs and are therefore less susceptible to fishing pressure.

CREEL & POSSESSION LIMITS

Without creel limits anglers wouldn't quit catching and keeping walleye until their freezer was full. Obviously there has to be reasonable limits established to protect fish stocks. How biologists come up with limits is based as much on reason as scientific or biological data.

Most states have a walleyes limit of five fish per day. A few states allow six fish in the creel. In Lake Erie 10 fish per day can be taken from U.S. waters. Creel limits are set depending on the fish population and the number of anglers who will potentially fish.

Many states combine limits on popular fish. For example in Michigan anglers can have a combined total of five fish per day including walleyes, largemouth bass, smallmouth bass and pike. Such a creel limit makes fishing regulations easy to enforce and provides a degree of protection for all species involved.

Possession limits are a little more difficult to enforce. Technically, possession limits are set to prevent anglers from stockpiling fish in the freezer by taking limit catches for several days in a row.

Some waters such as the Ohio waters of Lake Erie have no possession limits. In other words an angler can catch and keep a 10-fish limit every day of the year. Such generous fish limits are the exception, not the rule.

Most states have a possession limit that's twice the daily limit. In other words if you can have five walleyes per day, the total number of fish you can have in possession is 10. Many states have a possession limit that's the same as the daily limit.

Possession limits are tools that help to restrict the harvest of fish during peak fishing periods. Unfortunately, possession limits are more difficult for conservation officers to enforce.

STOCKING AS A MANAGEMENT TOOL

Limiting the number of walleyes that anglers can catch and keep is a vital fisheries management tool. But during the last decade stocking has also become a powerful management tool for biologists charged with the responsibility of establishing and maintaining walleye fisheries.

Compared to other species, walleyes are relatively easy to raise and stock. The survival rate on walleye fingerlings is as high as 60 percent in some waters, making the stocking efforts highly profitable.

Rearing ponds are used to raise walleyes. These ponds are shallow and they feature dikes or flood control devices that are used to raise and lower the water level as needed.

During the early spring when walleyes are spawning, adult fish are captured from the wild and the eggs and milt removed. The eggs are fertilized and held in the hatchery at optimum water temperatures until they hatch.

Meanwhile the ponds are being prepared for flooding. Organic fertilizers are spread on the dry ground to stimulate a rapid growth of plankton once the pond is flooded. Animal waste is a common source of fertilizer used in rearing ponds.

Once the ponds are flooded, plankton that's naturally in the water starts to multiply. Fueled by nutrient-rich water, plankton numbers skyrocket.

As soon as the eggs hatch into fry, they are released into the ponds. The timing of this adventure must be perfect. When the fry are released there must also be an abundant supply of plankton or the young walleyes will have nothing to eat.

The plankton is a rich food source and the young walleyes grow at an alarming rate. In just a few weeks the walleyes are 2 or 3 inches long and ready to be released into the wild.

Again the timing of this operation must be perfect. If the plankton levels start to drop, walleyes will begin to feed on one another. In a matter of days an entire pond can be wiped out.

The number of fingerlings raised per pond varies by size and how well the balance of nature swings. It's common for even small ponds to produce more than 100,000 fingerlings and many ponds yield several hundred thousand young walleyes.

Once the walleyes reach fingerling size they must be released. In some cases the ponds are built right on the shore of the lake or river into which the fish will be stocked. A flood gate is opened and the fish are simply flushed out of the pond and into the real world.

In other instances the ponds must be drained and the young walleyes netted and trucked to nearby lakes. This labor intensive job is more than many fish and game departments can handle. Volunteer help from local fishing clubs helps to insure the work gets done in a timely fashion.

Most stocking efforts are organized and monitored by the state game and fish department, but the funds to raise these fish often come from the private sector.

In some cases a modest number of young walleyes are held in the pond and grown to a larger size before releasing them. The larger the walleyes are when they are released the higher the survival or recruitment rate. Unfortunately, the cost of raising these fish also increases as does risk of disease increases.

Not all stocking efforts start with fingerlings or small fish. Sometimes the natural process of spawning is given a helping hand by workers at the fish hatchery. Eggs and milt are taken from wild fish and the fertilized eggs held in the hatchery at the perfect temperature for incubation. When the eggs hatch into fry, the fry are released to fend for themselves.

When the fry hatch they are barely 1/4-inch long. Typical fry plants dump millions and in some cases billions of tiny walleyes into a body of water. While these numbers sound impressive, the survival rate is less than one percent in most cases.

Fry plants sometimes produce strong year-classes of walleyes and other times they fail completely. A number of conditions must be ideal for fry plants to work. First off, there must be adequate levels of plankton available for the fry to feed on when stocked. Only the most fertile lakes or rivers are good candidates for fry plants.

Secondly, the fishery to be stocked must also support an abundant forage base of minnows or small fishes. This may sound elementary, but biologists are often pressured by fishing clubs to stock lakes that simply don't have enough natural forage to support a large population of walleyes. When fish are stocked into these environments growth rates are painfully slow and recruitment levels low.

Biologists have been known to stock fry in lakes to satisfy insistent demands from fishing clubs and lake associations, knowing full well the survival rate would make the action a waste of time. A political agenda and fishery management plans don't mix well. Walleye stocking efforts are projects that should be carefully managed by biologists who study various waters and carefully pick the best candidates. When the private sector uses political power to force plants in waters that are marginal, valuable man power, money and time is wasted.

The best candidates for stocking are fertile waters with both a large population of forage species and limited competition from other predators. It's also important that suitable habitat is readily available.

Generally, the best waters for walleyes are large lakes, rivers or reservoirs with an average water depth of 40 feet or less. Walleyes stocked into small bodies of water don't fare well and are usually fished out quickly.

Prime bodies of water for stocking should also contain a good mixture of structure and natural cover. Areas suitable for natural reproduction are also critical. It makes no sense to stock walleyes into waters where they will struggle to reproduce naturally.

WALLEYES OUTSIDE THE HEARTLAND

Walleyes are distributed widely across the United States and Canada, but this species is most sought after in a handful of northern states and Canada. Walleyes create the most fan fare in Michigan, Ohio, Pennsylvania, Wisconsin, Illinois, Minnesota, Iowa, North Dakota and South Dakota. The Canadian provinces of Ontario, Manitoba and Saskatchewan harbor the most walleyes.

Many of the reservoirs in Missouri, Arkansas, Kentucky and Tennessee have great potential as walleye fisheries. Some bodies of water already have excellent populations of fish, but ironically local anglers pay them little attention.

The western states are experiencing some of the fastest growth in walleye fishing. Great fishing is currently available in Wyoming, Montana, Colorado, Kansas, and Nebraska.

A limited fishery occurs during the spring when walleyes migrate up into creek arms and stack up below dams to spawn. During the rest of the year other species such as bass and crappies are more popular.

A small but growing number of walleye anglers in the near south suggests that this species may become a more important member of the sport fishing community.

In the east walleyes are gaining a foothold in some areas such as New York state, but much of the eastern seaboard has yet to appreciate the value of these fish. In the west things are much different. Walleye fishing is on fire throughout the western reservoir system. Montana, Idaho, Utah, Wyoming, Kansas, Colorado and Nebraska all offer first-rate walleye fishing opportunities.

Large bodies of water, unlimited forage supplies and limited angler pressure combine to create fabulous walleye fishing opportunities. No

doubt, the western states will soon rival the heartland when it comes to interest in walleye fishing.

Walleyes are one of the few species that are rapidly expanding both their range and population. It's easy to see why walleyes are so popular. It's hard to find a sport fish that is more challenging to catch, sporting at the end of a rod or tasty on the table.

Add in the fact that walleyes can be readily raised in rearing ponds and they adapt to a wide variety of waters and the future of walleye fishing gets even brighter. Walleyes also respond well to progressive resource management plans that provide anglers the opportunity to harvest a generous amount of fish, while insuring that breeding stocks remain strong.

Taking everything into consideration, walleyes are the perfect sport fish for the future. What other species offers anglers so much?

LURE THE FISH YOU WANT TO CATCH

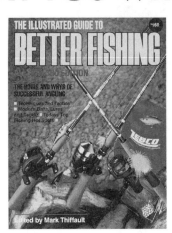

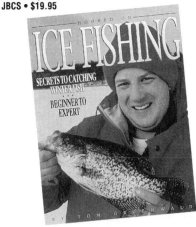
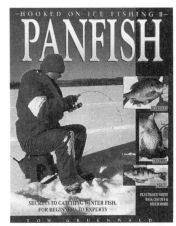

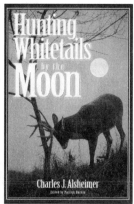

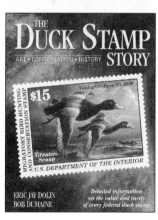

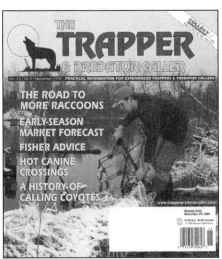